The Politics of Human Trafficking

The Politics of Human Trafficking

Lessons from Asia and Europe

Siddhartha Sarkar

LEXINGTON BOOKS

Lanham • Boulder • New York • London

Published by Lexington Books
An imprint of The Rowman & Littlefield Publishing Group, Inc.
4501 Forbes Boulevard, Suite 200, Lanham, Maryland 20706
www.rowman.com

6 Tinworth Street, London SE11 5AL, United Kingdom

British Library Cataloguing in Publication Information Available

Library of Congress Control Number: 2020930642

ISBN 978-1-7936-1169-7 (cloth)
ISBN 978-1-7936-1171-0 (pbk)
ISBN 978-1-7936-1170-3 (electronic)

Contents

Preface

The issue of human trafficking has been problematized as a threat to the sovereignty of states by transnational organized crime to its territorial and moral authority. This has led to its securitization—resulting in attempts to control migration—seemingly to limit the negative effects of globalization. Both state and non-state actors interact and play significant roles in the development of normative frameworks, legislation, policies, and processes to counter the phenomenon, as well as legitimating and perpetuating certain political agendas over others. The need to tackle the root causes of human trafficking has been recognized in the United Nations Protocol to Prevent, Suppress, and Punish Trafficking in Persons Especially Women and Children, supplementing the 2000 Convention against Transnational Organized Crime—the Palermo Convention. The Palermo Protocol emphasizes that root causes and political, social, and economic factors are all relevant to discourse regarding the vulnerability of potential victims to the risk of human trafficking. Questions of trafficking can thus be approached through attempts to grasp the significance of other macro issues of systemic significance—such as the nature of disintegration, "transition," managed democracy," "sovereign democracy," "corporate bureaucracy," political agenda-setting, uneven regional economic developments or changing life strategies, social attitudes, and public opinion.

Unsurprisingly, there is little official data on the economics of trafficking. In fact, the very notion of economic "value added" may seem inappropriate when applied to human trafficking and is sometimes rejected by anti-trafficking groups. The legality or illegality of human trafficking is irrelevant, as both legal and illegal production should be included in the systems of national accounts. Every country in the world today is affected by trafficking for buying and selling commodities or services illegally. Trafficking has been identified as the fastest growing criminal segment in the world. Slowdown economic situation coupled with robber barons can cause people to be even more vulnerable to human trafficking. The number of trafficking cases has increased particularly due to the significant lack of economic development. Likewise, the decline in the power of the government of any country during political crisis contributes to the rise in human trafficking. Most governments are doing nothing to crack down and try to end the illegal importing and exporting of commodities and services. Human trafficking market is classified as a monopolistic competition which consists of many sellers and buyers dealing in differentiated commodities and services. The ease of entry and exit rules out a monopoly or oligopoly market in human trafficking. The traffickers may have a number of political goals, apart from any financial gains. The political actors who purposely involve in trafficking for the benefit of their political gain may be called as political traffickers.

A typical strangeness of laundering the proceeds from cross-border human trafficking is the fact that the funds are generated over a long period of time in the territory of a foreign state. It is precisely for this reason that moving the money from the destination country presents the organizations with a major problem. Often traffickers make arrangements with a well-known agent with whom they have a close relationship to remit a large sum of money from the destination country. The traffickers consolidate the money earned by the sex workers so as to collect a larger amount. A regular practice of the traffickers includes buying or selling real estate in the fake names. Typically also, when traffickers acquire real estate property, they use it for laundering. For instance, they declare false purchasing and selling prices, they cheat on the actual turnover figures, when they are in retail, and so on. Oftentimes traffickers win public tenders for clear cutting, for example, by means of political protection and coercion. Entering into legitimate economy, the traffickers guarantee themselves clean money from subsequent transactions in those business spheres. Depending on the level and role they play in the criminal organization, the members receive different portions of the revenue generated from trafficking and henceforth sex trade. The actual distribution of funds does not solely depend on a person's position within the organization; people who hold the same position may not be paid the same.

Over the last couple of years, the online sex trade is flourishing and the websites display ads for sex services, and they also serve as online communities where clients, pimps, and victims can arrange business deals, share police sightings, and swap tips. The online trade has, in some ways, made sex trafficking and solicitation easier, while giving the police new insight into a historically hidden, underground culture. The distribution of images depicting the sexual exploitation is mainly facilitated by offensive use of the Internet. Furthermore, the relative vagueness offered by this means of communication makes it difficult to successfully locate and identify the offenders and to protect the victims from further exploitation. It must be emphasized that the discovery of illegal material is only the beginning of an investigation into the actual sexual exploitation of a woman or child. There is a clear distinction between specific legislation on the offenses related to the production, distribution, or sale and possession of sexual exploitation material and specific legislation on sexual offenses committed against victims. While there is no doubt that the sexual abuse and exploitation of women is a serious problem, there is a lack of accurate and reliable statistics on the nature of the phenomenon and the numbers of survivors involved, mainly due to differences in national definitions of different women and children sexual abuse and exploitation offenses.

Therefore, human trafficking is a politicized phenomenon wherein knowledge production is not always based on an analysis of phenomenology. This study, however, is an attempt to understand the politics and discourse of human trafficking, interactions, and roles played by state and non-state actors unfolding the basic structure of criminal organizations, various methods, and sophisticated technology used in trafficking business including principles of laundering and distributing the profit between the various levels in the organization based on the theoretical and empirical evidence from cross-country study.

Siddhartha Sarkar
January 31, 2020

Introduction

THE CONCEPT

Human trafficking as a global problem is located within the multilevel governance structure of the United Nations in terms of international law and transnational cooperation. States are simultaneously addressing the phenomenon within the confines of their borders, and through the harmonization of domestic legislation and policy. Moreover, human trafficking is an issue of foreign policy, or unilateralism on the part of the United States, in the form of its compliance and enforcement mechanism—the Trafficking in Persons Report. Thus, in order to study and understand how human trafficking is conceptualized and addressed—the actors, institutions, and processes involved—how they interact with one another, their agendas, the diverse and competing perspectives which exist, the impact and consequences of such actions—it is vital to study the complex network of human trafficking governance.

Human trafficking is a widely studied phenomenon, attracting academic interest across disciplines. However, until moderately of late there has not been much in the way of systematic, empirically, and theoretically grounded research on this socially complex problem. There are also numerous approaches to the study of human trafficking due to the plethora of definitions and conceptualizations of the phenomenon, its causes, its victims, the traffickers, and responses. Many approaches to the study of human trafficking are compartmentalized, operating in competition with one another, and based on conflicting political agendas. Most of the research conducted has been nonempirical and has focused almost exclusively on women and trafficking for sexual exploitation, to the detriment of other forms of trafficking and tends to exclude men as victims. Such research tends to be ideologically, morally, or politically driven. This has in part been due to the early prevalence or dominance of nongovernmental organizations, and international organizations, involved in advocacy and research on human trafficking as a form of sexual exploitation of women and girls and linked to transnational migration. The constraints on focus and emphasis on human trafficking research has resulted in a body of knowledge built on methodologically and conceptually flawed foundations, and has had a tangible effect on counter-trafficking responses by states and other actors. Much research on human trafficking is disconnected from theory. There has been a noticeable turnaround in the way human trafficking is conceptualized and addressed recently as more academics have applied their knowledge to the problem of trafficking through empirical research. Trafficking for the purposes of sexual exploitation combined within a narrative of organized crime and law enforcement/criminal justice remain the most commonly researched areas of human trafficking.

Human trafficking research is thus concerned with a range of intersecting and competing, or even contradictory issues. These are typically interwoven with the supremacy of the state, its sovereignty, and threats to its existence by the shadowy forces of globalization, porous borders and undocumented migration from the developing world. This is in turn stitched together with issues of human insecurity—the moral threat of prostitution and transnational organized crime. In this area of political science research, the state is once more elevated to the position of defender of its citizens and the integrity of its borders—the provider of political goods and certainty in an uncertain world. Studies on human trafficking from this perspective typically engage with concepts of security, transnational threats, and the role played by states and international institutions and normative regimes to prevent and combat the phenomenon which is seen as a threat to global security. Such an approach, however, only paints a partial picture of the phenomenon of human trafficking—the way it is or should be conceptualized, and responses to the phenomenon. Such an approach often fails to interrogate the causal relationship between legislation, policy interventions, and unintended consequences. It does not meaningfully take into consideration migrants or human rights. It is more concerned with protecting the state and by extension the international system from external threats posed by non-state actors and networks. Such an approach does not take into account the multifaceted nature of the phenomenon or the diversity of its victims, or the ways in which it can be problematized and examined, or the influence of actors on the discourse and thus responses. Instead, it tends to focus on seeking simple solutions from either a state-centric or criminal justice perspective to a complex problem. An uncritical, theoretically disconnected approach to the study of human trafficking, data and information provided, or which is limited by the dominant discourse or singular approaches, is thus rejected.

The study of human trafficking is increasingly being approached from a more holistic perspective which takes into consideration the political, social, cultural, historical, and economic dimensions of the problem. Human trafficking is thus studied "in the context of the illicit global economy, rising illegal migration, and as a regional and international policy issue." An approach which combines a human rights and law enforcement perspective is increasingly being followed, and allows for a more nuanced and fuller picture of the phenomenon and redirects focus to the victims of trafficking rather than the state. Research from this perspective tends to be more methodologically rigorous and empirically based. However, it remains focused on discourse and institutional analysis typically from feminist or gendered perspectives. The discursive narratives which define the international human trafficking discourse and the polarization of perspectives are unpacked, and the role played and influence exerted by counter-trafficking actors on institutions and the discourse is examined. However, such studies tend to be based on prescriptive theories and limited in scope and focus either on the international discourse and counter-trafficking institutions, or the influence of the United States and counter-trafficking actors. Moreover, there is a preponderance of research focused on the process of female migration, migrants' experiences and "the institutional ramifications and consequences for migrants." Such an approach is still limited in its ability to deal with the complexity and multidimensionality of human trafficking.

A relatively new approach to the study of human trafficking is a complexity approach. According to this approach, theorists critique the tendency of dominant discourses to be either state-centric and/or exclusionary of divergent perspectives, and thus only partially telling the story which does not take into account the myriad of ways actors interact within a complex system. A complexity approach provides useful conceptual tools to describe the changing nature of discourses, institutions, governance structures, laws and responses by counter-trafficking actors, and the "rich pattern of interactions" between them. A complexity approach is not predictive nor does it specify particular solutions. Moreover, theorists examine the way in which a plurality of shifting perspectives present in a group is facilitated and maintained through dialogue and critically reflect on the role and importance of diverse actors, and their multifarious interactions and relationships within the complex adaptive systems within which they are situated in order to generate fuller pictures of reality.

The human trafficking discourse that has emerged over the past decade is diverse and often contradictory and competitive due in part to competing viewpoints from a variety of actors, organizations, scholars, and their particular political and moral agendas. The issue of human trafficking has been problematized as a threat to the sovereignty of states by transnational organized crime to its territorial and moral authority. This has led to its securitization—resulting in attempts to control migration—ostensibly to limit the negative effects of globalization. Both state and non-state actors interact and play significant roles in the development of normative frameworks, legislation, policies, and processes to counter the phenomenon, as well as legitimating and perpetuating certain political agendas over others. This has had an impact on the way human trafficking is addressed. The politics of human trafficking and the human trafficking discourse, interactions, and roles played by state and non-state actors, as well as the forms of human trafficking governance which have emerged trans-nationally and locally in relation to both developed and developing countries.

The human trafficking discourse is constructed in a similar fashion, creating a distinctive set of definitions, understandings of the phenomenon, leading to anti-trafficking programs and initiatives—all of which appear logical—but maintain certain prohibitions on our definition and understanding of the phenomenon, and thus potentially skewing outcomes or resulting in outcomes that do not have the desired effect. The predominant position of sex trafficking within the human trafficking discourse, which it is often taken as being synonymous with, constitutes "an intersecting and fortifying set of prohibitions in a fluid and complex 'grid' excruciatingly enmeshed around sexuality and politics." It is this notion which drives the human trafficking discourse and our limited understanding of the phenomenon. This has resulted in most narratives of trafficking being somehow laced with sexual exploitation and organized crime. It has also led to a variety of draconian attempts by the state to bolster the security of its borders by trying to keep the "undesirables" (illegal migrants) out and an overly narrow focus on the supposed perpetrators of the crime—the "kingpins." Victims of trafficking are depicted as young, helpless, uneducated, and somewhat innocent. They are all in search of a better life, a better job opportunity in the destination country. The narrative accounts of these victims include how they were completely unsuspecting and deceived into thinking that they would enter into gainful employment upon arrival at their destination, only to be sold by organized criminals into prostitution, and beaten and raped repeatedly until they comply with the demands of their new keepers. This is the story told time and time again. This particular narrative, and variants on it, has succeeded in creating a discourse based on the trafficking of women and children into forced prostitution.

In the most general of term the word trafficking in persons is understood to explain the transportation of persons by means of coercion or deception into exploitative or slavery-like conditions which is currently viewed as a serious problem by a wide range of different agencies, organizations, and political actors. In November 2000 the UN Convention against Transnational Organized Crime was adopted by the UN General Assembly. The purpose of this convention was to promote interstate cooperation in the combating of transnational organized crime and to eliminate "safe havens" for its perpetrators. It is supplemented by three additional protocols which deal with smuggling of migrants, trafficking in persons especially women and children, and trafficking in firearms. The definition of trafficking in persons in the Protocol contains three elements—it is defined as an action, consisting of "the recruitment, transportation, transfer, harbouring or receipt of persons"; as one which occurs by means of "the threat or use of force or other forms of coercion, of abduction, of fraud, of deception, of the abuse of power or of a position of vulnerability or of the giving or receiving of payments or benefits to achieve the consent of a person having control over another person"; and as being undertaken "for the purpose of exploitation which includes, at a minimum, the exploitation of the prostitution of others or other forms of sexual exploitation, forced labour or services, slavery or practices similar to slavery, servitude or the removal of organs."

It is important to remember that the Palermo Protocol, as it is known, is not a human rights instrument. It is an instrument designed to facilitate cooperation between states to combat organized crime, rather than to protect or give restitution to the victims of crime. States are to strengthen border controls to prevent trafficking and smuggling. Border controls and police cooperation, not human rights protection, lies at the heart of both the smuggling and trafficking protocols. The emphasis is on intercepting traffickers and smugglers and on punishing and prosecuting them. While states are encouraged to offer protection to trafficked persons in particular to consider providing victims of trafficking with the possibility of remaining, temporarily or permanently on their territory, actual obligations are minimal and the protection provisions are weak. Though there do exist other more progressive legal instruments governing trafficking, even in these the protection of trafficked persons is dependent on their cooperation with authorities. The Palermo Protocol's concerns with crime and borders arose partly from a more particular concern about the prostitution of women and minors, and there is special reference made in the protocol to sexual exploitation and exploitation of the prostitution of others. Media, policy, and research on trafficking have for the most part focused exclusively on sex work, and trafficking is commonly associated with "sexual slavery" and organized crime. Journalists, politicians and scholars are quick to depict migrant women in the sex industry as victims of abuse and violence, and traffickers as Mafia like individuals and/or organizations that enslave women in prostitution. This helps to install the image of trafficking within a simplistic and stereotyped binary of duped/innocent victims and immoral traffickers. Trafficking appears as an activity that takes place outside any social framework—it is criminal individuals that are responsible.

POLITICAL DISCOURSE

Politics has often been defined in terms of who gets what, when, and how. The question of who gets what frequently boils down to political competition over the distribution of wealth and power. Politicians and political parties generate at least part of their support via their capacity to protect and promote the interest of key economic and social groups. In many countries, this often involves an expectation that politicians on the left will support the interest of workers and the public sector, while their counterparts on the right support corporations and the private sector. While not everything can be explained in terms of interest, there is no doubt that interest matters a great deal when it comes to shaping political behavior and political outcomes. This familiar model of politics can be usefully applied to recent efforts to combat human trafficking. Since the mid-1990s, a growing number of researchers have linked anti-trafficking efforts to larger political interests and agendas. These links are said to be strongest with regard to the relationships between trafficking and the legal status of prostitution, and between trafficking and the expansion of border protection measures.

In the most general terms trafficking in persons is understood to include the transportation of persons by means of coercion or deception into exploitative or slavery-like conditions, which is currently viewed as a serious problem by a wide range of different agencies, organizations, and lobby groups. And yet different groups identify trafficking as a problem for very different reasons and often have very different political agendas with regard to the issue. Three broad groupings are of particular significance for debates on trafficking:

- *Governments*: Their interest in trafficking is often grounded in concerns about irregular immigration and/or transnational organized crime, which are viewed as a threat to national security.
- *Feminist abolitionist NGOs*: Such organizations place trafficking high on their political agenda because they view trafficking as central to, and emblematic of, the increasing globalization of female sexual exploitation.
- *Migrant workers and other labor organizations, child rights NGOs, sex workers rights activists, and other human rights agencies and NGOs*: They approach trafficking on the basis of more general concerns about a range of human rights abuses and abusive working conditions to which particular groups are especially vulnerable.

Because the various groups that are involved in debates on trafficking view the issue through the lens of different political concerns and priorities, attempts to produce a precise definition of "trafficking in persons" and to identify appropriate policy responses to it have provoked, and continue to provoke much controversy. There are two key strands to the "trafficking" debates—one concerns anxiety between governments' obligations to protect and promote human rights, and their desire to restrict irregular forms of migration which is often regarded as a matter of state sovereignty; the other centers on conflicting views of the relationship between trafficking and prostitution. States have many different and often competing agendas concerning trafficking. However, from a governmental and intergovernmental perspective, trafficking has been framed as a crime control and prevention issue. It is linked to transnational organized crime through the Vienna process and the United Nations' Protocol to Prevent, Suppress, and Punish Trafficking in Persons, and it is also linked to violation of immigration laws. Governments clearly have many important and legitimate concerns about transnational crime and immigration. Yet crime and immigration are both also widely recognized as issues that can be manipulated by politicians and other actors in pursuit of less than altruistic ends. The mention of the words "organized crime" has the power to draw the press, win votes, acquire law enforcement resources, gain public support for various legislative or enforcement crackdowns (Beare and Naylor 1999). To mention "organized crime" alongside "illegal immigration" is a still more potent and populist formula. Fears and prejudices concerning "illegal immigration" are given fresh basis, and clampdowns on irregular migration are justified and humanized. As a result, those who view trafficking through the lens of concerns about human rights issues are often doubtful so far as the interest of governments and law enforcement agencies in trafficking is concerned. It must be emphasized that migration is the general phenomenon, and trafficking is only a mode of migration. Overemphasizing trafficking and taking it out of context in relation to migration is strategically counterproductive in the fight for human rights because (a) trafficking puts migration in a crime control, crime prevention context, rather than talking about human rights of the migrants first and then talking about trafficking in the context of human rights; and (b) trafficking is being used by governments as a vehicle to develop more restrictive approaches to migration in general (AMC 2000). While state actors often hold that trafficking can be combated through tougher immigration controls and enforcement, many non-state actors argue that the reverse is true. Strengthening efforts against human trafficking is essential in the fight for fundamental human rights, restrictive migration policies actually fuel markets for smuggling and trafficking of migrants (ILO 2002). Although many NGOs fear that governments could "hijack" or have already "hijacked" the issue of trafficking in order to pursue their own domestic agendas concerning asylum and immigration, governments' interest in the topic also means that trafficking is now a focus of national and international concern and debate. This in turn means that resources and media attention are increasingly available to those working on trafficking issues, and this provides human rights and child rights NGOs with an incentive to develop programs and initiatives in this area. Trafficking thus becomes a vehicle for pursuing more general human rights concerns.

While qualitative change in the global order implies a lack of global authority, the emergence of the notion of global governance has accounted for these changes described in the global political modus operandi of "governance without government" (Rosenau and Czempiel 1992). Moreover, as has commonly been pointed out, addressing cross-border issues in a globalized world requires solutions that transcend the porous and interdependent levels of governance. Here, the enhancement of global governance capability through new forms of multilevel governance targets particular (victim) groups who are at the margins of global politics. The spread of failed states and global slums have created security risks and risk groups at the margins of the globalized world whose experience of governance has generated a "state of exception" that resonates with a modus of "anarchical governance" expressed in particular forms of a "targeted governance" (Tosa 2009). The victims of trafficking represent a group at the periphery of global politics from whose perspective the qualitative shift of global order expressed in the deterritorialization of the nation-state and the advancement of globalization can be observed in full scope, and which requires a form of governance that takes into account the current vectors of global change pointed toward increasingly porous state borders accompanied by a lack of government capacity in response to cross-border problems.

Sexual Abuse

Global trafficking in persons particularly for the purpose of sexual exploitation victimizing mainly women and girls has been recognized as the most well-known form of modern slavery. The entrenchment of sex trafficking as the dominant narrative within the human trafficking discourse has led to a sense of panic among state and non-state actors alike. This becomes apparent when one delves into the history and evolution of the modern human trafficking discourse which has been built upon the foundations of prohibition, sexuality, and politics particularly statecraft. This discourse in turn has been manipulated by various actors predominantly advocacy organizations to suit particular ideological or political agendas.

Negotiations over the Palermo Protocol brought together states and feminists who were particularly concerned with prostitution, and until recently the policy discussions and research on trafficking have been very much focused on attitudes to sex work rather than migration. The discussions around the Protocol itself were affected by the polarized debate between those who are "feminist abolitionists" and who argue from the view point of "rights of sex workers." Abolitionists argue that prostitution reduces women to bought objects, and is always and necessarily degrading and damaging to women. Thus they recognize no distinction between "forced" and "free choice" prostitution, and hold that in tolerating, regulating, or legalizing prostitution, states permit the repeated violation of human rights to dignity and sexual autonomy. Prostitution is a "gender crime," part of patriarchal domination over female sexuality, and its existence affects all women negatively by consolidating men's rights of access to women's bodies. All prostitution is a form of sexual slavery, and trafficking is intrinsically connected to prostitution. From this vantage point, measures to eradicate the market for commercial sex are simultaneously anti-trafficking measures, and *vice versa*.

Feminists who adopt what might be termed a "sex workers' rights" perspective reject the idea that all prostitution is forced and intrinsically degrading. They view sex work as a service sector job, and see state actions that criminalize or otherwise penalize those who make an individual choice to enter prostitution as a denial of human rights to self-determination. They also strongly challenge the simple equation by feminist abolitionists of the demand for trafficking and the demand for prostitution. From this standpoint, it is the lack of protection for workers in the sex industry, whether migrant or not, rather than the existence of a market for commercial sex in itself, that leaves room for extremes of exploitation, including trafficking. The solution to the problem thus lies in bringing the sex sector above ground, and regulating it in the same way that other employment sectors are regulated.

The proposal to criminalize prostitution in order to combat sex trafficking and the exploitation of migrant workers in the sex sector is often based on a simplistic view of the sex industry and the way the sector operates. To focus anti-trafficking efforts and policies on the buyers as those causing the demand, and/or on "traffickers" as exploiting migrants' labor, diverts attention from the much wider economic, social, and political context within which the sex industry is located; and in particular, it diverts attention from the role played by residency and employment regulations in the destination states. This approach also reduces women's migration and participation in the sex industry to the idea of (sex) slavery, and simplifies social relations by viewing them exclusively in terms of patriarchal oppression or criminal activity, leaving no space for sex workers' agency. Moreover it adds force to the idea that trafficking equals coerced and illegal migration, and fosters an imaginary clear-cut separation between "legal" and "illegal" forms of migration. Finally, a focus on sex work as the main feature of trafficking does little to dissipate the moral panic that feeds fears of illegal migration. On the contrary, it strongly reinforces the idea that increasing restriction is called for. Those advocating the criminalization of clients are failing to consider that it is precisely the tightening of immigration controls and restrictive labor laws that create the conditions for the proliferation of illegality and labor exploitation.

Corruption

Trafficking in persons and corruption are closely linked criminal activities, whose interrelation is frequently referred to in international fora (UNDOC 2011). Still, huge challenges remain, notably the serious lack of accurate and reliable information on the scale and scope of trafficking, which makes it difficult to measure the effectiveness of anti-trafficking policies. The gap between the legal framework and the enforcement of relevant laws at the national level poses problems as well. Despite political will, law enforcement agencies lack the skills, knowledge, and resources to understand and respond to the evolving complexities of human trafficking. Collusion between corrupt government officials and criminal networks is another severe problem. Traffickers are known to enlist the help of corrupt officials in recruiting victims and moving them across borders. In fact, despite the scarcity of specific official data on corruption and trafficking, there are consistent indications that corruption does play an important role in facilitating and fostering the crime of trafficking in persons. Information and data gathered for other purposes, for example, investigation of cases of human trafficking, through accounts of victims and perpetrators indicates unequivocally that the corrupt behavior of law enforcers may help traffickers to recruit, transport, and exploit their victims; corrupt criminal justice authorities may obstruct the investigation and prosecution of cases, and/or impede the adequate protection of victims of the crime. Furthermore, corruption involving the private sector, such as employment agencies, travel agencies, model agencies, marriage bureaus, hotels, construction companies, and others may also contribute to human trafficking.

Public officials can directly participate in human trafficking playing an active role in the recruitment, transportation, and exploitation of their victims. Direct involvement of officials in trafficking encompasses both sex and labor trafficking. These officials actively participate in trafficking by owning or operating brothels holding trafficked adults and children; forcing victims into domestic servitude; or owning or operating factories that hold workers in forced labor. Across the globe, public officials have been found to participate directly in sex trafficking, recruiting victims, and profiting from their exploitation. The officials' positions often give them a measure of protection from prosecution. In addition, their proximity to vulnerable populations

Table 0.1 Opportunities for Corruption in Trafficking Chain

"When": The trafficking chain consists of the recruitment of victims, the provision of documentation (identity papers, visas, permits etc.), the transport of victims, which may include border crossing, their exploitation, as well as the laundering of the proceeds of the crime.
"Who": Corrupt actors within this chain of activities may include police, customs officers, embassies/consulates, border control authorities, immigration services, other law enforcement agencies, intelligence/security forces, armed forces (national or international), local officials, persons/groups/parties with influence on public officials, political actors as well as private sector actors, such as travel agencies, airlines, transportation sector, financial institutions etc.
"What": Corrupt acts include ignoring, tolerating, participating in, and organizing trafficking in persons, ranging from violation of duties or corruption and involvement in organized crime.

allows them to target victims. Public officials may act alone or in concert with trafficking rings. Public officials have also been found guilty of labor trafficking. Public officials may also misuse their positions to operate labor recruiting schemes. Increasingly, diplomats and officials of international organizations face allegations of direct involvement in trafficking for forced labor and domestic servitude. Under existing rules of international law, diplomats are generally permitted to bring domestic workers to their place of posting. In some cases, diplomatic officials use the privileges and immunities of their position to engage in corrupt practices that facilitate the trafficking of domestic workers for the purposes of forced and exploitative labor. Across the globe, diplomats have trafficked domestic workers, committing visa fraud, confiscating passports, threatening abuse of legal process and, in some instances, engaging in physical and sexual violence against the women trapped in the diplomatic households. Diplomats frequently hide behind their immunity to escape punishment for trafficking crimes. Although diplomatic immunity does protect these officials from prosecution, it is possible to hold diplomats criminally accountable. Unfortunately, this rarely occurs, allowing officials with full diplomatic immunity to commit these crimes with impunity.

Most often, administrative corruption is present in destination countries and in regards to sex trafficking, where prostitution is legal and regulated. There are different examples of administrative corruption in such countries. Consular staff could be bribed to facilitate obtaining of entry visas and secure the stay of the victim in the desired destination country. Labor authorities could be approached for work permits in order to legalize the status of the victim. Municipal authorities are targeted in order to avoid zoning requirements, to change the classification of real estate in order to be operated as a brothel, or to issue a license for night club.

Police corruption is the most widespread type of corruption in relation to trafficking in human beings and is particularly used in cases of trafficking for sexual exploitation. Organized crime groups in destination countries bribe police officers to turn a "blind eye" or even protect venues where sex services are procured. Corrupt police officers could leak information on starting or ongoing investigations or even obstruct investigations. Organized crime groups also bribe border guards in origin and transit countries in order to evade strict border control procedures. Bribes may take the form of direct payments or free sex services. These interactions between traffickers and law enforcement officers in certain cases entirely dissolve the boundaries between criminals and police and influence law enforcement officers to turn to criminal practices, such as racketeering sex workers, directly participating in trafficking rings or setting up and running brothels.

The representatives of the judiciary are much less targeted by organized crime in relation to human trafficking. The reasons why traffickers target judges and prosecutors are to obtain some kind of protection, to avoid investigation, or to gain influence over the outcome of trials against trafficking ring members. Corruption pressure is often achieved through extortion involving prostitutes or by exerting pressure through professional, social, and political networks.

The different extent of political corruption in destination and origin countries could be partially explained by the larger shares of proceeds from trafficking laundered in the legal economy in destination countries, as well as with the specific context of emerging and development of organized crime in these countries. It is not uncommon for ring leaders in destination countries to become wealthy local businessmen with substantial influence and links to local political elites or even with political positions. In this respect, elite prostitution rings and escort services provide either direct access to politicians or access through influential businessmen.

States should put in place strategies that address both trafficking in persons and corruption. A first step would be to include corruption issues in anti-trafficking policies, procedures, and training. This could be accomplished "by modifying anti-corruption tools or by including corruption issues in existing anti-trafficking measures." States should broaden the mandates of existing anti-corruption agencies to include a focus on trafficking-related corruption. Countries should form specialized multi-agency units and establish multi-agency training regimes with anti-corruption and anti-trafficking experts. These institutions should be entrusted with responsibility for detecting, investigating, and prosecuting corruption offenses related to human trafficking. Independence and autonomy are essential to the effective functioning of such agencies. The investigations should have the capacity to lead to both criminal and administrative penalties. An anti-corruption agency could investigate corruption cases; cooperate with prosecutors to bring criminal cases; raise public awareness of the problem; and facilitate interagency cooperation including security, law enforcement, and financial/ bank institutions. The agency could also be charged to disseminate statistical and comparative findings through a public awareness campaign. A corruption risk assessment is a useful starting point for developing a risk mitigation strategy or action plan. Any plan must be continually "monitored, tested and refined." Law enforcement and other state actors should be subject to constant review and vetting. Anti-corruption strategies will vary depending on the type of corruption. Promoting professional standards of integrity has been successful in addressing both street-level corruption (bribery, extortion, kickbacks) and bureaucratic corruption within police forces. Criminal corruption, such as protection, collusion or direct involvement in criminal activities has been successfully addressed through the investigation, prosecution and removal of corrupt officials. States must build mechanisms to detect and punish police involvement in any aspect of human trafficking, such as internal disciplinary measures, accountability mechanisms, and integrity management system.

CONCLUSION

Human trafficking is a phenomenon that encompasses so much more than a perceived threat to the sovereignty and security of states and their citizens. It is the ultimate manifestation of many of the systemic social, structural, economic, cultural, and political problems which continue to entrench discrimination, inequality, exclusion, and exploitation across the globe. In general, human trafficking is conflated with other problematized and politicized issues to further particular political, moral, or ideological agendas. Men are viewed primarily as active agents who seek out smugglers to assist them to cross transnational borders illegally. Whereas women and children are agentless victims who do not migrate out of choice rather they are trafficked into situations of extreme exploitation, primarily into the sex industry. Moreover, the securitization of human trafficking by states has resulted in an uneasy union of humanitarian—"politics of pity" and security—"politics of risk" discourses (Aradau 2004). The hallmarks of the "politics of pity" are that it relies on a so-called "emotional" governmental model that configures suffering, in relation to victims, "as recognizable, something the spectators can identify and sympathize with." In this sense, the politics of pity is strategically used to reveal "a defect, flaw, a disorder, a chaos, either in the organization of society or in the constitution of the individual." From a governmental perspective, concerned with security, and as such law enforcement responses to human trafficking, it would seem almost "natural" that the politics of risk has been wedded to this constructed problem framework. The politics of risk is utilized within the human trafficking discourse to market governmental prevention and protection. Victim profiles are thus crafted, in order to facilitate risk identification and categories "high-risk" groups. Moreover, trafficked women also mutate into a risk to the state/society. In other words, the trans-border trafficked individual represents an uneasy duality—a victim worthy of pity and a risk to the state and/or society, created by the risk posed by that individual's migration or potential to be re-trafficked.

A common critique of anti-trafficking regimes is that most efforts have focused on criminalizing and prosecuting traffickers, as opposed to preventing the crime and protecting its victims. The focus on criminalization and prosecution may have increased awareness, but more should be done to prevent trafficking through effective law enforcement and efforts to educate vulnerable groups about its dangers. Similarly, there must be greater effort to address the needs of victims. In addition to personal safety and security, victims need access to legal protection, health care, and temporary shelter, as well as assistance with repatriation and integration. The fight against human trafficking requires better national criminal justice systems to effectively enforce anti-trafficking laws, and these efforts must be part of a broader, multi-track approach that addresses the socioeconomic and political dynamics of trafficking. The complexity of the challenge means it cannot be tackled by any one actor, such as the state, or by focusing only on one aspect of the issue, such as sexual exploitation or forced labor. A comprehensive, more human-centered approach compels us to delve deeper into the other drivers of human trafficking, including poverty, severe exploitation, and political repression. This requires active participation and partnership between government and civil society groups, the private sector, and international foundations.

REFERENCES

AMC. 2000. *Asian Migrant Yearbook 2000: Migration Facts, Analysis and Issues in 1999*. Hong Kong: Asian Migrant Centre.

Aradau, C. 2004. "The Perverse Politics of Four-letter Words: Risk and Pity in the Securitization of Human Trafficking." *Millennium: Journal of International Studies* 33(2): 251–277.

Beare, M. and Naylor, R. T. 1999. *Major Issues Relating to Organized Crime: Within the Context of Economic Relationships*. York University, Ontario: Nathanson Centre for the Study of Organized Crime and Corruption.

ILO. 2002. *Getting at the Roots: Stopping Exploitation of Migrant Workers by Organized Crime*. Paper Presented to International Symposium on the UN Convention against Transnational Organized Crime: Requirements for Effective Implementation, February 22–23, Turin.

Michaelis, L. 2001. "Politics and the Art of Suffering in Hölderlin and Nietzsche." *Philosophy and Social Criticism* 27(5): 89–115.

Rosenau, J. N. and Czempiel, E. O., eds. 1992. *Governance without Government: Order and Change in World Politics*. Cambridge: Cambridge University Press.

Tosa, H. 2009. "Anarchical Governance: Neoliberal Governmentality in Resonance with the State of Exception." *International Political Sociology* 3(4): 414–430.

UNODC. 2011. *The Role of Corruption in Trafficking in Persons*. Issue Paper. Vienna: United Nations.

Chapter 1

Role of Technology in Trafficking

Sex trafficking which is associated with exploitation comes in many forms, including forcing victims into prostitution, subjecting victims to slavery or involuntary servitude, compelling victims to commit sex acts for the purpose of pornography, and misleading victims in to debt bondage. It is a modern-day form of slavery in which a commercial sex act is induced by force, fraud, or coercion (United Nations 2001). Legalization of prostitution expands the market for commercial sex, opening markets for criminal enterprises and creating a safe haven for criminals who traffic people into prostitution. Organized crime networks do not register with the government, do not pay taxes, and do not protect prostitutes. Legalization simply makes it easier for them to blend in with a purportedly regulated sex sector and makes it more difficult for prosecutors to identify and punish those who are trafficking people (Limoncelli 2009; Finkenauer 2001). However, there are many controversial issues related with legalization or criminalization of prostitution when it comes to sex trafficking. Some argued that criminalization of prostitution have enhanced sex worker's risk to dangers of trafficking, exposing prostitutes to more dangerous clients and less safe sex practices. Instead legalizing prostitution gives chances for trafficked people to testify against the smuggler and build confidence to ask legal protection. The other dimension also pointed out that criminalization of prostitution discourages trafficking if the law is effectively implemented. It gives slight chance for the pimps and traffickers to exercise their work and discourage potential perpetrators due to the fear of taking risk against the law (US Department of State 2004).

The advancement of information technologies have been accompanied by rise in illegal exploitation and misuse of technology for criminal activities. With respect to cyberspace, the Internet is increasingly used as a tool and means by criminal organizations. While the rapid dissemination of digital

1

technologies such as smart phones, social networking sites, and the Internet has provided significant benefits to society, new pathways and opportunities for exploitation have also come out. Increasingly, the trade in human trafficking is taking place online and on mobile phones. But the same technologies that are being used for trafficking purposes can become a dominant instrument to combat trafficking. The defined role that digital technologies play in human trafficking still remains blurred, however, and a closer examination of the phenomenon is crucial to identify and respond to new threats and opportunities (Latonero 2012).

On January 29, 2013, a total of 103 persons were surmised of being part of a people-trafficking network throughout Europe (Europol 2013). Ten European countries and European Union Rule of Law Mission in Kosovo were engaged in the common action supported and coordinated by Europol. In the early hours the suspects were arrested in Croatia, Czech Republic, France, Germany, Greece, Hungary, Poland, Slovak Republic, Turkey, and Kosovo region. Other coercive measures were taken in Switzerland; Austria also supported the common action. All arrested persons were alleged of being involved in the clandestine nature of trafficking of a large number of women and girls into and within the European Union mainly passing through Turkey and the Western Balkan region. These trafficked women were recruited largely in Afghanistan, Iraq, Pakistan, Syria, and Turkey by the criminal networks. The traffickers used technology-based various modus operandi to transfer them illegally into and within the European Union. The women and children are often trafficked in brutal and risky conditions, such as in very petite hidden compartments in the floor of buses or trucks, in freight trains or on boats. This is one of the largest coordinated actions against traffickers made at a European level, involving more than 1200 police officers who seized many smart phones and huge cash from the perpetrators (Europol 2013).

Nepal is a source country for men, women, and children who are subjected to forced labor and sex trafficking. Nepali women and girls are subjected to sex trafficking in Nepal, India, the Middle East, and China (US Department of State 2013). In addition, trafficking takes place for the purpose of organ transplant to India; to Korea and Hong Kong for the purpose of marriage and to other Asian countries including Malaysia, Hong Kong, and South Korea (National Human Rights Commission 2012). The Trafficking in Persons Report 2009 provided an estimate of 10,000 to 15,000 Nepali women and girls are trafficked to India each year (US Department of State 2009). Trafficking in women and children—both as a root cause and manifestation of poverty and human deprivation—is a major challenge to all stakeholders in Thailand. Thai women and children are trafficked to Australia, South Africa, Japan, Bahrain, Taiwan, Europe, and North America for sexual exploitation.

Internal trafficking also occurs in Thailand, involving victims from Northern Thailand. The most common trafficking routes within Thailand are from North to South and from rural areas to Bangkok (Sarkar 2011). Therefore, the main victims of trafficking are women and children and the phrase especially women and children is frequently added, in order to emphasize the links between trafficking and sexual exploitation, pornography and paedophilia.

The online sex trade is blooming even though extensive campaigns and squeeze from government leaders. The sex for pay sites exhibit ads for sex services, and these also serve as online communities where customers, pimps, and victims can arrange business transactions. The online trade has, in some ways, made sex trafficking and solicitation easier, while giving the police new insight into a historically hidden, underground mores. Challenging the sites legally has proven difficult since the websites are protected by the Communications Decency Act of 1996, which states that website owners are exempted from responsibility for the content of their users (Walter 2012).

In this study "sex trade" refers to the sexual exploitation of women and children. Among other things, it includes the production of abuse images and their online diffusion as particularly serious forms of crime committed against women and children (Buzatu 2010; Holt and Blevins 2007; Limoncelli 2009; Quayle and Taylor 2002; Quinn and Forsyth 2005). The distribution of images depicting the sexual exploitation is mainly facilitated by offensive use of the Internet. Furthermore, the relative vagueness offered by this means of communication makes it difficult to successfully locate and identify the offenders and to protect the victims from further exploitation. It must be emphasized that the discovery of illegal material is only the beginning of an investigation into the actual sexual exploitation of a woman or child. There is a fair distinction between specific legislation on the offenses related to the production, distribution or sale, and possession of sexual exploitation materials and specific legislation on sexual offenses committed against victims. While there is no doubt that the sexual abuse and exploitation of women is a serious problem, still there is a lack of accurate and reliable statistics on the nature of the phenomenon and the number of survivors involved, mainly due to differences in national definitions of precise women and children sexual abuse and exploitation offenses (Europol 2012).

Various technological advances such as social networking, micro-blogging and smart phones have enabled people to connect and transfer their activity from a private space into a public space (Kaplan and Haenlein 2009; McCartan and McAlister 2012; Moreno et al. 2012; Wood 2009). The movement of sex trafficking to a digital space can both make the crime more public, but also get rid of it from places where it has been traditionally recognized and identified. These complications present challenges for accurate identification and assessment of the nature and frequency of sex trafficking. Although the observation of technology intensifying sex trafficking has been made by scholars and professionals in the field, little research has been executed to measure the effect of technology on sex trafficking (Latonero 2012; Sykiotou 2007). The reasons for this may be several. While the crime has itself been brought more into the forefront, it is still challenging to identify. It is a crime that traditionally occurs with hidden victims who are often in transit (McGough 2013). Furthermore, it remains a very underreported crime. This continuous underreporting can be the result of many factors. One such factor could be the personal nature of the victimization consistent with that of any other sexual crime. However, the public nature of commercial exploitation can also compound the trauma of the victimization. Often victims panic revenge from their traffickers. Traffickers can be ruthless in their victimization using physical and psychological violence. In addition to legitimate fear, the underreporting can also be related to the dynamic between victim and trafficker which can inculcate anxiety (Clauson 2008), conflicting allegiances, or confusion causing the victim to fail to self-identify as victims. Furthermore, even if the crime occurs in the open, it can be difficult for both the general public as well as the inexperienced law enforcement members to recognize due to its dynamic adaptability to detection efforts.

Over the last couple of years, overall use of online social networking has steadily enhanced across the world. Social networking is a set of online sites and applications, which at least consist of three parts—users, social links, and interactive communications (Ahn et al. 2007; Wilson and Nicholas 2008). Social networks exist in a cyber space, thereby allowing individuals to create their profiles and share texts, images, videos, blogs, and links with other website members; in fact, they are currently the world's fastest growing personal networking tools (Lin and Lu 2011). A steady and considerable increase in online social network usage among teens and young adults is identified in various studies (Boyd 2004, 2007). According to the most recent Pew Internet and American Life Project report (Madden and Zickuhr 2011), 83 percent of young adults (aged 18 to 29) who surf the Internet use social networking sites. Although this represents a small decrease from 2010 (86 percent), usage of social networking sites among this age group has overall increased consistently and significantly in the past six years, from 9 percent in 2005, to 67 percent in 2008 (Madden and Zickuhr 2011). Among teens (defined in much of the literature as users between the ages of 12 and 17), use of social networking sites is also relatively high. As Lenhart et al. (2010) described in a recent Pew Internet & American Life report, 73 percent of wired American teens now use social networking websites, which represent a sharp increase from prior studies which documented social networking sites usage at 65 percent of teens in February 2008 and 55 percent of teens in November 2006. The research indicates that social networking among online teens has risen at a steady swiftness over the last several years, a trend that has been replicated in various countries around the world. For instance, a cross-national survey of the online practices of children and teens across the European Union found that 77 percent of internet users aged 13–16 years reported using a social networking site, with 46 percent identifying Facebook as the one they used the most (Livingstone, Ólafsson, and Staksrud 2011). Kaiser Family Foundation report, which reveals that in 2009 the average time spent on social networking among 8–10-year aged was 5 minutes, compared to 29 minutes for 11–14-year aged, and 26 minutes for 15–18-year aged (Rideout, Foehr, and Roberts 2010). Research by Lenhart et al. (2010) shows that female and male adolescents are equally likely to use traditional social networking sites such as Facebook, yet qualitative studies suggest important differences in the ways and places boys and girls engage online (Livingstone and Helsper 2007; Lin 2008; Fields and Kafai 2010). In March 2013, 1.11 billion people using Facebook site each month, slightly more than the 1.06 billion reported in December 2012 (The Associated Press 2013). Having surveyed teenagers in 30 countries, it was revealed that the number of teenagers claiming to be active on Facebook had 56 percent in the third quarter of 2013 (Parmy 2013). More recently, researchers began to shift their attention to self-presentations in less anonymous online environments such as Internet dating sites (Gibbs, Ellison, and Heino 2006; Yurchisin, Watchravesringkan, and McCabe 2005). Unlike Internet dating participants who are primarily looking for romantic relationships among people previously unknown to them, Facebook users are looking for friendships as well as passionate relationships among two types of people: those they know in person, and those they do not know in person (Zhao, Grasmuck, and Martin 2008). Social networking features are increasingly integrated into other types of media tools and online communities. Social networking sites invite convergence among the hitherto separate activities of e-mail, messaging, website creation, diaries, photo albums, and music or video uploading and downloading (Livingstone 2008). It should be hassled that traffickers also operate through unsolicited e-mails, luring users into revealing sensitive data via so-called phishing e-mails. Donath (2007) observed that whether face-to-face or online, much of what people want to know is not directly observable. She contended that much of human interaction consists of signals that communicate the status and characteristics of an individual. Signaling theory examines how one's self-presentation in social networking sites develops identity and trust with others. For example, when a user displays a contact as a friend he or she is, in an indirect way, vetting that that person is in fact who they claim to be. Thus, members who indiscriminately add any and all friend requests, including fake profiles or people they do not know, in an effort to seem popular may instead damage their credibility and trustworthiness to others.

ONLINE MODUS OPERANDI IN TRAFFICKING

There may be a few official records on the use of new information technologies for sexual exploitation purposes by traffickers, but there is no reason to
think that they are not using the latest technologies for trafficking purposes.
The Internet offers traffickers unprecedented opportunities, which they have
been swift to exploit. Internet, and other telecommunication technologies,
gives the sex industry and individual users new ways of finding, marketing and delivering women and children into appalling conditions of sexual
exploitation and modern-day slavery (Buzzell 2005; Hughes 2001; Lane
2000; Sharpe and Earle 2003).

Traffickers now have an effective, unrestricted means of recruiting their
victims. Online employment and marriage agencies can all be used to lure
victims (Europol 2006; Latonero 2011; Sykiotou 2007). Internet chat rooms
are often used to befriend them. For young people, the danger of falling
into the traffickers' clutches has substantially increased. Job offers through
various channels, both formal and informal, seem to be the main approach
to recruitment. Its nature being what it is, the Internet offers a broader range
of approaches to recruitment from offers aimed at a broad spectators, such
as employment opportunities basically in abroad, through the use of search
engines or pop-ups to publicize tempting offers, all the way to more targeted
spaces, for example, chat rooms, spam mail, and Internet dating, where victims can be recruited. Privacy is at risk from spyware, spread by e-mail or
software, which tracks and reports on users' behavior. Digital cameras and
recorders enable the making of images that don't need to be professionally
processed, thereby eliminating the risk of detection. These new types of
equipment also make it technologically easier for people to become producers
of pornography. Digital media formats are no longer static and independent.
One format can quickly be converted online into another. Videos are still the
primary production medium for child pornography, and the static images for
the Internet are produced from video capture (Taylor 2001). The traffickers
aggressively adopt every new communications and information technology
for the marketing, selling and transmitting pornographic materials and live
sex shows. Perpetrators also take advantage of each new technology and
application to trace victims, transmit illegal materials, and avoid detection by
law enforcement.

The traffickers and pimps use many unethical practices to draw attention
to their online sex trading sites, and trap users once they are there. They post
ads on search engines and websites with free pornography and use techniques
such as page jacking and mouse trapping to pull in people who had no intention of visiting a pornographic sites, then trapping them there as page after
page of pornography opens up when the viewer tries to go away the site.

Page jacking is a technique the perpetrators use to misdirect users so they mistakenly come to their website. There is a certain consistency in production of the sites which are mainly used to recruit victims for sexual exploitation abroad. The traffickers often set up sites in the countries of origin and in the languages of potential victims, such sites then spawn others, often building up to form national recruitment networks. The material collected via the first site is then used on a second, aimed at attracting clients. Information on the recruited victims is translated into English and the languages of other sex markets where the traffickers desire to handle. At this stage, escort service sites begin seeking subscriptions from clients, who are provided the option of paying online to visit the girls in their own countries or, alternatively, import them. If a client wants to bring a girl to his own country, a local go-between makes sure that she gets in and out safely. The same process may apply if a local trafficker wants to bring in victims advertised on the Internet and exploit them in his own business. Often, this involves contacting a broker—which can be the case with most forms of trafficking in human beings, from domestic slavery to sexual exploitation. Traffickers in these two groups may be identical (the same person) or, more often, the second may act as accomplice to the first. The third type is the trafficker who recruits victims and exploits them directly without broker via online booking with clients. A distinction should obviously be made between traffickers who set up sites themselves and then exploit the victims recruited, and operators who are paid by traffickers to set up sites, thus becoming their accomplices. These people play a key role in trafficking in human beings via the Internet, since they have the technical knowhow needed to create sites, and hide electronic traces from the police (Sykiotou 2007).

Traffickers adopt mainly two methods of online recruitment—spurious advertisements for employment, marriage, dating agencies and chat rooms. The recruitment sites often used by traffickers include marriage agency sites, escort service sites, dating clubs, employment sites seeking, for example, home helps, waitresses, hostesses, people to work in construction sites, people to take educational courses, people to work in tourism, and so on (Skrivankova 2007). The victims are normally, but not always, recruited in their own countries. There, a recruiter from the employment agency persuades them to sign an incomplete or incomprehensible job contract. The necessary documents (visa, work permit, etc.) are then procured by the agency, which normally charges a fee or makes the victim a loan to cover costs. Persons recruited are often assisted by agency representatives and, on reaching their destination, are taken over by a local contact. Supposedly for their own protection, their papers are often taken from them. Without papers, and often without knowing the local language and environment, they are easily exploited. Marriage agency, often operating online, also play a potentially significant role in recruiting victims; it is no coincidence that many are located in the main source countries, or specialize in providing women from them. On account of poverty and joblessness many women prefer to go abroad, and once a woman decides to go abroad, she will try every agency or strategy, regardless of the risk. However, this does not give us the true measure of the recruitment of victims of trafficking in human beings through marriage agencies. Cultural differences, which make recourse to marriage agencies more popular in some countries than in others, must also be considered (Sykiotou 2007).

METHOD

This study was an attempt to undertake field survey comprising interviews with victims of trafficking, traffickers, and clients to understand the role of information and communication technology in human trafficking. The survey was carried out using semi-structured questionnaire mostly open-ended question were developed for the interviews. Three different questionnaires were designed. In addition to several socio-demographic questions, the first questionnaire was targeted for trafficked survivors, with questions predominantly on how did they use technological devices under pre- and post-trafficking circumstances, and how did they advertise themselves. The second questionnaire was targeted for the traffickers who could give insight into how were diverse services and technologies used to trade in sexually exploited trafficked women. The last questionnaire was intended for the clients to identify how did they explore, communicate, and pay for their sex transaction. The framing of the questionnaire led the researcher to realize that entirely different ways would be needed to interview traffickers and clients. It was, therefore, decided to revise the questions in the questionnaire accordingly.

Locating respondents was by no means an easy task. In the case of rescued victims, some were found in rescue homes but the researchers had to search for repatriated trafficked "survivors" in the places they had been rehabilitated. In certain states where the research partners were unable to locate the respondents, the help of NGOs was sought. Interviewing victims who were still trapped in commercial sexual exploitation was the most difficult. Segregating the trafficked victims from the non-trafficked ones in the brothels was certainly no simple matter. Moreover, as they were under the complete control of the exploiters, it was not easy to get them to speak the truth. The researchers had to make repeated visits to the brothels to interview the victims and clients. Traffickers, of course, were the most difficult to find. They were interviewed with the assistance of the police higher-ups and officials from home departments or offices in the surveyed countries. Interviewing respondents raise a number of ethical questions and safety concerns for the both interviewee and interviewer. Having a sound understanding of the risks, ethical considerations, and the practical realities related to trafficking can help minimize the dangers and increase the likelihood that a participant will disclose relevant and accurate information. In this study, WHO ethical and safety recommendations for interviewing trafficked women (World Health Organization 2003) and ethical standards for counter-trafficking research and programming (United Nations 2008) were considered.

The field survey was conducted in India, Nepal, Thailand, Hungary, and United Kingdom in different time periods from November 2010 to November 2013. A total number of 246 individuals were interviewed in five countries consisting of 97 victims, 64 traffickers, and 85 clients. Since this study was designed, executed and recorded over a lengthened time period, its nature was necessarily exhaustive and exploratory. This study utilized a non-probability convenience sample and, therefore, its findings should be taken at best as indicative rather than decisive. However, findings from this study are significant, and lead the way with regard to understanding the needs of further research on technology security in combating trafficking. The findings, therefore, may be applicable for practice and policy considering the impact of technology in human trafficking.

The study involved both descriptive and generic methods. The textual data was systematically organized and analyzed. Open coding of data was used and the data were subsequently organized or grouped into concepts and later developed into contextual themes. Once the data was collected from the field, codebooks were developed based on the responses in the interview schedules. Thereupon the data in all the schedules was duly filled in and coded. The task included feeding in the data, verification, computation, and validation to facilitate data analyses and interpretation. The coded data was processed using the SPSS package. The findings are grounded with the use of direct quotes from participants. In order to be representative in selecting comments for inclusion, all responses that represent diverse thought, actions, or decisions associated with the research questions are reported. All the respondents agreed to take part when they were approached and any immediate concerns that participants may have had about the research or using interpreters were addressed prior to arranging date and time for the interview. Participants were assured that their involvement is voluntary and would not impact the support, relationships with the access to any of the services. Furthermore, participants were also informed that they could change their minds about participating or stop the interview at any time. The interviews ranged from 30 to 45 minutes with an individual respondent. In order to ensure the safety and console of participants, the interviews took place at the secured places. The interview was conducted with the help of a language interpreter for participants who preferred or spoke a different language other than English.

RESULT AND DISCUSSION

With the advancement of new technology, everyone may have unrestricted use of the Internet on their mobile phones as well as the use of applications, both of these advancements possible to make mobile phones more likely to palm of their hand laptops. Nowhere is the impact of technology on sexual violence, especially sexual abuse of trafficked victims, been more distinct than through the advent of new technology, specifically social networking sites. Creating, collecting, and distributing indecent images of women and children victims is not a new phenomenon; neither the Internet nor mobile phone technology can be held responsible for the invention of offensive images. The offensive images are now widely used by those who advocate for gender rights in relation to sexual abuse through photography and videography. Mobile phones, especially smart phones, can be used to generate and circulate sexually offensive images and video; meaning that a sexual assault can be recorded, stored, altered, uploaded, and downloaded on to the Internet to related network at a lower cost, which does not necessarily require a personal computer or laptop and can be operated easily on the victims at any time in any place.

The study shows that there was a sharp variation of using technologies among the participants before and after they were trafficked. Only 32 percent had a mobile handset in their home for emergency uses and they rarely used it due to lack of sources of monetary support for using and maintaining mobile phones but after they were trafficked and compelled to work in sex service, the survey reveals that all respondents possessed at least one mobile phone. Forty-nine percent had more than one mobile phone, and 11 percent used BlackBerry phones. The number of respondents used tablet was seven and twelve women had either personal laptop or notepad. Many respondents (74 percent) preferred their existing cell phones and the thought of upgrading is not a pleasant one. They liked their phone's features and ease of use. They didn't want to have to get used to another phone. However, there are times when upgrading a cell phone is the best option to reach maximum number of the clients at a time. Next, the users were asked to respond about the reasons why they should upgrade their cell phone. Around 25 percent of the respondents liked to have the latest features and technology, while others (14 percent) used their phones to make and receive calls because they did not prefer to work online. Eighty-three percent of the women enjoyed unlimited Internet data access facility while 56 percent had unlimited text messaging option in their mobile. However a few women (5 percent) often used the computer with Internet access. One victim from Nepal reported: "I do not know how to use Internet on mobile phone; moreover I do not have any internet facility on my mobile, my pimp contacts with client and update me their details." Survey shows that victims always did not enjoy freedom to take their individual decision; rather it was guided by their pimps.

According to the respondents (54 percent), Facebook was the most commonly used and most effective social networking site. They reported using Facebook to keep in touch with clients whom they already shared an offline connection. Facebook, Twitter, and LinkedIn were the social networking tools of choice among the participants to communicate with the clients (82 percent) while 12 percent contact with their clients by mobile calls. The motives for using these social networking among the participants were to maintain existing offline relationships (44 percent), to meet new clients (56 percent), to express or present oneself updating status or profile and express emotions to reach maximum number of the targeted clients (67 percent). The participants surfed online social networking on an average 4–6 hours a day in search of intended clients. About 73 percent reported that Facebook and Twitter was not only the best way to market themselves to rich clients but also to siphon off losers. Using partner categories for Facebook ads targeting one can reach a very specific group of clients. Many used (68 percent) sex dating sites to promote themselves by way of uploading their explicit profile pictures and video clippings and using online video chat. Facebook recently has extended its advertiser tracking capabilities into the real world through the partnership with big data brokers like Acxiom, Datalogix, and Epsilon. This data sharing will let advertisers know if people who see their ads online on Facebook. They piece together offline and online activities through personal information. They also link users' online and offline lives through their phone number or zip code. One victim from the UK described how to attract a potential client online. According to her "I post photos on websites along with my prices. I first review details of the client online who wants to buy sex. Learning more about the client beforehand helps me to make an idea of what specific he needs to get from me if we meet. I use this opportunity to get to know more about my client and let him know that he can trust me." Another woman from Hungary noted that "the first client I met was a very young guy from out of city. He was very nervous in the e-mails we transmitted, and I wasn't sure he would actually keep the date we fixed online. We met in the next evening in a pub. I wasn't flattered, but I did feel more in control."

The human trafficking is dynamic, adapting as populations become vulnerable and as areas of demand shift. The trafficker may never meet the ultimate users of the trafficked victims. The traffickers may be men and women. They are often relatives or friends. Sometimes pimps play a dual role—trafficker as well as employer. In fact, when recruiting the victim, a woman traf- ficker may appear more trustworthy than a male—especially in the case of recruiting children or young women for forced sexual exploitation. They lure their victims by using attraction, love and affection, promising a better life and opportunities to make money. Victims of human trafficking, having placed their trust in the traffickers, soon discover that those promises are false. These words of expectation might sound so reliable to poor parents wishing the best for their child. It is also the case that their circumstances may justify selling their child so that past debts can be repaid or the family can be supported for a while. Traffickers may be linked to highly organized international criminal networks, they may be involved in domestic networks, or they may operate local in a very small scale. They may be the owner of a business such as bar, pub, massage parlor, factory or farm, recruitment or marriage agency. Sometimes traffickers may become the lover or the legal spouse of a victim. In some cases, human traffickers use kidnapping as a means to procure their target. Having successfully lured their victims, the traffickers then use physical and psychological threats, humiliation, beatings, sleep-deprivation, and malnutrition in order to control them. Trafficking is the most lucrative illicit network-business with potential opportunity to the traffickers to get long-term return on investment once victim starts selling sex. An overwhelming majority of traffickers operated their business in a group (97 percent). There are a few traffickers who worked individuality (3 percent). Of the total traffickers interviewed (64 cases), 35 percent reported that they had two members in their group, 24 percent reported as three mem- bers, 21 percent as four members and another 17 percent as five or more members engaged in trafficking. Trafficking networks extend from village or working places to destination. Forty-three percent of traffickers had links with politicians, businesspersons, state officials, police officers, customs officers, border security officers, overseas recruiters, travel agents, and trans- port agencies. According to the respondents, parent (5 percent), friends (48 percent), relatives (26 percent), and villagers/local people (21 percent) were the major agents. One trafficker stated that "the lover boy approach is one of the trafficking strategies to lure the young girls. Young guy hangs around school or nearby locality, looking for vulnerable girls. He starts talking to the girl, giving her gifts, taking her around in his motorbike or car. The boy keeps the girl's family and friends away until the boy gains complete trustworthiness from the girl." Most of the traffickers (92 percent) generally adopted mobile phones to contact with these commission agents to finalize the deal. One trafficker from Thailand reported that "in addition to using the Internet, I typically use prepaid cell phone to do my business as prepaid ser- vice providers do not require that the customer should disclose their identity which eventually allows us to network without any definite record of our activities." Others (8 percent) preferred a face-to-face conversation with the agents due to fear of call tapping, but they were not scared of using Internet calling. One participant from India stated: "I always avoid calling from my prepaid mobile phone and I never use my mobile for doing this business as my identity proof and other details are kept by the service providers." Most of the traffickers (72 percent) had a propensity to change frequently their mobile number. The traffickers (92 percent) often operated their business either through a recruitment agency or marriage agency. They used online ads offering attractive jobs or imaging handsome guys in various social net-working sites to grasp the optimal number of young girls and children. For those who would like to travel abroad with the hope of higher earnings, fake employment, or marriage agency is another trap. Once the mutual negotiation is done, the traffickers hold passport and air ticket of the anticipated victim and at the last moment the agency demands money to finish it up. So people either try to sell their jewelry, land, and house or borrow money against mort-gage of property. Once the victim enters into the sphere of sex trafficking, she is used to luring friends from her native place. For young girls, the danger of falling into the traffickers' clutches has substantially increased.

In domestic trafficking, selling of the victims is comparatively trouble-free compared to cross-border trafficking. In cross-border trafficking, most of the traffickers (87 percent) used trivial airport of an intermediate country to transfer the victims, others (13 percent) handed over the victims to an Inter-national agency at the domestic airport. Mobile phones and Internet is widely used by all respondents surveyed for selling the victims to intended buyer. Generally traffickers send out all descriptions of the victims to the buyer well in advance through social networking sites where the business deal is made. Once the deal is settled, then traffickers send the victim to the potential buyer. The agent transfers the money electronically deposited to an account of the trafficker using the quick money transfer services or online banking. A highly placed trafficker makes arrangements with a well-known agent with whom he has a close relationship to remit to him a large sum of money from the destination country.

The clients often use Internet and mobile phones to search, contact and pay online for sex deal with the victims. The data indicates that the costs for sexual services borne by the clients vary widely, and the users are geographi-cally movable. In fact, clients may visit the same providers in similar regions, and know and interact with each other online and offline. Specifically, clients spend considerable time online in searching the various sexual services and prostitution available in a particular location. Clients provide information on ways to directly contact sex workers in addition to their locations. Pimps provide websites for contact information and pictures of specific sex work-ers. These websites are primarily used for access to pictures and short video clipping of different categories and age group of sex workers. Users also supply phone numbers or e-mail address that would give them direct access to a female for sex trade. Our survey shows that most of the clients (81 percent) who used Internet to search women for the purposes of sexual exploitation appeared to be traveling businessmen, tourists, and teenagers.

Among the participants, 23 percent of the clients searched for victims in chat rooms, especially those "chats" that are specifically focused around young people's interests. Client with an interest in trafficked victims sometimes worked together online with other client to help each other to find a suitable victim. This was reported by 11 percent of the clients interviewed. Client looked for potential victims by going through personal websites (4 percent). 21 percent of the clients used social networking sites. Clients often moved between different cyber-technologies as they position themselves for abuse (43 percent). They might select a victim from a picture and profile they found online from a social networking site. They then might meet the victim in an open chat room and then go into a private chat room, where they start exchanging e-mails, messages, pictures, and videos. After this, they even send the victim their mobile phone number that they can keep in secret to talk with the client for fixing the deal. The study also reveals that 25 percent of the clients had online profiles on dating sites. 11 percent of the clients were found who bought sexual services once they are away from home on either official or business trips. They preferred to search victims through a local agent. The study discloses that 56 percent of the clients paid online for the service while 27 percent made payment by cash, 7 percent did not report anything about their mode of payment. One guy from UK explained: "I was tempted by online dating, but knew that anyone I might meet would be more sexually experienced than me, and this became a major impediment" Another client from Thailand reported: "I never use online to direct communicate with girl for paid sex. I visit many places frequently for my business trips and prefer to get an escort service via agency to feel confident myself."

CONCLUSION

Traffickers use Internet in exactly the same way as formal businesses—to advertise and attract clients. They transmit their communications through a series of haulers, each using different communications technologies. In effect, such technologies have enabled them to more easily distance themselves from the offenses they perpetrate, and provide a degree of anonymity and disguise which allows them to commit their offenses with a reduced risk. The rapid expansion in the use of the Internet and mobile phone has added a new dimension to trafficking in human beings. The Internet is a fast, convenient, and cost-effective means of connecting people even without disclosing personal identity. There is a basic link between the Internet and the provision of sexual services, and it is essential to make monitoring of the Internet an integral part of any action taken against trafficking in human beings. The traffickers no longer need to put in their victims in outdated red-light districts or lay them on the streets, when clandestine arrangements can be made anonymously online, allowing clients to go to nondescript addresses in cities not previously allied with the sex trade. In such settings, victims are less likely to draw police attention, and can be strictly supervised at all times. This clearly has implications for law enforcement, which is no longer just a matter of trawling the well-known areas, arresting traffickers and rescuing victims—unfortunately, things are now a great deal more complicated (Sykiotou 2007). Some trafficking cases begin with the traffickers making contact with the potential victims on social networking sites such as Facebook and Twitter. The techniques used by the traffickers to grow faith fluctuate widely. Another type of trafficking effort starts with an online employment search and results in an unsuspecting victim moving from her place on the promise of an unbelievable job opportunity.

Traffickers are now scrutinizing on hidden pathways where limited access is permitted only to the selected clients. The traffickers and their networks make more and more use of sophisticated software in order to protect their anonymity, to make use of online storage and hosting services and to use advanced encryption techniques to counteract digital forensic investigation by police. Commercial distribution of sexually abuse material of child victim on the Internet is currently executed through the use of several, in some cases less conventional, payment systems such as money remitters and electronic money. The selection is performed by the channel's owner or managers based on the amount, nature and quality of images or video that can be shared, and even based on trust. Illegal material is increasingly self-produced by the victims who share their images or video files mainly through social media or video-enabled instant messaging among potential clients. Online grooming and the solicitation of sexual messages through mobile phones and multimedia devices are also used by the victims to lure the clients.

Certainly, the Internet is not evenly used in all the member state. One must not forget that equipment availability and infrastructure differ between states, chiefly for economic reasons. However, one should not miscalculate the velocity at which Internet use is rising (Sykiotou 2007). Unless suitable action is taken, this may lead on to an increase in victim recruitment and eventually sexual exploitation. Technology moves fast, and traffickers are always the first to exploit new developments. At the same time, sexual exploitation is not the only kind practiced via Internet. Increasingly, victims of labor exploitation are being lured by fraudulent job offers online. Combating forced sexual exploitation, including the proliferation of sexual exploitation material on the Internet, is a constant challenge for law enforcement, due to technological innovations which provide easier and faster access to the material to the offenders, while strengthening their ability to remain anonymous. It is argued that this development has created a wider market and demand for such illegal material which has inevitably led to rise in sexual exploitation of the victims. It is clear, though, that an effective partnership approach is required between law enforcement agencies, judicial authorities, the information technology sector, mobile and Internet service providers, the banking sector and nongovernmental organizations.

REFERENCES

Ahn, Y. Y. et al. 2007. "Analysis of Topological Characteristics of Huge Online Social Networking Services." Proceedings of the 16th International Conference. *World Wide Web* 2(6): 835–844.

Boyd, D. 2004. *Friendster and Publicly Articulated Social Networks*. Conference on Human Factors and Computing Systems, Association of Computing Machinery, Vienna.

Boyd, D. 2007. "Why Youth (Heart) Social Network Sites: The Role of Networked Publics in Teenage Social Life." In *MacArthur Foundation Series on Digital Learning: Youth, Identity, and Digital Media Volume*, edited by D. Buckingham. Cambridge, MA: MIT Press.

Buzatu, C. 2010. *Transnational Cooperation against Human Trafficking*. Budapest: Passzer Kft.

Buzzell, T. 2005. "The Effects of Sophistication, Access and Monitoring on Use of Pornography in Three Technological Contexts." *Deviant Behavior* 26: 109–132.

Clauson, H. 2008. *Identifying Victims of Human Trafficking, Inherent Challenges & Promising Strategies from the Field*. Washington, DC: US Department of Health and Human Services.

Donath, J. 2007. "Signals in Social Supernets." *Journal of Computer-Mediated Communication* 13(1): 231–251.

Ellison, N., Heino, R., and Gibbs, J. 2006. "Managing Impressions Online: Self-presentation Processes in the Online Dating Environment." *Journal of Computer Mediated Communication* 11(2): 415–441.

Europol. 2006. *Organised Crime Threat Assessment Report 2006*. The Hague, Netherlands.

Europol. 2012. *Child Sexual Exploitation Fact Sheet 2012*. The Hague, Netherlands.

Europol. 2013. *Major People Smuggling Criminal Network Dismantled Across Europe*. Press Release, 30 January, The Hague, Netherlands.

Fields, D. A. and Kafai, Y. B. 2010. "Knowing and Throwing Mudballs, Hearts, Pies, and Flowers: A Connective Ethnography of Gaming Practices." *Games and Culture* 5(1): 88–115.

Finkenauer, J. O. 2001. "Russian Transnational Organized Crime and Human Trafficking." In *Global Human Smuggling: Comparative Perspectives*, edited by David Kyle and Rey Koslowski. Baltimore: The Johns Hopkins University Press.

Gibbs, J. L., Ellison, N. B., and Heino, R. D. 2006. "Self-presentation in Online Personals: The Role of Anticipated Future Interaction, Self-disclosure, and Perceived Success in Internet Dating." *Communication Research* 33(2): 152–177.

Holt, T. J. and Blevins, K. R. 2007. "Examining Sex Work from the Client's Perspective: Assessing Johns Using Online Data." *Deviant Behavior* 28: 333–354.

Hughes, D. M. 2001. *The Impact of the Use of New Communications and Information Technologies on Trafficking in Human Beings for Sexual Exploitation: A Study of the Users*. Council of Europe.

Kaplan, A. and Haenlein, M. 2009. "The Fairyland of Second Life: Virtual Social Worlds and How to Use them." *Business Horizons* 52(6): 563–572.

Lane, F. S. 2000. *Obscene Profits: The Entrepreneurs of Pornography in the Cyber Age*. New York: Routledge.

Latonero, M. 2011. *Human Trafficking Online: The Role of Social Networking Sites and Online Classifieds*. Los Angeles, CA: University of South California.

Latonero, M. 2012. *The Rise of Mobile and the Diffusion of Technology-facilitated Trafficking*. Research Series on Technology and Human Trafficking Center on Communication Leadership & Policy. Los Angeles, CA: University of South California.

Lenhart, A., Purcell, K., Smith, A., and Zickuhr, K. 2010. *Social Media & Mobile Internet Use among Teens and Young Adults*. Washington, DC: Pew Internet and American Life Project.

Limoncelli, Stephanie A. 2009. "The Trouble with Trafficking: Conceptualizing Women's Sexual Labour and Economic Human Rights." *Women's Studies International Forum* 32(4): 261–269.

Lin, H. 2008. "A Cultural Geography of Gaming Experiences in Homes, Cybercafés and Dormitories." In *Beyond Barbie and Mortal Kombat: New Perspectives on Gender and Gaming*, edited by Y. B. Kafai, C. Heeter, J. Denner, and J. Sun. Cambridge, MA: MIT Press.

Lin, K. and Lu, H. 2011. "Why People Use Social Networking Sites: An Empirical Study Integrating Network Externalities and Motivation Theory." *Computers in Human Behavior* 27: 1152–1161.

Livingstone, S. 2008. "Taking Risky Opportunities in Youthful Content Creation: Teenagers' Use of Social Networking Site for Intimacy, Privacy, and Self-expression." *New Media & Society* 10(3): 393–411.

Livingstone, S. and Helsper, E. J. 2007. "Gradations in Digital Inclusion: Children, Young People and the Digital Divide." *New Media & Society* 9: 671–696.

Livingstone, S., Ólafsson, K., and Staksrud, E. 2011. *Social Networking, Age and Privacy*. London: EU Kids Online.

Madden, M. and Zickuhr, K. 2011. *65 Percent of Online Adults Use Social Networking Sites: Women Maintain their Foothold on SNS Use and Older Americans are Still Coming Aboard*. Washington, DC: Pew Internet and American Life Project.

McCartan, K. F. and McAlister, R. 2012. "Mobile Phone Technology and Sexual Abuse." *Information & Communications Technology Law* 21(3): 257–268.

McGough, M. 2013. "Ending Modern Day Slavery: Using Research to Inform US Anti-trafficking Efforts." *National Institute of Justice Journal* (271): 1–7.

Moreno, M. A. et al. 2012. "A Pilot Evaluation of Older Adolescents' Sexual Reference Displays on Facebook." *Journal of Sex Research* 49(4): 390–399.

National Human Rights Commission. 2012. *Trafficking in Persons, Especially on Women and Children in Nepal*. National Report 2011. Lalitpur, Kathmandu: National Human Rights Commission.

Parmy, O. 2013. *Here's Where Teens are Going Instead of Facebook*. http://www.forbes.com/sites/parmyolson/2013/11/12/heres-where-teens-are-going-instead-of-facebook/.

Quayle, E. and Taylor, M. 2002. "Child Pornography and the Internet: Perpetuating a Cycle of Abuse." *Deviant Behavior* 23: 331–361.

Quinn, J. F. and Forsyth, C. J. 2005. "Describing Sexual Behavior in the Era of the Internet: A Typology for Empirical Research." *Deviant Behavior* 26: 191–207.

Rideout, V. J., Foehr, U. G., and Roberts, D. F. 2010. *Generation M2: Media in the Lives of 8 to 18 Year Olds*. California: A Kaiser Family Foundation Study.

Sarkar, S. 2011. "Trafficking in Women and Children to India and Thailand: Characteristics, Trends and Policy Issues." *International Journal of Afro-Asian Studies* 2(1): 57–73.

Sharp, K. and Earle, S. 2003. "Cyberpunters and Cyberwhores: Prostitution on the Internet." In *Dot Cons: Crime, Deviance and Identity on the Internet*, edited by Y. Jewkes. Cullompton, UK: Willan Publishing.

Skrivankova, K. 2007. *Anti-slavery International*. Presented at the Council of Europe Seminar on the Misuse of the internet for the recruitment of victims of trafficking in human beings, 7–8 June, Strasbourg.

Sykiotou, A. P. 2007. *Trafficking in Human Beings: Internet Recruitment*. Council of Europe: Directorate General of Human Rights and Legal Affairs.

Taylor, M. et al. 2001. "Child Pornography: The Internet and Offending." *Canadian Journal of Policy Research* 2(2): 94–100.

The Associated Press. 2013. *How Facebook has Grown: Number of Active Users at Facebook over the Years*. http://news.yahoo.com/number-active-users-facebook-over-230449748.html.

United Nations. 2001. *Protocol to Prevent, Suppress and Punish Trafficking in Persons, Especially Women and Children*. New York: United Nations.

United Nations. 2008. *Guide to Ethics and Human Rights in Counter-trafficking: Ethical Standards for Counter-trafficking Research and Programming*. Bangkok: United Nations Inter-Agency Project on Human Trafficking.

US Department of State. 2004. *The Link between Prostitution and Sex Trafficking*. Washington, DC.

US Department of State. 2009. *Trafficking in Persons Report 2009*. Washington, DC.

US Department of State. 2013. *Trafficking in Persons Report 2013*. Washington, DC.

Walter, S. 2012. "Online Sex Trade is Flourishing Despite Efforts to Curb it." *The New York Times*, March 16: A21A.

Wilson, M. and Nicholas, C. 2008. "Topological Analysis of an Online Social Network for Older Adults." *Proceeding of the 2008 ACM Workshop on Search in Social Media* 2(6): 51–58.

Wood, C. 2009. "The Power of Social Media: From Bolt-on to the Centre of the Universe." *The Hospitality Review* 8(3): 18–19.

World Health Organization. 2003. *WHO Ethical and Safety Recommendations for Interviewing Trafficked Women*. Geneva: World Health Organization.

Yurchisin, J., Watchravesringkan, K., and McCabe, D. B. 2005. "An Exploration of Identity Re-creation in the Context of Internet Dating." *Social Behavior and Personality* 33(8): 735–750.

Zhao, S., Sherri, G., and Jason, M. 2008. "Identity Construction on Facebook: Digital Empowerment in Anchored relationships." *Computers in Human Behavior* 24(5): 1816–1836.

Chapter 2

Financial Flows in Trafficking

The rise of sexual exploitation has been rapid and in fact a global phenomenon, depicting increasing numbers of children and young women into this domain. The growth of this crime is hasty due to nonexistence of certainty or severity of punishment. Human trafficking gains public attention as a result of economic and demographic inequalities in the world, the upswing of conflict and gender discrimination. Typical regional differences in trafficking are not a contemporary experience. In the past, there was no single model of slavery. Just as the trade in human beings was warped in the past by cultural, geographic, and economic forces, today's human trafficking is also shaped by these forces as well as historical traditions. Slavery is illegal throughout the world, yet more than twenty-seven million people are still lured in one of history's oldest social institutions (Shelley 2010).

Trafficking in persons is not only a threat to the individual, but to entire communities that come across themselves at risk, because of poor socioeconomic factors. Additionally, in transition societies, trafficking in persons also constitutes a threat to the system of law and order, which is *per se* a threat to the essential components of the state, since by evading the law and corrupting state officials the traffickers threaten citizens' larger interests of security and protection. Trafficking in persons is a human rights violation and is so "damaging to its victims, which it has become a cause of human insecurity" (Bales 1999).

First, trafficking in persons represent a threat to the individuals and their inherent basic human right and freedom. Regardless of the form of exploitation, vulnerable people around the world end up in the webs of traffickers for whom each represents a continuous source of profit, as victims are sold time and again, unlike the one-time trade in drug and arms. Paradoxically, they are

21

at the same time highly expendable, easily replaceable assets (Miller 2006), because victims are considered by the criminals to be disposable goods, it makes the former' situation extremely dangerous and uncertain. In the case of external trafficking, the victims are in a particularly vulnerable situation because of their illegal status of residence.

The involvement of organized criminal networks is equally damaging to the fabric of a community and eventually the general society. The presence and power of organized crime networks can influence the community behavior in two ways that are each equally perilous to the principle and practice of democracy. First, because they locally provide "jobs" and a sort of social safety net, people tend to view them sympathetically and support their activities instead of fighting them. Second, because they succeed in corrupting officials and weakening the enforcement system, many citizens lose the trust in their country's government and more severely in the rule of law. Moreover, because they have a stake in maintaining a country unstable and lawless, they have an incentive to oppose return to normality in post-conflict societies. Consequently, this is not only just a form of forced labor and a violation of the human rights of the people, but it is also a crime that weakens the socioeconomic and legislative bases of the state (Woodward 2005). Increasingly, due to the fact that restrictive migration policies and immigration controls imply much more sophistication than the individual operators and the small gangs can provide, large transnational organized crime networks have been claiming a monopoly over smuggling and cross-border trafficking in human beings. Furthermore, the "low risk high profit" characteristics of trafficking are highly attractive for organized criminal networks who use the money thus obtained to finance other criminal activities like extortion, racketeering, money laundering, drug and arms trade, loan sharking, and the bribery of state functionaries. Thus, traffickers are threatening the state and undermining its authority and legitimacy, and they do so by using its powers, and by corrupting officials and law enforcement officers (Väyrynen 2005).

Being a complex phenomenon, problem of trafficking is profoundly entrenched in the socioeconomic, political, and cultural reality of the context in which it occurs, although this may not be its immediate cause. The perpetrators are the traffickers about them relatively little are known. This gap has to be urgently addressed, along with the demand factors, which drive trafficking. It is a fundamental violation of the rights of human beings and shows a blatant disregard for the dignity of a person (Sarkar 2011a). The scale of the phenomenon of trafficking is difficult to judge. It is very difficult to collect data on trafficking because of the clandestine nature of the operations. The trade is secretive, the women are silenced, the traffickers are dangerous and not many agencies are counting (Hughes 2000). Human trafficking trade generates sizable amounts of funds that need to be laundered (Savona 1997).

Money is the root cause of many evils like corruption, black marketing, smuggling, drug trafficking, tax evasion, and the buck does not stop here; it goes to the extent of sex tourism and human trafficking (a human selling another human in the era of human rights). Money laundering has a close nexus with organized crime (Moneyval 2005; US Department 2009). Money launderers accumulate enormous profits through sex trafficking. Cash trans- actions are predominantly used for money laundering as they facilitate the concealment of the true ownership and origin of money. It is well recognized that through the huge profits the criminals earn from sex trafficking and other illegal means, by way of money laundering could contaminate and corrupt the structure of the State at all levels, this definitely leads to corruption. Further, this adds to constant pursuit of profits and the expansion into new areas of criminal activity.

INDIA AND UK RESPONSES TO SEX TRAFFICKING

Among the most quoted figures are the United Nations estimates that 4 mil- lion people in a year are traded against their will to work in some form of slavery, in which many of them are children. In the last thirty years, traf- ficking in women and children for sexual exploitation in Asia alone has victimized more than 30 million people. Asia is mainly an origin region as well as a destination for trafficking in persons. Asian victims are reported to be trafficked from Asia to Asian countries, in particular to Thailand, Japan, India, Taiwan, and Pakistan (United Nations 2006). The US Department of State estimates that 600,000 to 800,000 (of which around 250,000 in Europe) women and children are trafficked for sexual purposes across international borders each year, of which approximately 80 percent are women and 50 percent are minors. In addition to sex trafficking, 12.3 million people are trafficked worldwide for labor exploitation annually as reported by the Inter- national Labour Organization (ILO) (US Department of State 2006).

India is located in the golden triangle which is the most vulnerable region for the trafficking of women and children for flesh trade (Westwood 1998). Literature on trafficking in India is completely dominated by the issue of commercial sexual exploitation, so much so that trafficking as a distinct separate crime does not get highlighted. At times it is almost reduced to insignificance in comparison to commercial sexual exploitation. Even though there seems to be considerable information available, one is unable to form a picture which reflects the reality of trafficking in women and children in India (Sen and Nair 2004). The trafficking definition legally explains exploitation, the exploiter and the exploited for the first time in India's Independent his- tory. Exploitation is defined as forced labor or services, slavery, or practices similar to slavery, servitude, forced removal of organs and prostitution, or other forms of sexual exploitation (Sarkar 2011b).

Calculations of trafficked people are generally made with reference to commercial sex exploitation. In India, the stigma attached to prostitution and the clandestine nature of operations makes it doubly difficult to arrive at authentic numbers (Gupta 2003). Increasing incidence of trafficking has threatened the social fabric of the country. Girls under eighteen are being lured from Nepal, Bangladesh to Indian metropolitan cities. In India, traffickers also lure girls and young women from Assam, West Bengal, Bihar, Rajasthan, Jharkhand, Madhya Pradesh, Chhattisgarh, and Uttar Pradesh. The counterfeit promises of jobs and better living standards push these girls and young women into prostitution (Sarkar 2011a).

Bangladesh is a major country of origin and transit for trafficking in persons, especially forced labor and forced prostitution. There is internal trafficking within the country, but a large proportion of trafficking is cross border. Often such transactions are carried out with ease. There are many enclaves between the border of India and Bangladesh. There are 111 Indian enclaves in Bangladesh and 51 enclaves in Bangladesh in India. Traffickers often use these enclaves as recruitment and collection sites. Many border areas are frequently used as land routes for trafficking. A large proportion of cross-border trafficking of women and children in Bangladesh is due to illegal migration in search of better employment to India. Recruiting agencies acting as middlemen in such cases often charge exorbitantly, and there have been a number of cases of recruitment fraud where such female migrants are misled about terms of employment including payment. They find themselves being forced to work in prostitution.

Movement of persons from Nepal to India is quite easy considering the long border it has with India. There are fourteen legal entry points, but illegal cross-border movement without documents often takes place as India has an open border policy with Nepal. Nepalese have free access to enter India, and, therefore, trafficking becomes difficult to identify. Nepal's concerns also include making it less economically lucrative to go to India providing alternatives within Nepal considering the poverty, the lack of educational and job opportunities available in Nepal. These concerns need to be addressed in order to tackle push factors, which make vulnerable female victims of trafficking (Sarkar 2011b).

Therefore, female trafficking and illegal migration, which works through social network in Bangladesh, Nepal, and India, are a very complex and multi-casual phenomenon. Trafficking involves deep-rooted process of gender discrimination, lack of female education, ignorance of rural folk, poverty and lack of economic opportunities. Woman's lack of empowerment or lack of information about what may happen if they migrate—these factors can be assumed to increase vulnerability to trafficking. Hence economics of illegal female migration can be linked with economics of trafficking.

Besides, during 2011, 946 potential victims of human trafficking in the UK were referred to the National Referral Mechanism (NRM). Of these, 634 were females and 312 were males, 712 were adults and 234 were children. The majority of potential child victims were reported to be in the 16–17-year-old age category (UK Home Office 2012a). The most prevalent source countries for potential victims who were referred into the NRM were Nigeria, China, Vietnam, Romania, and Slovakia. The most prevalent exploitation type recorded through the NRM, for adults, was sexual exploitation however it is recognized that the incidence of labor exploitation and criminal exploitation is increasing. The most prevalent type of exploitation reported for children was labor exploitation. The recently published Serious Organized Crime Agency (SOCA 2013) Intelligence Assessment report suggests that there are 2,250 potential victims of human trafficking were encountered during 2012 in the UK, which represents an increase of 178 (9 percent) compared to those reported in 2011. Of the 2255 potential victims 1246 (55 percent) were female, 910 (40 percent) were male and the gender of 95 (5 percent) of potential victims was unknown. 1607 (71 percent) of all potential victims were adults, 549 (24 percent) were children and the age of 99 (5 percent) of potential victims was unknown. Potential victims were from seventy-eight different countries of origin. Where identified, the most frequently recorded countries of origin were Romania 272 (12 percent), Poland 240 (11 percent), Nigeria 209 (9 percent), Vietnam 133 (6 percent), Hungary 125 (6 percent), Albania 107 (5 percent), Slovakia 103 (5 percent), UK 86 (4 percent), Lithuania 77 (3 percent) and the Philippines 53 (2 percent). The country of origin of 333 (15 percent) potential victims was unknown. Sexual exploitation (35 percent) and labor exploitation (23 percent) were the two most prevalent exploitation types as assessed by SOCA (SOCA 2013).

Because of the covert nature of human trafficking, the crime is difficult to detect. Organized criminals are involved in the exploitation of people for profit with the largest number of Organized Crime Groups (OCGs) reported to be from Romania. The UK uses a range of intelligence tools to understand the threat of human trafficking and deploys a range of tactics to deter and disrupt trafficking activity. Understanding the recruitment methods used by traffickers is important in mitigating the risk to individuals, and closing down identified trafficking routes and practices. Risk profiles are also used by Border Force to help facilitate the identification of more potential trafficking victims and assist in carefully targeted operational activities against trafficking.

The UK Government published its Human Trafficking Strategy in 2011 which aims to take a comprehensive approach by focusing on preventing trafficking activity and maintaining effective care for victims. Actions have been taken forward to improve the awareness of frontline professionals so that they can better identify, support, and protect victims. Effective adult care arrangements for human trafficking victims are in place across the UK.

Increased international engagement is helping the UK to gain a better understanding of the human trafficking landscape, to raise awareness, and to assist in strengthening law enforcement and justice systems in priority source countries. Concentrated efforts have been made by a range of agencies to work together to share information and maximize capabilities to provide an effective response at the border. Law enforcement agencies across the UK also work collaboratively and with their counterparts in other countries to share intelligence and collectively target traffickers. Raising public awareness of human trafficking, working in partnership with NGOs, and tackling the demand for cheap services and goods are also key aspects of the UK's strategy.

Tackling human trafficking in all its forms is vital and the UK is committed to continually shaping and tailoring its response to mitigate the threat. Although the UK has already achieved significant progress in the fight against trafficking, it recognizes that any response must be able to quickly adapt and evolve to keep pace with the traffickers. Three key areas have been identified where further concerted effort is needed to improve and strengthen the UK's approach: data capture and intelligence sharing, training and awareness raising for frontline professionals, and coordinating prevention activities. The UK is not complacent about the efforts required to stop people from being trafficked for exploitation or punishing the perpetrators and will continue to work collaboratively with stakeholders and key agencies as well as supporting source countries in tackling the issues that fuel the demand for human trafficking. Human trafficking is an abhorrent crime which affects communities throughout the world. The international nature of human trafficking means that it knows no boundaries. The UK Government recognizes the importance of working collaboratively with partners both in the UK and overseas, and of using all the available tools in the fight against organized criminals who seek to exploit others.

However, harsh legislation in itself is not the answer. To rely solely on prosecuting and convicting the perpetrators means that a failure to tackle the core issue, protecting the vulnerable people who are susceptible to traffickers in the first place. Stopping traffickers by deterring and disrupting their activities will help to protect the men, women and children who may fall prey to these despicable acts.

The UK already works with international partners to ensure that, where possible, the threat of trafficking is reduced. Law enforcement agencies in the UK work with their counterparts in other countries to pool resources to tackle trafficking and to bring the perpetrators of this terrible crime to justice, often through joint investigations. It is this kind of collaborative action that will certainly perk up national and international response to human trafficking. From 2013, the new National Crime Agency is also playing a key role in the fight against traffickers through its enhanced intelligence capabilities and its coordination and tasking functions (UK Home Office 2012b).

For Indian government to respond more effectively and carry out the counter-network and counter-market strategy, they need to set up a system that looks remarkably similar to the one they are trying to destroy. It looks initially at the limits of governance, both in general and specifically in relation to combating human trafficking. It then suggests that the networks involved in human trafficking are agile and difficult to combat, especially because they operate within a dynamic market characterized not only by a high demand for forced labor and commercial sex but also a ready supply of trafficking victims. In short, human trafficking poses enormous challenges to governance and law enforcement, and, at times, these challenges seem to be overwhelming. Even if it is something, which is unlikely to be eliminated, however, more effective steps can be taken to contain or even reduce the scope of the problem. This, in turn, has to be manifest in more effective laws against human trafficking. Many countries continue to have inadequate laws, enforcement is often both problematic and misguided (e.g., treating women who have been trafficked for commercial sex as criminals rather than victims, or simply failing to provide adequate levels of protection and assistance), and on those occasions when penalties are enforced they are often ridiculously low. The fact is that too many states continue to provide safe havens for traffickers and trafficking further reduces the effectiveness of the modest efforts at international law enforcement cooperation, which are currently in place. These issues can only be overcome by a concerted effort to raise the priority of combating human trafficking and by both exerting pressure on and enhancing capacity in country like India, which still lack legal instruments and serious anti-trafficking activities.

LAUNDERING MECHANISM

Human trafficking market is a monopolistic competition consisting of many sellers and buyers dealing in differentiated products. Traffickers transcend some barriers to enter the market when they perceive profit being made by other perpetrators or exit the market immediately when there is less possibility of making any profit. The ease of entry and exit rules out a monopoly or oligopoly. Despite the huge number of suppliers in the market, product differentiation (in this market, trafficked individuals with different personal attributes) allows monopolistically competitive sellers to have some control over the price at which they offer their products.

The monopolistic competition model best fits the market for human trafficking for a number of reasons. First, there are numerous sellers in the market. Whether human trafficking is by organized groups of criminals or by tiny, loose networks of entrepreneurs, the benefits so greatly offset the costs that a willing cadre of traffickers is assured. Second, many buyers demand human trafficking victims for employment for a variety of reasons. Employing trafficked individuals is by nature exploitative. In many cases, the trafficked individual does not have the right to decide whether to work, how many hours to work, or what kind of work to perform. Third, the human trafficking market is characterized by product differentiation.

Human traffickers partake in a monopolistically competitive market supplying a product in many forms. The price the trafficker will get is based on availability of the desired product, characteristics of the product, the number of similar products available, and the negotiating acumen of the human trafficker. At very low prices, human traffickers will be unwilling and unable to supply trafficked individuals because costs exceed revenue. If the trafficker's costs do not change, an increase in the price received leads to increased profit and thus an increase in the number of trafficked individuals supplied.

In the human trafficking market, traffickers act as intermediaries to provide employers, who use trafficked labor, with workers who have the desired characteristics. The successful human trafficker's business is dynamic, adapting as populations become vulnerable and as areas of demand shift. The trafficker may never meet the ultimate users of the trafficked victims. Human traffickers offer differentiated products; limiting the number and type of individuals they traffic to employers (or use as employers). This means that each human trafficker faces an individual demand curve for his product. This demand curve depends partly upon how unique consumers perceive the supplier's product to be in comparison with similar products available from other suppliers.

There is a rational economic calculus underlying traffickers' involvement in the trade. Kelly and Regan (2000) describe how traffickers view women and children as commodities, from which they seek to profit. Salt and Stein (1997) state that "the migration business may be thought of as a system of institutionalized networks with complex profit and loss accounts, including a set of institutions, agents and individuals, each of which stands to make a commercial gain." The revenue from human trafficking is large, an annual estimated average of US$ 13,000 per trafficked victim totaling US$ 32 billion (Belser 2005). Trafficked individuals are assessed as much as US$ 100,000 each in the United States (Zakhari 2005). Human traffickers face monetary (operational), physical (risk to life and health), psychological, and criminal (risk of being caught and severity of punishment) costs. In addition to the cost of moving individuals from one place to another, transportation costs include the costs of outfitting individuals for travel and falsified documents.

There are also reports of traffickers presenting a sum of money to the families of children they traffic as signs of goodwill. Hughes (2000) weighs the low risk faced by traffickers with the potentially high profits due to "computer communication of international financial transactions, political and economic weakening and collapse, and the desire to migrate." In the short run, the human trafficker gains economic profit (total revenue minus total cost, including the opportunity cost of using inputs) by selling at a price above average total cost of trafficking persons. Average total cost includes average fixed costs (an average of those costs that have been paid and cannot be recovered) and average variable costs (costs that vary depending upon the individuals and circumstances necessary for trafficking). Average fixed cost includes the cost of establishing routes, recurring bribes, and forged travel documents. Because of these high fixed costs, average total cost is high at low quantities of trafficked individuals and decreases as operations increase in size, up to a certain point. Average variable cost consists of specific travel arrangements that vary based upon the individuals and changing characteristics of transportation. As the quantity of trafficking by an individual trafficker increases, the average total cost begins to rise due to the increase in average total costs brought about by the complicated logistics of illegally transporting larger numbers of people. Thus the average total cost curve is at first downward sloping and then upward sloping. The marginal revenue (additional revenue from the last unit supplied) curve for a human trafficker is downward sloping. At very low quantities, the trafficker can charge very high prices to those employers who demand trafficked workers. Employers are willing to pay lower prices as more trafficked workers become available in the human trafficking market. Thus the marginal revenue curve is downward sloping.

Marginal cost is the additional cost to the trafficker of the last unit (trafficked person) supplied. The cost of supplying the first unit of trafficking is high because of the (fixed) costs of setting up the trafficking network in addition to the variable costs of transporting the individual. The additional cost of supplying the second trafficked person is much lower because the fixed costs have already been taken into account with the first person. We assume, therefore, that the marginal cost is very low for each of the first few trafficked individuals after the first one. As the trafficker increases the number of individuals supplied, marginal cost increases to account for the increased costs of providing documentation, housing, and transportation to a larger group of people. This means that the marginal cost curve in figure 2.1 is upward sloping (Wheaton et al. 2010).

A trafficker will choose the quantity of individuals to traffic based upon maximizing profit. This occurs at the point (Quantity* on figure 2.1) where marginal revenue equals marginal cost. At any quantity above this point, the cost of supplying the individual is greater than the revenue received from the

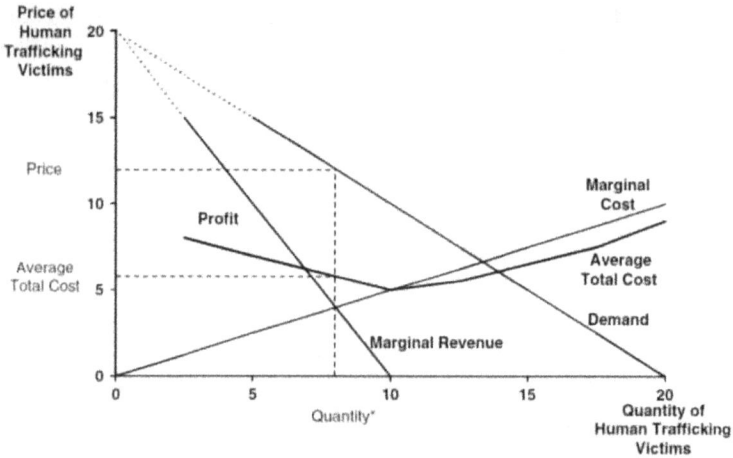

Figure 2.1   Short-run Supply of Human Trafficking by an Individual Trafficker in a Monopolistically Competitive Market. *Source*: Wheaton, E. M. et al. 2010, 125.

sale of the individual, thus driving down profit. The profit is shown as the area below the demand curve between price and average total cost. Faced with an average total cost greater than price, suppliers will exit the market. When other entrepreneurs find that there is economic profit in the human trafficking market, more suppliers enter the market. When there is an influx of a certain type of trafficked individuals (an increase in supply), there is greater competition and differentiated products become more similar, which drives down prices. In the long run, this means the individual trafficker's demand curve will shift left showing a decrease in the part of the entire human trafficking market provided by that trafficker. Suppliers will continue to enter and exit the market based on the possibility of profit until economic profit (which takes into account the opportunity cost of using inputs) is zero. Although economic profit is zero, accounting profit (revenue minus monetary costs, excluding opportunity costs) is positive for those traffickers remaining in the market. For an individual supplier, this is the point where price equals average total cost for the individual trafficker as shown in figure 2.2. It is reasonable to assume that traffickers who accept the lower profit include those who have the lowest costs, are desperate for money, have networks in which the victims can be resold, or are involved in multistage operations in which there are different uses of the trafficked victims. A trafficker knows that he is taking a risk in his chosen business and that his liberty and safety are constantly threatened.

The profits made by traffickers may be computed as in equation [1], total profits (π) can be broadly defined as the total economic value added (VA)

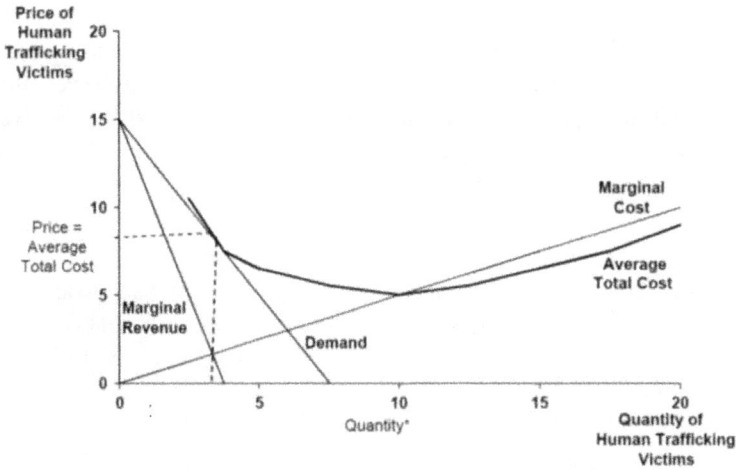

Figure 2.2 Long-run Supply of Trafficking by an Individual Trafficker in a Mono-politically Competitive Market. *Source*: Wheaton, E. M. et al. 2010,127.

minus total wage payments (W) excluding rents and interest or capital depreciation.

$$\pi = VA - W \qquad [1]$$

In the case of trafficking, wages are usually below market rates and many victims are paid just enough for their subsistence. In the most extreme cases, traffickers and other perpetrators have complete discretion over the payments to trafficking victims. Hence, it is difficult to consider whatever payment the victims receive as a "wage" in its standard definition, that is, the compensation obtained by voluntary workers in the labor market. This, however, does not change the fact that the expenditures for the subsistence of workers reduce the profits of the perpetrators and, hence, must be deducted from value added. Thus, whenever possible, we use equation [1] to estimate profits.

If data on value added is not available, profits can be estimated by using information on turnover and intermediate expenditures. Equation [1] can be rewritten as shown in equation [2], where profits (π) are equal to the difference between the total turnover (T)—that is, the total value of goods or services produced and the sum of wage payments (W) and intermediate consumption (C), which is the expenditure for all necessary inputs, such as rent for example.

$$\pi = T - (W + C) \qquad [2]$$

As shown in equation [3], turnover (T) is equal to the number of workers (N) multiplied by the average value of the goods and services produced by each worker (t)—which is itself equal to the physical number of units of goods or services produced by each worker (q) multiplied by the average price of the goods or services produced (p).

$$T = t. N = (q. p). N \tag{3}$$

It follows from this last equation that global profits (π) made from trafficking victims are ultimately equal to the average number of units of goods or services produced by each worker (q) multiplied by the average price of these units (p), minus the sum of average wage (w) and intermediate consumption (c), and multiplied by the number of forced laborers (N).

$$\pi = \left[(q. p) - (w + c) \right]. N \tag{4}$$

These equations show that the profits are not restricted to the earnings of networks who act only as intermediaries, recruiting and trafficking people across borders and "selling" them to criminal enterprises. The calculations refer to the broader annual profits made by the criminal agents or enterprises that exploit trafficked persons at the point of destination (and out of which the intermediaries are being paid). That is, profits are the whole net value created by the work of trafficking victims (Belser 2005).

METHOD

This study was designed to understand the basic structure of criminal organizations and principles of distributing the proceeds between the various levels in the organizations based on the empirical information obtained through the field survey from India and the UK. Since this study was designed, executed and recorded over a six-month period starting from June 2013 to November 2013, its nature was necessarily limited and exploratory, and its findings should be taken at best as suggestive rather than decisive. Semi-structured interviews with the exploiters of trafficking survivors were conducted in India and the UK. Recruiting a sample for research on the demand for commercial sex workers presented great methodological challenges. There was no sampling frame listing everyone who used sex trafficking and it was, therefore, impossible to obtain a random or probability sample of these particular population groups. Accessing clients or pimps who broke the law or engaged in practices regarded as socially undesirable (for instance, buying sexual services where it is illegal to do so, or who contravene legislation regulating the employment of sex workers after they have been trafficked) was even more difficult. It took time to find people willing to be interviewed about personal and sensitive topics and since we had very little time, we recognized that it would be realistic to aim for at least fifty individual interviews in both the countries. This meant that the interview research was not, nor could have been, undertaken with a representative cross-section of either. Because we were keen to generate comparable, cross-national data, the research design included the exploring demand for commercial sex to be undertaken in each country. Ultimately, it proved impossible to standardize the sampling techniques used in each country in the time available. Though the survey on trafficking for sexual servitude produced some very interesting data, unfortunately they were not fully comparable. The survey comprised total of 124 respondents from India and the UK, with 68 from India (37 victims and 31 exploiters) and 56 (31 victims and 25 exploiters) from the UK. A standardized questionnaire was used for both the countries. The multistage stratified sampling technique was undertaken. The survey covered rural, semi-urban, and urban areas in each of the sample countries. In each area, interviews were proportionally distributed according to the size of settlement. Within each group, settlements were randomly selected applying probabilities proportional to size.

The findings from each of the country studies cannot necessarily be generalized as representative of the country as a whole. The markets for commercial sex are extremely diverse. This means that there is no one single type of employer or client. Therefore, the findings from interview research with a small and non-random sample of employers and clients in each given location cannot be taken as providing a snapshot of all forms of demand in that location. Although we aimed to standardize research on clients and employers in the countries involved to make data sets from each country comparable, this proved to be impossible in the time frame and resources accessible. Instead of a comparative cross-national study, we have a series of studies in two countries, elements of which are comparable. This means that the data need to be treated with immense prudence.

RESULTS AND DISCUSSION

Unsurprisingly, there is little official data on the economics of trafficking. In fact, the very notion of economic "value added" may seem inappropriate when applied to sex trafficking and is sometimes rejected by anti-prostitution groups. The legality or illegality of sex trafficking is irrelevant, as both legal and illegal production should be included in the systems of national accounts.

By excluding illegal or underground activities, national accounts would simply exclude monetary transactions that actually take place and hence would provide a distorted picture of reality. It should be clear that by referring to the activity and to the revenue it generates, the ILO does not endorse or legitimize it. The lack of data on the economic value added of sex trafficking is largely explained by the fact that trafficking for sexual exploitation is usually part of the non-observed economy (Belser 2005). In view of these facts, the basic structure of criminal organizations and principles of distributing the proceeds between the various levels in the organizations based on the empirical information obtained through the field study in India and the UK has been come out. The study also shows the various investment practices, typical money laundering schemes for proceeds generated from sex trafficking in India and the UK.

A typical strangeness of laundering the proceeds from cross-border human trafficking is the fact that the funds are generated over a long period of time in the territory of a foreign State. It is precisely for this reason that moving the money from the destination country presents the organizations with a major problem. Several methods of repatriating the money have been identified in the study. Each one of these methods has its own characters and variations. Thus, the prostitutes may propel the money directly to the pimp in India and UK using the quick money transfer services or bank institutions. But these methods may be as well complex. A highly placed trafficker makes arrangements with a well-known agent with whom he has a close relationship to remit to him a large sum of money from the destination country. The trafficker consolidates the money earned by the sex workers so as to collect a larger amount. Thereafter, he delivers the money to the agent, who deposits it into a bank account of his own in the destination country. Besides this, a loan agreement for the same amount as the sum delivered in advance is concluded between the participant and the trafficker. Apart from serving as a supporting document for the transaction to be presented to the bank, the agreement enables the trafficker to legitimize the money he holds. The agent transfers the money deposited to an account of the trafficker in India and the UK. As a result of these transactions, the trafficker repatriates to India and the UK the money earned by the prostitutes and makes it appear as if this money has been borrowed. Another method of repatriating the earnings of the sex workers to India and the UK is purchasing various goods in the destination country, which are then imported and sold either in India or UK. In the study, this stands out as one of the most commonly used methods. In the specific cases, traffickers purchase used and new cars, laptops, electrical appliances, gold etc. Quite often the pimps own retail establishments in India and the UK, where the imported goods are sold. These are car dealerships, boutiques, outlets, stores, and so on. When traffickers use this scheme, they try to sell the goods as quickly as possible so as to recover the money invested in the goods, as well as make room for new merchandise from the future exploitation of the prostitutes. To achieve these goals, the retail establishments used by the traffickers very often sell branded goods far cheaper than the normal economic operators, which undermine the competitive environment.

Depending on the level and role they play in the criminal organization, the members receive different portions of the revenue generated from trafficking and prostitution. The actual distribution of funds does not solely depend on a person's position within the organization; people who hold the same position may not be paid the same. The most variation exists with regard to the net profit that the prostitutes receive. It can differ even among girls working for the same organization. The difference depends on the individual experience of the girl. If a girl is very experienced and earns in a lot of money, traffickers need to offer her a higher percentage in order to keep on her. The survey shows that the deal was negotiated between sex workers and employer in advance between 40 percent and 50 percent of the earnings. Based on the information from the respondents, the researcher identified cases in which the girls were promised a start-up salary of £1,500–2,000 (₹10,000–15,000) per month, with the possibility of reaching £2,500 (₹20,000). The researcher was able to confirm only a few cases in which the girls received the percentage they had initially negotiated. The organizations that tend to be accurate with prostitutes are primarily those who control the most lucrative locations. In some instances, the prostitutes received extra money; if they work in an erotic bar, they get 20–25 percent of the money for the sexual service, 12–15 percent of the money for a dance and 8–10 percent of the money for the drinks on the client's tab.

Still, the prostitutes do not get the money that was initially promised to them. One reason is the numerous fines they have to pay for all kinds of violations—tardiness, improper clothing, and so on. Their income drops significantly on account of these fines. Furthermore, the girls themselves cover most of the living expenses and all job related expenses. They pay a fee for the location where they work, for food and accommodation, for transportation to and fro work, clothing and condoms, and so on. So even if the girl were to receive the percentage initially agreed upon, the end amount would be much less than that. Some of the respondents reported receiving only a small portion of the initially determined percentage: they were given only 15–20 percent of their earnings instead of the 50–60 percent they had been promised. In other cases, the traffickers and the prostitute shared only the amount of the earnings which exceeded the fixed daily rate. Once the rate was set, it all went to the trafficker, and the prostitute received half of the amount over that. Another tactic of the traffickers is to tell the girls that before they can start getting any money they have to pay for the expenses incurred in preparing their travel documents, and for their transportation and accommodation. Once they have paid it back, they receive their percentage. The same holds true when a girl is sold. Her new boss tells her that before receiving her share, she must recover the money he paid for her. How long the prostitute has to work without money is up to the traffickers. The study shows that in many cases, during the first months up to half of a year the girls received very little if any money, between 4 percent and 8 percent, under the pretense of a debt they owe the traffickers.

As gathered from the interviews, there were cases in which the girls did not receive any money during the entire period of exploitation they spent. The study reveals that, in reality, after covering expenses, the survivors received between 15 percent and 18 percent, and most often between 10 percent and 13 percent of the money they earned. The rest of their earnings were distributed up the ladder. In addition to the money from the victimized girls, the criminal organizations drew money from the independent pimps through racketeering.

The pimps were required to pay a fixed amount per girl monthly, in the range of £900–1,200 (₹4,000–6,000); in some cases this amount is as much as £2,000 (₹10,000). These dues added to the revenue distributed within the criminal organization. There was no single pattern of distributing the money at the middle level, either. The bottom girls did not receive a percentage of the money earned by the other girls. But they had the privilege to take a bigger percentage of the money they themselves earned. The recruiters typically received lucrative money for each new girl. The controller, the resident, and the country supervisor were on a payroll with a fixed monthly salary in most cases, plus bonuses if the profit was good. Sometimes instead of a salary or percentage, they had a girl working for them and they were not required to share the proceeds with other members of the organization. Under this arrangement, the controller, the resident, or the country supervisor received the basic portion of their pay from the turnover of their girl. Based on the information from the interviews, the hooligan team was on a fixed income as well. Frequently they were bonded by debt to the boss, and they ultimately received only small amounts.

The foreign nationals, who are the owners of the sex establishments where the prostitutes work, received a percentage of the turnover, usually between 15 percent and 35 percent. That amount sometime reached to 60 percent, but only in exceptional cases. Because a substantial portion of the money goes to the foreign owners, organizations look for ways to avoid paying. They employ two strategies: one involves outdoor prostitution, which is less costly, and the second is acquiring property in the foreign country. This helps eliminate the foreign owners from the scheme and saves on assets. Usually, the leader received 10–15 percent of the revenue and the regional boss took up to 30–40 percent. A number of respondents confirmed these figures and the principles of distribution, even though the interviews did not provide exact data about the percentage of commission received by the national boss. The national boss may receive a large portion of the money earmarked for him. Members of the top levels of the criminal organization get the key share of the money and have the opportunity to make investments. However, it seems that they first spend the money on golden necklaces, luxury automobiles, and houses and think of investment options last. One explanation of their behavior may be the desire to show off the economic power they have amassed. Power must be easily recognizable, but since the power of prostitution bosses must remain hidden, luxury cell phones and cars are its rightful proxy.

In most of the reported cases (72 percent), the traffickers invested the money generated from sexual exploitation in real estate property. The traffickers buy hotels, motels, bars, and so on to be used as sex establishments or apartments and houses for the accommodation of traffickers during their stay abroad. At the same time, as property owners they eliminate the need to pay rent for business facilities, which is, as mentioned, a substantial expenditure for them. There are countries where the Indian and the British traffickers control large segments of the sex markets and own many bars and apartments, which are used for sexual exploitation. The traffickers also lease the property they buy. In two such cases, the traffickers bought an old residential building, renovated it, and put the apartments up for rent. In a few other cases, the traffickers invested in factories for sports clothing, furniture, and wooden flooring in the foreign countries. A regular practice includes buying or selling real estate in the fake names. Typically also, when traffickers acquire real estate property, they use it for laundering. For instance, they declare false purchasing and selling prices, they cheat on the actual turnover figures, when they are in retail, and so on. Oftentimes traffickers win public tenders for clear cutting, for example, by means of political protection and coercion. Entering into legitimate economy, the traffickers guarantee themselves clean money from subsequent transactions in those business spheres. Here is the difference between the integration phase (as described in the literature), which typically involves the investment of funds whose illicit origin is hidden, and the process of laundering the money from human trafficking where the participation in legitimate business is the main phase, with the most concentrated efforts to conceal the illegal genesis of the proceeds (Petrunov 2011).

CONCLUSION

Money laundering has a close nexus with organized crime. Money launderers accumulate enormous profits through sex trafficking. Cash transactions are predominantly used for money laundering as they facilitate the concealment of the true ownership and origin of money. It is well recognized that criminals earn huge profits from sex trafficking and other illegal means; this way of money laundering could contaminate and corrupt the structure of the state at all levels, which definitely leads to bribery. Further, this adds to constant pursuit of profits and the expansion into new areas of criminal activity. Combating money laundering is a dynamic process because the criminals who launder money are continuously seeking new ways to achieve their illegal ends. Through money laundering, organized crime diversifies its sources of income and enlarges its sphere of action. The social danger of money laundering consists in the consolidation of the economic power of criminal organizations, enabling them to penetrate the legitimate economy. In advanced societies, crime is increasingly economic in character. Criminal associations now tend to be organized like business enterprises and to follow the same tendencies as legitimate firms; specialization, growth, expansion in international markets and linkage with other enterprises. The holders of capital of illegal origin are prepared to bear considerable cost in order to legalize its use (Savona 1997).

Money laundering is a largely secretive phenomenon. The exact number of launders that operate every year, how much money they launder in which countries and sectors, and which money laundering techniques they use is not known (Unger 2007). However, there is growing evidence that criminals are turning to trafficking in human beings to a greater extent as this crime is perceived as highly profitable (Moneyval 2005; Sarkar 2014). As regards financial gains of criminals, typically traffickers operate smartly and minimize risk by splitting their financial gains into differing investments. Transfer of funds may occur by way of bank transfers, but for the most part it is done through informal channels, via personal transfers or couriers—persons traveling back to the home country may take the criminal proceeds as cash. Cash courier is often used for facilitating payments and moving money back to source countries in these types of offences. In general they seem to be used for the movement of the larger amounts. Sometimes intermediaries are used to perform different types of transactions, whether in the banking system or in relation to transfer using wire remittance services. Therefore, the issue of money transfer services appear to be particularly critical in the context of combating money laundering from sex trafficking and immediate defensive measures in connection with these services need to be seriously considered by India and the UK.

REFERENCES

Bales, K. 1999. *Disposable People: New Slavery in the Global Economy*. Berkeley and Los Angeles, CA: University of California Press.

Belser, P. 2005. *Forced Labour and Human Trafficking: Estimating the Profits*. Working Paper No. 42, InFocus Programme on Promoting the Declaration on Fundamental Principles and Rights at Work. Geneva: International Labour Organization.

Gupta, G. R. 2003. *Review of Literature for Action Research on Trafficking in Women and Children*. New Delhi: Institute of Social Sciences.

Hughes, D. 2000. "The 'Natasha' Trade: The Transnational Shadow Market of Trafficking in Women." *Journal of International Affairs* 53(2): 1–18.

Kelly, L. and Regan, L. 2000. *Stopping Traffic: Exploring the Extent of, and Responses to, Trafficking of Women for Sexploitation in the UK*. Police Research Series, Paper 125. London: UK Home Office.

Miller, J. R. 2006. "Slave Trade: Combating Human Trafficking." *Harvard International Review* 27(4): 70–73.

Moneyval. 2005. *Proceeds from Trafficking in Human Beings and Illegal Migration/ Human Smuggling*. Council of Europe.

Petrunov, G. 2011. "Managing Money Acquired from Human Trafficking: Case Study of Sex Trafficking from Bulgaria to Western Europe." *Trends in Organized Crime* 14: 165–183.

Salt, J. and Stein, J. 1997. "Migration as a Business: The Case of Trafficking." *International Migration* 35(4): 467–494.

Sarkar, S. 2011a. "Trafficking in Women and Children to India and Thailand: Characteristics, Trends and Policy Issues." *International Journal of Afro-Asian Studies* 2(1): 57–73.

Sarkar, S. 2011b. "Engendering Trafficking and Human Security: A Comparative Study of India and Hungary." *International Journal of Development Research and Quantitative Techniques* 1(2): 25–42.

Sarkar, S. 2014. "Trans-border Sex Trafficking: Identifying Cases and Victims in the UK." *Migration and Development* 3(1): 95–107.

Savona, E. 1997. *Responding to Money Laundering: International Perspectives*. Amsterdam: Harwood Academic Publishers.

Sen, S. and Nair, P. M. 2004. *A Report on Trafficking in Women and Children in India 2002–2003*. Volume I, NHRC - UNIFEM - ISS Project. New Delhi: National Human Rights Commission.

Shelley, L. 2010. *Human Trafficking: A Global Perspective.* New York: Cambridge University Press.

SOCA. 2013. *UKHTC: A Strategic Assessment on the Nature and Scale of Human Trafficking in 2012.* Intelligence Assessment Report, London.

UK Home Office. 2012a. *First Annual Report of the Inter-departmental Ministerial Group on Human Trafficking.* London.

UK Home Office. 2012b. *Report on the Internal Review of Human Trafficking Legislation.* Policy Paper, London.

Unger, B. 2007. *The Scale and Impacts of Money Laundering.* Cheltenham, UK and Northampton, MA: Edward Elgar Publishing.

United Nations. 2006. *Trafficking in Persons: Global Patterns.* New York.

US Department of State. 2006. *Trafficking in Persons Report.* Washington, DC.

US Department. 2009. *Trafficking in Persons Report.* Washington, DC.

Väyrynen, R. 2005. "Illegal Immigration, Human Trafficking and Organized Crime." In *Poverty, International Migration and Asylum*, edited by George J. Borjas and Jeff Crisp. New York: Palgrave Macmillan.

Westwood, D. 1998. *Child Trafficking in Asia.* World Vision Briefing Paper No.4, World Vision International.

Wheaton, E. M. et al. 2010. "Economics of Human Trafficking." *International Migration* 48(4): 114–141.

Woodward, S. L. 2005. "Enhancing Cooperation against Trans-border Crime in Southeast Europe: Is there an Emerging Epistemic Community?" In *Fighting Organized Crime in Southeast Europe*, edited by E. Athanassopoulou. Oxon: Routledge.

Zakhari, B. 2005. "Legal Cases Prosecuted under the Victims of Trafficking and Violence Protection Act of 2000." In *Human Traffic and Transnational Crime: Eurasian and American Perspectives*, edited by S. Stoecker and L. Shelley. Lanham: Rowman and Littlefield.

Chapter 3

Sexual Exploitation in Poland

Poland has turned into one of the significant European buffer states between the West and rest of the world. It is located very close to various migrant communities in major cities of the European Union area; for example, Berlin can be reached from Western Polish border at less than one hour drive. For illegal migrants coming from the East and South, Poland can be entered from six countries. It is estimated that up to about 15,000 people illegally cross the territory of Poland every year (Helsinki Foundation for Human Rights 1996). Two main transit routes lead through the country. The "Balkan trail" is used by Romanians, Bulgarians, and citizens from former Yugoslavia who enter legally because regulations allow a one-month stay without a visa. They then try to cross into Germany illegally. Strong cooperation between German and Polish border guards is now discouraging many illegal travelers. The second emigration trail via Poland runs from the Lithuanian border to Germany. This route, mainly used by Asian people, is dominated by citizens from Afghanistan, Iran, Iraq, India, Pakistan, and Sri Lanka. The number of illegal migrants caught at this border has almost doubled since 1996 (Subhan 1996). The trafficked people across this eastern border is apparently constantly rising, is increasingly better organized and seems to be linked to the opening of the Russia-Belarus border, which means there is no control. Between 2011 and 2012, the overall migration flow along the eastern land border increased significantly. This migration flow was particularly apparent at the Polish-Russian border with an increase of 70 percent, but also to a lesser extent at the Norwegian-Russian, Finnish-Russian, and Polish-Ukrainian borders (Frontex 2015). The growth was driven by expanding legal travel channels and longer-term economic developments in the Russian Federation which stimulate increased cross-border movement of people and goods. Worth noting are years 2009 and 2011–2013 when the Polish-Belarusian border saw exceptionally high numbers of Georgians arriving in Poland by train and filing asylum claims—a process during which many applicants quickly absconded from the asylum centers in Poland and headed to other European Union countries including Germany, Austria, and Belgium. In 2014 visa fraud and counterfeit border crossing stamps, as well as cross-border crime were predominant features on this route—more so than detections of illegal border crossing, which remained fairly low throughout the year (Frontex 2015). Along the land borders with Ukraine, the number of detections of illegal border crossing remained very limited (less than 150) despite the armed conflict in Eastern Ukraine. The impact of the Ukrainian conflict is however still felt in the growing number of asylum applications, mostly made inland within the European Union, as well as in the growing number of detections of illegal stay by the European Union Member States.

Traditionally, Poland has been serving as a country of origin for trafficking victims who are typically sexually exploited women in Western Europe (European Commission 2012), but it is also considered as a transit country especially for victims from Lithuania, Latvia, and Moldova (Ministry of Interior and Administration 2008). Sexual exploitation remains the prevalent and most commonly identified form of trafficking in human beings in Poland. Recently, Polish sex industry is being partially taken over by Bulgarian organized crime groups, which transfer part of the profits to Polish criminal groups. The majority of victims are Polish women and women from Ukraine and Belarus, providing sexual services in brothels and private apartments. Therefore, Poland is a source, transit, and destination country for women and children subjected to sex trafficking. Women and children from Poland are subjected to conditions of sex trafficking within the country and also in Austria, Germany, Italy, Japan, Malta, Morocco, the Netherlands, Sweden, and the United Kingdom, and from Belarus, Bulgaria, Moldova, Romania, and Ukraine. A lesser number of women from Africa, including Cameroon, the Democratic Republic of the Congo, Djibouti, and Uganda are subjected to forced prostitution in Poland. Additionally, there are more frequent incidents of trafficking in human beings for criminal activity, and an increase in trafficking in children for both begging and sexual exploitation (US Department of State 2013, 2014).

The National Crime Agency of UK (NCA) has found that Poland provided the second largest number of "potential victims of trafficking for exploitation" to the UK followed by Romania in the year 2013 (NCA 2014). The most recent figures available from the Attorney General, that helps prosecute cases of human trafficking, show that between 1997 and 2007 there have been 2,885 reported cases of human trafficking in Poland (Jensen 2009). Data from the General Prosecutor's Office show that in the years 2009–2011 there were in total 1,524 victims of trafficking in human beings, of which the vast majority

(81.7 percent) were Polish citizens (1,245). Other victims (279 people) were foreign nationals. This proportion is a stable trend—the percentage of foreigners (22.7 percent) is slightly lower than compared to 2006–2008 (Council of Ministers 2013). In the years 2010–2011, the Police concluded thirty-one proceedings of which twenty-five concerned sexual exploitation, eight cases concerned trafficking in children, four were about forced labor, one about exploiting for begging and two cases were about taking out loans fraudulently. In six cases, which concerned exploiting foreigners in Poland (sexual abuse of citizens of Ukraine and Bulgaria, using citizens of Bangladesh for forced labor, and using Romanian citizens for begging), 30 foreigners were granted the status of a victim. When forcing foreigners to beg in Poland is concerned, mainly citizens of Romania, Moldova, and sometimes Ukraine are used (Council of Ministers 2013). That number, one must remember, takes into account only those instances where the victims of trafficking have been able to get to a police station and report their cases. This sort of situation is, however rare and it is almost impossible to measure just how many people are trafficked in or through Poland accurately, though organizations like La Strada International and the International Migration Organization, both of whom work tirelessly to raise awareness about and combat human trafficking, claim that the real numbers are much higher.

Poland's accession to both the European Union and the Schengen zone has transformed it into both a transit and destination country for human trafficking (Ekstedt 2013). The scale of trafficking is already serious in Poland but has become aggravated in the past five years due to joining the European Union and the Schengen zone. The endemic forms of trafficking in Poland include, but are not limited to, trafficking for labor exploitation, for prostitution, and other forms of sexual exploitation. Poland has ratified key international and human rights treaties, including the Protocol on Trafficking in Persons to the 2000 UN Convention against Transnational Organized Crime (Palermo Protocol), under which States are required to take action to ensure the protection of trafficking victims, prevent trafficking and bring traffickers to justice (United Nations News Centre 2009).

The Government of Poland fully complies with the minimum standards for the elimination of trafficking. In 2012, authorities increased the number of trafficking investigations, prosecutions, and convictions, although half of all convicted offenders continued to receive suspended sentences. The Government of Poland improved its anti-trafficking law enforcement efforts in 2012. In 2012, Polish police investigated sixty new cases of human trafficking, an increase from thirty-seven in 2011. The border guard began four additional investigations. The government initiated prosecutions of twenty-four suspected trafficking offenders and convicted thirty-nine in 2012, an increase from seventeen prosecutions and twenty-eight convictions in 2011

(US Department of State 2013). The Government of Poland increased its anti-trafficking victim protection efforts in 2012, providing assistance to more victims, although the majority of child victims of sex trafficking did not receive specialized care. Government agencies reportedly lacked adequate tools and expertise to identify and assist potential victims of sex trafficking. There were no trafficking shelters designated specifically for male trafficking victims. The victim assistance program is highly centralized, and some academic experts believed it would be more effective if local NGOs were more directly involved in working with local authorities in the victim referral process and providing assistance. Although multiple government agencies and NGOs collected data on trafficking victims and related law enforcement actions, no central mechanism existed to consolidate these statistics, leading to difficulty in assessing the scope of trafficking in Poland and the efficacy of law enforcement efforts. The government did not organize any programs to reduce the participation of Polish citizens in child sex tourism. The government did not run any programs specifically designed to reduce the demand for commercial sex acts, although several of its awareness campaigns discussed the potential sexual exploitation of trafficked women, as well as penalty for the sexual exploitation of women and children.

OBJECTIVE, APPROACH, AND METHOD

In Poland, a detailed depiction of the dimensions and mechanisms of trafficking flows is missing. Empirical data on the involvement of criminal groups, smuggling routes used by such groups, and the prevailing modalities of transport are inadequate. Only scattered data on the dimensions of trafficking and the institutional responses to trafficking practices, especially the role of law enforcement and criminal justice system in countering human trafficking, are available. Therefore, the overall objective of the study was to comprehend the current trends and patterns of cross-border trafficking victims in Poland and the major areas of trafficking for sex-based exploitation within the current international security debate. While survey instrument was primarily focused on demographic characteristics but also a number of socioeconomic questions were asked to the respondents. The study was intended to identify the process, context, and experiences of victims of sex trafficking and designed to analyze demographic and social characteristics of the victims. Each potential respondent is given a brief explanation as to the purpose of study and they may be assured that their response to the questionnaire would be anonymous.

Women and girls who have been trafficked for sexual exploitation are a hidden population, largely due to the illegal nature of sex trafficking and sex work. Employers of sex trafficked women and girls may keep them hidden from public view and edge their contacts with the outsiders. Women and girls who have been sex trafficked may not identify themselves as such through fear of revenges from their perpetrators; panic of social stigma from involvement in sex work and ignominy of their activities being revealed to the family members. Therefore, identifying sex trafficked women and girls and obtaining access to them for interview is highly uncertain. It is only once these individuals have left their trafficked situation that they may be identified through contact with the key informants. Any interview with sex trafficked women and girls is, therefore, likely to be a "post-trafficking" situation either in transit homes, rehabilitation centers or in brothels. In view of these difficulties, the target population for this research was women and girls who had been sex trafficked into Poland. In response to this study, much of the available information on trans-trafficking in Poland was obtained from the National Police in Poland, NGOs like La Strada Foundation against Trafficking in Persons and Slavery; The Nobody's Children Foundation; Caritas Poland and Association Help-Full for Women and Children of Immaculate Mary and Polish Border Guard.

The researcher encountered various problems in obtaining hard data on sex trafficking in Poland, mainly because of poor documentation and lack of a database on human trafficking in Poland. In Poland it was difficult to obtain data, as most law enforcement agencies had little information and facts on sex trafficking beyond what they had heard in the media or from discussions as very few cases have been brought to the courts for prosecution. Little effort had been made to document movements of victims outside Poland. Thus, for those who agreed to complete the questionnaire, their answers reflect their opinions about the situation, and not any hard facts.

This study was based on quantitative research aiming to propose a comprehensive understanding of the determinants of women's exposures to sex trafficking in Poland. For this study, interviews were conducted with ninety-six female victims and survivors of human trafficking in Poland. Researcher gathered data using a semi-structured questionnaire that queried about barriers and success factors related to victims' services and coalition operations. Fieldwork was conducted during March 2015. A strict ethics and safety protocol was implemented based on the World Health Organization ethical and safety recommendations for interviewing trafficked women. The ethics protocol included, for example, guidance on informed consent, anonymity, confidentiality, privacy, responding to distress, knowing when to terminate an interview, and referral procedures. Participation in this study was completely voluntary, and participants could end their interviews at any time. Specific steps were taken to ensure that the participants' identities were protected. Open coding of data was utilized and the data were subsequently organized or grouped into properties and later developed into contextual themes around the research questions. Descriptive statistics were employed to analyze the data using the statistical packages for social sciences (SPSS).

THE STATE OF HUMAN TRAFFICKING
IN POLAND: WOMEN AT RISK

There is no official estimate of the total number of human trafficking victims in Poland. The Polish authorities have not provided the exact numbers on trafficking for sexual and other types of exploitation. As regards foreign nationals trafficked to Poland, GRETA (a group of experts on human trafficking from the Council of Europe) identified that trafficking of women for the purpose of sexual exploitation remains predominant which is about 80 percent of all identified cases (Council of Europe 2013). As regards Polish nationals trafficked abroad, the types of exploitation in recent years have involved sexual exploitation, forced labor in the agricultural sector, domestic service, benefit fraud, and using victims' documents to set up fake bank accounts and credit agreements.

Around 1990 when systematic flow of the trafficked victims across Polish borders instigated, the Polish law and judiciary institutions were hardly prepared to cope with it. The changes started late in 1990, when two important acts were passed by the Parliament concerning setting up of the Border Guard and the protection of state boundaries, and they were finally completed with coming into force of the Aliens Act in December 1997 and the Penal Code in the mid of 1998. A major route of trafficking in Poland is supposed to direct from East Belarus and Ukraine to West Germany and onwards (Okólski 1999). It is mainly chosen by the people, who are from Afghanistan, Bangladesh, India, Pakistan, and Sri Lanka. They often first take off from metropolitan towns of their native countries to Moscow or travel to Moscow by road or train, next they are transported by road to the vicinities of Minsk, Kiev or other large cities in countries adjacent to Poland, and ultimately are trafficked through Poland. Very frequently the final step before arriving in Poland is being made from the territory of Lithuania. Two routes of lesser importance are those leading from East to South and from South to West. The former features similar initial stages although after crossing eastern Polish border, it turns South to the Czech Republic. This route is often used by those migrants who on their earlier attempt had failed on getting directly to Germany. The latter route brings to Poland citizens of Iran, Turkey, and certain North African and Middle East countries who usually first fly to Istanbul and next use road transportation to reach the Polish-Czech (or Polish-Slovak) or a South corner of the Polish-Ukrainian border. The trafficked migrants for whom the ultimate destination is Poland get in through Germany (Vietnamese), Slovakia (Romanians and Ukrainians), the Czech Republic (Vietnamese) and Ukraine (Armenians and Ukrainians). As far as the cross-border trafficking is concerned, foreigners apprehended on illegal border crossing are subject to a legal action in Poland, and eventually to a penalization, detention, and expulsion. The same pertains to foreign citizens whose stay in Poland is found to be unauthorized or who during their stay in Poland commit a crime. All related judiciary and administrative procedures are clearly specified, and currently they seem to meet the European standards.

Therefore, Poland is the focal point of a transnational human trafficking network that currently spans the entire European continent. Situated at the center of Europe, its borders are contiguous with six countries, including Germany on the west and Ukraine in the east. This proximity to the poverty of Eastern Europe and the comparative prosperity of Western Europe makes Poland a prime transit and destination country for trafficked persons, specifically those from Ukraine, Moldova, Romania, and Bulgaria. Indeed, this situation reflects a tragic paradox at the core of human trafficking in search of a better life, victims ultimately have their hopes crushed, and find themselves in a far worse situation than they ever would have imagined. In spite of the tremendous likelihood, some victims really run away from the traffickers. However, a few go to the police station, either because they are illegal migrants, unable to prove their identity, or afraid of vengeance from their former traffickers. For those daring enough to come forward, Poland offers a number of support services legislated under the Act on Foreigners and the Act on Providing Security. Together these acts provide victims the right to a two-month stay whether they are legal or illegal migrants. The two-month duration intends to provide victims enough time to convalesce so they can make an informed decision about whether they want to assist investigating authorities. During this reflection period women can receive psychological counseling, safe housing, and other basic social support from La Strada. After two months, most choose to return home because they want to move on with their lives and put their ordeal behind them. This means only a small fraction of trafficked women decide to press charges or act as witnesses. Those choosing to assist the authorities receive a six-month residential permit or tolerated stay (based on the decision of the voivods, Poland's local administrative councils) that can be extended up to three additional months. Yet this permit fails to cover the length of most investigations and proceedings which often go on for at least a year and only guarantees that a victim won't be deported. Other basic provisions, such as public medical access and social assistance, are not permitted for foreign victims. Equally alarming is the fact that no official witness protection program exists in Poland for victims of trafficking, though such programs are in place for criminals. Without long-term safety and support, women who want to testify inevitably opt out, making it nearly impossible to identify and prosecute the perpetrators.

Given that a little number of trafficked women come to the police, the responsibility falls on the police to search for victims of sex trafficking and to rescue them. Yet throughout Poland, many police officers do not know how to identify a victim of trafficking or what options for assistance are available to her. Because police officers often detain trafficked women during brothel raids or street patrols, they are in a position to dictate the fate of these women. All too often, officers will assume a woman as an illegal migrant if she does not speak Polish and lacks a passport, identity documents or other belongings. The fact that she has been working as a prostitute will further validate their judgment and likely convince them to deport her within the requisite forty-eight hours. But the same signs suggesting a woman is an illegal migrant can also indicate that she has been trafficked. This lesson is just one of several on human trafficking that police officers are learning in workshops conducted by the Warsaw-based Central Unit on Combating Human Trafficking. Established in March 2006, the Central Unit is the only division of the National Police devoted exclusively to monitoring and preventing human trafficking in Poland. Alongside its anti-trafficking operations, the Central Unit is using public outreach within the Warsaw Police Headquarters to train officers to recognize and assist victims of human trafficking.

The Council of Europe made a meaningful step when it adopted the Convention on Action against the Trafficking of Human Beings in Warsaw in May 2005. Several articles of this document are devoted to the assistance of victims, which reflects the importance of victims' protection for preventing and fighting human trafficking. This document obliges its signatory states to provide persons who are trained and qualified in identifying victims to the authorities investigating and prosecuting the trafficking of human beings. But for all its merits, the convention has yet to be ratified by the Polish government, no less than because of its own negative attitudes about the victims of human trafficking. Like the rest of Polish society, Poland's national lawmakers regard the victims as unwanted persons, based on the fact that many of the victims are illegal migrants in addition to being former prostitutes. For these officials, ratifying the convention entails earmarking funds for assistance programs that will allow the victims to stay in Poland and benefit from state welfare—no matter how meager that welfare actually is. Rather than supporting the victims, officials are trying to relieve themselves of any further obligations to those whom the state never permitted to enter or reside in Poland, and in the process, rid their nation of the social plague brought by these women's engagement in prostitution. Simply put, victims of sex trafficking do not exist for Poland's government; their suffering and abuse fail to be properly acknowledged as a nationwide epidemic, while their sexual mores are deemed as such. This makes the problem of sex trafficking invisible to the government, thus creating a triangle shaped by the invisibility of victims that in turn upholds the impunity of the perpetrators.

Even more problematic is the fact that the Polish criminal code lacks a precise definition for human trafficking. Article 204 of this code, usually used to indict perpetrators of human trafficking for sexual exploitation, is actually devoted to the offense of forced prostitution. This means that the difference between prostitution and human trafficking is not properly distinguished in the Polish legal system. Furthermore, it is essential to mention that although the code has no definition of human trafficking, it does contain an article 253 that states the criminal penalty for committing the crime of human trafficking. This suggests that the Polish criminal law system is not prepared nor reformed enough to prosecute human trafficking as an independent crime. Prosecutors also use article 204 more frequently than article 253 when prosecuting traffickers. Accusations based on article 253 require very specific evidence of trafficking, such that validates that an exchange of money was made in order to come into the possession of a person. Prosecutors do not seem to be interested in investigating very difficult cases of human trafficking if they are not obliged to. This same attitude carries over to the courts, where article 253 is likewise underutilized. In Poland, then, the definition of human trafficking used in criminal sentencing often fails to comply with that recognized by the international community. This means the current definition for human trafficking can be used against innocents, while allowing countless traffickers to evade prosecution. Another difficulty is that there is no one person who specifically deals with human trafficking in the Ministry of Justice. However, it is important to note that every two years the Committee for Combating and Preventing Trafficking in Human Beings, established in the Ministry of Interior and Administration, formulates a National Program for Combating and Preventing Trafficking in Human Beings. But despite its momentous efforts, the Committee still has not developed a long-term, government-wide strategy for suppressing human trafficking in Poland.

When it comes to combating sex trafficking, it is clear that Poland's government condones glaring gaps in its policy. While the 2007 Trafficking in Persons Report lauds Poland's government for providing quality assistance to trafficking victims, witness protection and other state-provided services have yet to reach foreign victims (US Department of State 2007). Though Poland is the nexus for Europe's trafficking epidemic, Poland's current government continues to discount 29 of its peers by refusing to sign the Council of Europe's anti-trafficking convention. And despite the fact that tens of thousands of people are trafficked into Poland and across its borders each year, no clear definition of human trafficking exists in the Polish criminal code. Such shortcomings reflect a status quo of neglect toward sex trafficking, largely because of what the victims are: female, foreigner, and impoverished. Due to the invisibility of the victims, the silence of legislators, and the stigma attached to prostitution, a climate of impunity currently surrounds the trafficking of women and girls in Poland. Although the Polish government's disregard for sex trafficking may now seem fixed, it's not impossible to imagine that in the six to twelve months before the tournament, international media will hone in on Poland's sex trafficking dilemma and embarrass the government into action. But whether government leaders choose to finance an information campaign or step up funding for another anti-trafficking effort, they will not be the ones on the front lines.

The system of support and protection for victims of trafficking in human beings in Poland came into existence at the beginning of 2006. Since that time the system has been thoroughly improved and developed both in the legal and practical fields. The main objective of the system is to identify victims and to refer them to the proper institutions for assistance and support. National Consulting and Intervention Centre for Victims of Trafficking (KCIK) is the core of polish victim support system. It was established in April 2009 in order to improve the standards of assistance offered to victims and to make the assistance more available. KCIK is fully financed from the State's budget as a public task commissioned by the Minister of the Interior to NGOs. Currently the task is carried out jointly by two NGOs—La Strada Foundation against Trafficking and Slavery and Association Po MOC. The Center is addressed to victims identified by law enforcement agencies, but also to potential victims who have not been officially identified yet may suffer from the threat of being re-victimized. The KCIK is also dedicated to all institutions and organizations assisting victims of trafficking (table 3.1). The assistance offered by the Centre is unconditional and irrespective of the victims' cooperation with law enforcement agencies. With regard to the system of support and protection of minor victims of human trafficking there is no shelters dedicated specifically to identify underage victims. In case of emergency, victims who are under eighteen years of age are placed in foster care facilities having jurisdiction over the territory where the child was identified. The Programme of voluntary returns of victims of trafficking in human beings is done by the International

Table 3.1   Number of Victims Received Support from KCIK

Year	Victims, Supported by KCIK in 2011–2013
2011	133 persons (81 Polish citizens, 52 foreigners)
2012	198 persons (89 Polish citizens, 109 foreigners)
2013	222 persons (103 Polish citizens, 119 foreigners)
Total	553 persons (273 Polish citizens, 280 foreigners)

Source: European Commission 2015.

Organization for Migration on the basis of Agreement between the Ministry of Interior and the International Organization for Migration on the cooperation in the field of voluntary returns of foreigners leaving the territory of Poland. Owing to the amendment to the agreement which was implemented in 2011 all foreigners (including the EU-citizens) who are officially identified as victims of trafficking by Polish law enforcement agencies are entitled to a voluntary return organized by the International Organization for Migration. The Police established special anti-trafficking structures both at the central and regional levels. In the period of 2011–2013 at the level of the National Police Headquarters the Central Unit for Combating Trafficking in Human Beings was come into force and table 3.2 shows trafficking in human beings as per Police records during 2011–2013. Furthermore, permanent teams for combating trafficking in human beings were set up within criminal divisions of regional Police headquarters. The Border Guard, similarly to the Police structures, comprises the Trafficking in Human Beings coordinator at the level of the National Border Guard Headquarters and at the regional levels (at each division of the Border Guard). The regional Border Guard coordinators are in charge of official identification of victims of trafficking and of referral them to the assistance institutions (table 3.1).

Therefore, Poland is gradually getting rid of the problem of human trafficking, according to a report by GRETA, which reviewed the Polish government's implementation of the Convention on Action against Trafficking in Human Beings 2005 (Council of Europe 2013). The convention has been in force in Poland since March 2009 and has been enshrined in national legislation from September 2010, when human trafficking was officially criminalized. Since

Table 3.2 Data of Human Trafficking as per Police Records

Year	Crimes Detected	Persons Suspected	Victims	Polish Victims	Foreigners Victims
2011	427	13	166	165	1
2012	61	23	18	16	2
2013	186	23	141	133	8
Total	674	59	325	314	11

Source: European Commission 2015.

Table 3.3 Proceedings Carried Out by the Border Guard

Year	Proceedings	Victims
2011	5	11
2012	7	31
2013	9	54
Total	21	96

Source: European Commission 2015.

then, various measures have been adopted to combat and prevent the crime. Poland is one of six member states that fully accepted the European Union directive 2011/36 (the other countries were the Czech Republic, Lithuania, Finland, Hungary, and Sweden). But despite its efforts, much remains to be done. There is still a notable gap between the number of abuses reported and the number of prosecutions and convictions. Furthermore, it is still necessary to improve the knowledge and sensitivity of judges, prosecutors, investigators and other professionals in the field of victims' rights (Orlandi 2013).

FINDINGS

There is a common perception that women and children are more vulnerable than adult men to becoming victims of trafficking in human beings. This perception is reflected in the "protocol to prevent, suppress and punish trafficking in persons, especially women and children, which singles out the trafficking of women and children" as issues of particular interest. An analysis of the data collected for this research, which covered the profile of ninety-six female trafficked victims from Belarus, Bulgaria, Romania, Moldova, and Ukraine into Poland. The majority of the victims surveyed were Ukrainian, Lithuanian, and Belarusian women (55 percent), two were Romanian, and the other foreign victims came from Russia, Latvia, and Moldavia. In short it can be said that the traffickers have a huge potential market for Lithuanian, Latvian, Moldavian, Belarusian, Bulgarian, Russian, Romanian, and Ukrainian girls and women in Poland.

Victims of sex trafficking can be any age, race or gender, however young girls are most vulnerable and at risk to be coerced into the sex trade. Traffickers target children at a higher rate than adults because children are easier to control, coerce, and manipulate. Therefore, age and gender can have a significant influence on the ways that individuals are exposed to and experience with sex trafficking. The trafficked victims interviewed during the survey (n=96) were predominantly young women and children between 13 and 20 years of age with mean age of 17, while sixteen of the respondents were in the age group of above 20 years when they were trafficked. The study reveals that presence of elderly victims was comparatively low. At the same time, thirteen victims were virtually girl child in the sense that they were in the age of below 14. The study explains that only fifty-six of the respondents completed their primary school, twenty-two completed their secondary school education, and the rest were either totally or almost illiterate. Therefore, trafficked victims in Poland had a particularly low level of education and that less educated women were more vulnerable to sex trafficking. Only twelve victims were married. The presence of maidens and divorced or separated victims were forty-eight. Seventy-four victims were unmarried at the time of survey. The survey includes information about the types and extent of abuse victims had experienced prior to being trafficked. Of those ninety-six surveys of victim of trafficking, 64 percent indicated that victims had experienced multiple forms of abuse such as substance abuse, abusive relationship, parental neglect, and sexually abused by relatives prior to being trafficked. The forms of abuse reported to have been experienced by victims are predominant that presents childhood abuse or neglect and trauma as a significant risk factor in human trafficking. Of the ninety-six surveys with information about the victims' living situations prior to being trafficked, 13 percent indicates that victims had been homeless and 21 percent indicates that victims had run away from home or been forced out.

The victims of trafficking used land border crossing points—thirty with valid documents and sixty-six without having any valid travel documents, though they could not specify the names of the areas where they crossed the border. When crossing the border, 24 out of 96 respondents walked, while 42 used vehicles. Thirty women were sent to Poland by air. Out of forty-two women, twenty-six were transported by car; ten victims went by bus and six girls by train. The data is indicative of weak border management as well as established human trafficking networks, particularly along the Poland borders with Russia (Kaliningrad), Belarus, Moldova, and Ukraine. All the victims unanimously claimed that the main reason why they and other women with similar experiences traveled Poland was because they had been suffering from acute financial crunch, and there no jobs were available in their home country. Even when some got jobs, the income from such jobs were not adequate, some could not get suitable jobs nor had sufficient money for education, hence the desire to travel outside the country for better employment and security (22 percent). Other reasons were low level of education of girls; large family size; polygamy; poverty, and lack of good moral upbringing of children nowadays (47 percent).

Based on the survey findings the general aspects of trafficked women's living conditions in Poland can be classified into—the practice of the profession inside apartments (call girls or escorts); in brothel based, in public or private places (hidden prostitution, such as in the case of hostesses, dancers); or on the street (street prostitutes). Key elements which affect the trafficked women's living and working conditions include the existence or not of experience of prostitution before arrival into Poland; the different types of consent; the extent of any deceit, coercion or violence that caused emigration; and the amount of contracted debt and the mode of repayment; the duration, since first entering into Poland, and the different phases that mark the experience—either a strengthening of subordinate relations to the detriment of the prostitute, or a progressive process of relief from bondage; the modes and the degrees of autonomy that the women are able to acquire or attain in the course of their work, either by mutual agreement, or through the establishment of an acceptance of partners' roles and functions, or, in contrast, in open or latent conflict with the protector. The survey discloses that 21 percent of trafficked women engaged as call girls in Poland while 48 percent was brothel based. Call girls usually lived in a private flat, where they stayed alone. Women as hidden prostitutes are often recruited by traffickers for the types of work which, at least on paper, are legal, but which in practice involve prostitution. Hidden prostitution is covered by socially accepted professions such as hostesses and dancers in public or private clubs (nightclubs), beauticians, masseuses, strippers, pornographic video actresses, entertainers, and so on. It has been found that 18 percent of the victims involved in hidden prostitution. The practice of street prostitution is very different from the previously stated typologies. According to the survey, 13 percent of trafficked women belonged to street prostitution.

Trafficking victims are often recruited into the sex trade by someone they know. Victims may misinterpret the lifestyle as attractive at first, but soon come to find that they are unable to escape their situation. Traffickers will also befriend victims and manipulate them into thinking they are involved in a romantic relationship. The trafficker then coerces the victims into performing commercial sex acts. Trafficking victims are also recruited on the Internet. The study shows that traffickers used social media sites to gain contact with young girls and coerce them into joining the sex trade (23 percent). Social media websites allow traffickers to befriend on the Internet and slowly gain their trust. Often, the traffickers lure them into the sex trade under false pretenses and false promises. Women were also recruited through classified advertisements on the Internet (14 percent). Traffickers use popular classified advertising websites to pose advertisements claiming to offer work such as modeling or dancing. However, the women are forced to perform commercial sex acts and are never given the jobs offered in the advertisements. Making false promises of modeling jobs and other types of work is a common technique used by traffickers to recruit victims. Victims of sex trafficking in Poland may be forced to work as street prostitutes, call girls, and strippers to make money. In addition, study shows that some might be forced into pornography, live sex shows, or sold as mail-order brides (11 percent). Sex traffickers advertise women and girls over the Internet. Traffickers may utilize the Internet in a variety of ways, such as forcing victims to perform strip shows or sex shows on videos or webcams. Furthermore, social networking sites and classified advertisement sites have been used as a portal to advertise prostitution and sell trafficking victims. The study shows that 30 percent of victims were recruited by a boyfriend, 26 percent by a friend, and 12 percent by a family member. Women fall victim to trafficking through various means such as coercion, deceit and abuse of power as defined in the trafficking protocol. In this study, between the two options, thirty-four respondents answered that they followed the traffickers based on false promises and the remaining sixty-two said that they were taken by force. Among victims entrapped through false promises, all were lured by the promise of well-paid jobs.

In regard to the question whether they experienced any violence at the destination, sixty-six victims were able to respond; twenty-one women reported that they were subjected to threats, while forty-five were subjected to physical violence. The cases of sexual exploitation collected during the survey cover three different patterns of violation—forced prostitution where the victim is forced into prostitution and the perpetrator makes profit out of the act, sexual servitude and assault where the victim is physically molested or raped by the traffickers, and sham marriage. Therefore, trafficking victims are exposed to a wide range of violence and physical and mental abuse. Many victims experienced violence at the hands of traffickers and clients. Victims reported incidents of beatings, sexual assaults, and the use of weapons in assaults. This study finds that as many as fifty-two of sex trafficking victims reported being sexually assaulted and thirty-five reported being physically assaulted. Other forms of violence, such as kidnappings and torture were reported by nine sex trafficking victims. The reported forms of torture include burning, hanging, piercing, mutilation, being bound and gagged, or being penetrated with objects. The study reveals that 40 percent of trafficked women reported using substances to cope with the trauma they experienced as a result of their victimization. Traffickers use a variety of means to control victims, such as physically restraining victims, holding them captive in locked rooms or facilities, controlling their money, isolating them from friends and family, and taking forms of identification. Traffickers may threaten physical harm to the victim or victim's family, or demonstrate violent acts on others. Furthermore, traffickers demeaned and degraded victims (83 percent) through verbal assaults and emotional abuse. Many (72 percent) trafficking victims were forced to live in traumatic environments characterized by high levels of control, exposure to chronic stress and threat, isolation, provocation of fear, and the creation of a sense of helplessness in victims. Victims become dependent on their traffickers and fear the consequences of rebelling or leaving. The traffickers provoke feelings of fear, disconnection, dependency, and helplessness in their victims. The constant threats and environment of fear prevent victims from leaving or seeking help. The study reveals that thirty-two victims were branded by their traffickers through tattoos in order to label and further control them.

It was found during the survey that all categories of trafficking cases included coercive elements such as physical abuse, for example, beating, burning, and forcible use of drugs; psychological abuse, for example, threat of violence and killing, restricted or no freedom of movement, partial or no payment of salary, and debt bondage occurring in all stages of the trafficking process—during recruitment, transport, and at the destination. As a result of these elements, the victims are enslaved without any control of their own fate until they have a chance to run away or be rescued by the authorities. None of the victims interviewed during the survey paid any amount of money to the traffickers in advance, but instead were indebted during the process and unable to keep any of their earnings while working. Among the fourteen women who were able to recall the exact amount of their debts, the average amount was 370 euro. Twenty-four respondents said that they had limited or no freedom of movement at the destination and eighteen of them were denied of any form of movement.

The survey shows that trafficking victims experience constant trauma and stress as a result of their victimization. Individuals who have been exposed to complex trauma often develop lasting psychological disorders as a result of their victimization. Seventy-two percent of trafficking victims who had experienced continuous psychological, physical, and sexual abuse might develop disorders such as depression, anxiety, bipolar disorder, and post-traumatic stress disorder. Many victims might also develop dissociative disorders and personality disorders as a result of the extensive trauma they experienced during childhood and as victims of trafficking. They may have feelings of guilt, shame, and worthlessness as a result of the acts they were forced into, as well as the psychological and emotional abuse they experienced from their traffickers. Furthermore, victims may experience lasting feelings of fear and anger, as well as low self-esteem, boundary issues, suicidal ideation, and issues with intimacy.

Sex trafficking victims also suffer from a variety of physical health problems. Many victims (78 percent) had limited access to health care while being trafficked. Victims suffered from injuries such as broken bones, bruises, and head trauma as a result of the violence they experience while being trafficked (29 percent). Victims reported other physical health problems such as gastrointestinal problems, vaginal bleeding, pelvic pain, malnutrition, fertility issues, and dental problems (12 percent). Five victims of sex trafficking were also at high risk of contracting sexually transmitted diseases and HIV.

DISCUSSION

Poland is a source, transit, and destination country for women and children subjected to sex trafficking. Women from Poland are subjected to sexual exploitation in Europe, primarily Belgium, the Czech Republic, Italy, the Netherlands, the Scandinavian countries, and the United Kingdom. Women and children from Poland are subjected to sex trafficking within the country and also in Austria, Germany, Italy, Japan, Malta, Morocco, the Netherlands, Sweden, and the United Kingdom. Women and children from Belarus, Bulgaria, Moldova, Romania, and Ukraine are subjected to sex trafficking in Poland. Foreign children, particularly Roma children, are recruited for forced begging in Poland.

The Government of Poland fully complies with the minimum standards for the elimination of trafficking. During the reporting period, authorities expanded the mandate of the border guard to investigate more trafficking cases and designated police investigators at the national and provincial headquarters to specialize in trafficking investigations. The government continued to provide training to border guard and police officers on trafficking; however, judges lacked adequate training opportunities. A large proportion of convicted traffickers continued to receive suspended prison sentences. The government increased funding for victim assistance and amended laws to improve available protections for identified victims. However, the Polish government did not systematically provide specialized services to child victims of trafficking, and authorities lacked a trafficking-specific shelter for men. Systematically provide child victims of trafficking specialized care; continue to increase the shelter system's capacity to assist victims, including men and children; improve efforts to identify trafficking victims proactively among vulnerable populations, particularly unaccompanied children and irregular migrants; continue to vigorously investigate and prosecute trafficking offenses and take steps to ensure that trafficking offenders receive sentences commensurate with the severity of the crime; improve victim identification procedures and training on such procedures to better identify victims of labor trafficking; increase training for prosecutors and judges; incorporate the victim compensation process into criminal proceedings; amend the criminal code to ensure that identified victims of trafficking are not penalized for acts committed as a direct result of being trafficked; consider establishing an independent national rapporteur to monitor the government's anti-trafficking progress; ensure all victims are given access to and encouraged to use the reflection period; and conduct additional awareness campaigns to reduce the demand for commercial sex acts and deter child sex tourism.

The Government of Poland improved its anti-trafficking law enforcement efforts during the reporting period through establishing trafficking-specific police investigators and empowering the border guard to investigate more trafficking cases. Poland prohibits all forms of both sex and labor trafficking through several articles of its criminal code, including Articles 115.22, 115.23, 189a, 203, and 204.3. Prescribed punishments under these statutes range from one to fifteen years imprisonment; these sentences are sufficiently stringent and commensurate with those prescribed for other serious crimes, such as rape. In 2013, Polish police investigated sixty-eight new cases of human trafficking, compared to sixty in 2012. The border guard began nine additional investigations. The government prosecuted forty-eight suspected trafficking offenders and convicted thirty-five in 2013, compared to twenty-four defendants prosecuted and thirty-nine traffickers convicted in 2012. In collecting data, the government only considered sentences issued after appeals to be final. In 2012, the most recent year for which post-appeal sentences were available, sixty-four traffickers were sentenced, compared to sixty-three in 2011 (US Department of State 2014). Sentences ranged from suspended sentences to less than one year to eight years' imprisonment. Similar to the previous three years, approximately half of the convicted offenders received suspended sentences. The government did not report the investigation or prosecution of any public officials for alleged complicity in human trafficking-related offenses. Polish authorities collaborated on human trafficking investigations with counterparts in several European countries. The government continued to include a module on human trafficking in the basic training for all police officers and invited civil society to assist in training. During the year, the government continued to offer limited optional trainings on human trafficking to prosecutors and judges; according to the GRETA, prosecutors and judges often lacked expertise in labor trafficking cases. Government officials acknowledged that police were less adept at identifying forced labor victims as compared to sex trafficking victims. In December 2013, an amendment to the Law on Aliens expanded the border guard's authority to investigate potential trafficking cases that did not involve another border-related offense, such as possession of false documents. In January 2014, the police established a department in its national headquarters that will have eight officers focused exclusively on human trafficking investigations. In addition, the police continued to designate forty officers in provincial headquarters to handle trafficking offenses. Regional prosecutorial offices continued to designate specially trained prosecutors to assist local prosecutors with trafficking cases and assume lead responsibility for particularly complicated cases.

The Government of Poland improved its anti-trafficking victim protection efforts during the reporting period through increased funding and legal changes, although authorities did not systematically provide specialized care for child trafficking victims. The police and border guard identified 218 possible victims of trafficking in 2013, compared to ninety possible victims identified in 2012. Observers reported that Polish authorities did not conduct sufficient outreach and proactive identification among unaccompanied children and irregular migrants held in detention. The government increased funding for victim assistance, allocating the equivalent of approximately $329,400 in 2013, compared to the equivalent of approximately $256,300 in 2012 (US Department of State 2014). The government continued to completely finance the NGO-run National Intervention-Consultation Center for Victims of Trafficking (KCIK) to provide assistance to foreign and Polish victims of trafficking, which provided assistance to 222 victims in 2013, compared to 198 in 2012. Of the 222 victims, 161 were women and 61 were men. Slightly more than half of these victims were foreign nationals and 31 of those assisted were child victims. Government-funded NGOs offered trafficking victims medical and psychological care, legal assistance, food, clothing, and employment-related training. Local governments also funded and operated 178 crisis intervention centers around the country, 16 of which were prepared to accept trafficking victims and had a capacity to accommodate approximately 200 persons (US Department of State 2014). Adult female victims of trafficking had access to trafficking-specific shelters, and they were allowed to leave the shelters abandoned and at will. KCIK was responsible for finding safe shelter for male trafficking victims and utilized crisis centers and hostels for this purpose, as there were no trafficking-specific shelters for men. The government placed child victims in orphanages and with foster families. The government did not systematically refer child victims of sex trafficking to KCIK for specialized care. GRETA reported that some unaccompanied minors disappeared from orphanages. The government provided training for social workers, consular officers, medical personnel, and other civil servants working with trafficking victims.

The government's witness protection program, which is implemented by KCIK, provided for a temporary residence permit, medical and psychological care, safe transportation, food, clothing, and shelter or lodging support for victims who cooperated with law enforcement. The government enrolled fifty-six trafficking victims into this program in 2013. The Law on Aliens offered foreign victims a three-month reflection period during which foreign victims can stay legally in Poland to decide whether to cooperate with the criminal process; however, no victims received a reflection period in 2013. GRETA reported that authorities do not systematically inform victims about the reflection period, particularly victims who chose not to participate in an investigation. Victims who decided to report the trafficking offense to law enforcement could apply for a temporary residence permit that enabled them to live and work in Poland. The December 2013 amendment to the Law on Aliens extended the duration of the temporary residency permit for victims of trafficking from six months to three years. The amendment also provided for the possibility of victims of trafficking to obtain permanent residency. The Interior Ministry continued to work with an international organization to repatriate foreign victims of trafficking, and in 2013, twenty-five trafficking victims were repatriated to their country of origin. During the reporting period, the government modified the code of criminal proceedings to establish special interview procedures for victims of sexual crimes and child victims to prevent re-traumatization. Victims may file civil suits against traffickers, but observers reported that very few trafficking victims have ever received compensation from their traffickers. There were no reports of trafficking victims punished for crimes committed as a direct result of being trafficked.

The government sustained its strong anti-trafficking prevention efforts during the reporting period. In May 2013, the government adopted a 2013–2015 national action plan for combating trafficking. The plan was developed in coordination with NGOs and prioritizes enhanced care for child victims, more training for those likely to encounter victims, and information campaigns targeting the most vulnerable populations. The Interior Ministry continued to lead the inter-ministerial anti-trafficking team, as well as a working-level group of experts, which met regularly to coordinate efforts and develop national policies. However, observers reported that Poland lacked effective central operational coordination for all anti-trafficking activities. The government did not have an independent national rapporteur to monitor anti-trafficking efforts. The government sponsored a number of information campaigns, including a festival featuring films that highlighted human trafficking. Government-funded KCIK also operated an anti-trafficking hotline. Authorities continued to produce and distribute information to Polish citizens seeking work abroad, and the Ministry of Labor operated a website in which Polish citizens could chat with experts about finding legitimate jobs abroad. Authorities also continued to distribute labor rights information to foreign workers in Poland and migrants at Poland's eastern border crossings. The government did not even organize any programs to reduce the participation of Polish citizens in child sex tourism. The government did not run any programs specifically designed to reduce the demand for commercial sex worker.

CONCLUSION

The magnitude of the sex trafficking in Poland is, according to all estimates, substantial. The importance of the exact number is not so much in its absolute order but rather in that each event of trafficking involves a complex of illegal activities that reach not just to Poland but also to many other countries, and, therefore, the negative effects of this phenomenon might be seen with a certain multiplier relative to the consequences of other illegal or irregular migration trends. The main root causes of migrant trafficking appear deep and complex enough to ensure a high plateau and durable character of that phenomenon. This is another argument (besides the current scale and ensuing direct effects) testifying that the problem is socially sensitive and vital from the political point of view. In spite of these arguments, the trafficking is largely perceived by the law enforcement agencies in Poland as a temporary and soft problem, as a nuisance rather than a structural illness. The actors dealing with this problem tend to focus on its current symptoms, and they aim at effectively dealing with its specific manifestations. By this rather than grasping the root causes and wide preventive activities pursued on national and international scale they see the way to cutting down of the incidence of trafficking. Although in Poland government and nongovernment organizations may have to cope with trafficked victims or trafficking networks, the by far major burden of everyday activities rests with the Border Guard. Since the trafficking networks (and the movements of the trafficked foreigners) are spread all around the country whereas, by law, the Border Guard acts principally in areas close to the state frontier, this implies a sort of incompatibility of competencies. In the absence of a legally designated central agency that would be entrusted with carrying out the tasks of immigration policy and coordinating the related activities of various organs, and bearing in mind the human, organizational and infrastructural potential of the Border Guard, such solution might be considered unavoidable. On the other hand, in view of the above mentioned incompatibility of competencies and an exclusive necessity of conducting other important statutory activities by the Border Guard, its all-embracing role in combating human trafficking in Poland would seem only provisional. Combating the phenomenon of trafficking might become easier and more successful provided the recognition of its organized, international, and criminal character and of its penetration into the interior of Poland become widespread (Okólski 1999).

Since 2006, the Programme for Support and Protection of Victims of Human Trafficking has been implemented based on the commission of the Minister of the Interior and Administration. Financed entirely from the state budget, the program is dedicated to foreign nationals—citizens of third countries identified as victims of trafficking in human beings in Poland. Since January 2010, the program has been a part of a new public service—the National Consultation and Intervention Centre for victims of human trafficking that offers help to Polish and foreign nationals who are victims of trafficking in human beings. Within this service, it was also possible to support alleged victims of trafficking in human beings, especially foreigners whose employee rights were violated. In the years 2009–2011, the Programme for Support and Protection of Victims of Human Trafficking helped ninety foreigners (Council of Ministers 2013). The number of victims supported by the National Consultation and Intervention Centre for victims of human trafficking shows, to some extent, the scale of the phenomenon—between April 2009 and December 2011, 619 people received direct support consisting of 328 Polish people and 251 foreigners (Council of Ministers 2013). Notwithstanding, in several cases, victims of trafficking in Poland were subject to more than one form of exploitation and it is difficult to decide which the dominant form is. This confirms the findings that the scope of organized criminal activity networks has been expanded in Poland.

REFERENCES

Council of Europe. 2013. *Report Concerning the Implementation of the Council of Europe Convention on Action against Trafficking in Human Beings by Poland.* Strasbourg: Council of Europe.

Council of Ministers. 2013. *National Action Plan against Trafficking in Human Beings for 2013–2015.* Resolution Number 3 of the Committee for Combating and Preventing Trafficking in Human Beings. Warsaw: Council of Ministers.

Ekstedt, A., Olsson, A. J., Mujaj, E., and Polatside, V. 2013. *Human Trafficking 2013: Baltic Sea Region Round-up.* Stockholm: The Council of Baltic States.

European Commission. 2012. *Together against Trafficking in Human Beings: Poland.* https://ec.europa.eu/anti-trafficking/content/nip/poland_en.

European Commission. 2015. *Poland 3: Implementation of Anti-trafficking Policy.* https://ec.europa.eu/anti-trafficking/member-states/poland-3-implementation-anti-trafficking-policy_en.

Frontex. 2015. *Eastern Borders Route.* http://frontex.europa.eu/trends-and-routes/eastern-borders-route/.

Helsinki Foundation for Human Rights. 1996. *Asylum and migration in Poland.* http://www.europarl.europa.eu/workingpapers/libe/104/poland_en.htm#N123back.

Jensen, M. 2009. *Human Trafficking in Poland.* http://beinghadii.blogspot.com/2009/01/human-trafficking-in-poland.html.

Ministry of Interior and Administration. 2008. *Trafficking Human Beings in Poland.* Warsaw: Ministry of Interior and Administration.

NCA. 2014. *NCA Strategic Assessment: Nature and Scale of Human Trafficking in 2013.* London: NCA.

Okólski, M. 1999. *Migrant Trafficking in Poland: Actors, Mechanisms, Combating.* Warsaw: Institute of Social Studies, University of Warsaw.

Orlandi, L. 2013. *Poland Working to Crack Down on Human Trafficking.* http://www.west-info.eu/poland-working-to-crack-down-on-human-trafficking-czech-republic-abuses/.

Subhan, A., ed. 1996. *Migration and Asylum in Central and Eastern Europe.* Luxembourg: European Parliament.

United Nations News Centre. 2009. *Poland Becoming Transit, Destination Country for Human Trafficking.* http://www.un.org/apps/news/story.asp?NewsID=30961#.VQW8a-GzmVI.

US Department of State. 2007. *Trafficking in Persons Report*. Washington, DC: US Department of State.

US Department of State. 2013. *Trafficking in Persons Report*. Washington, DC: US Department of State.

US Department of State. 2014. *Trafficking in Persons Report*. Washington, DC: US Department of State.

Chapter 4

Trafficking and Human Security in India and United Kingdom

The rise of sexual exploitation has been rapid and in fact a global phenomenon, depicting increasing numbers of children and young women into this domain. The growth of this crime is hasty due to nonexistence of certainty or severity of punishment. Human trafficking brings to the public attention as a result of economic and demographic inequalities in the world, the upswing of conflict and gender discrimination. Typical regional differences in trafficking are not a contemporary experience. In the past, there was no single model of slavery. Just as the trade in human beings was warped in the past by cultural, geographic, and economic forces, today's human trafficking is also shaped by these forces as well as historical traditions. Slavery is illegal throughout the world, yet more than twenty-seven million people are still lured in one of history's oldest social institutions (Shelley 2010). The trade in human beings received attention first and foremost in relation to the trade in women (Bertone 2000; Chuang 1998; Derks 2000), being associated with the phenomenon of the "white slave trade" that had been enthusiastically condemned by moral reformers and feminists in the late nineteenth century. Subsequent historical research revealed that there was little material basis for this crusade of purity (Corbin 1990; Doezema 2000; Rosen 1982; Walkowitz 1982), although Doezema (2000) refers to this question as the "myth of white slavery." This campaign in fact overlapped with an increase in the number of migrant prostitutes in Europe during that period (Guy 1992). According to some analysts, the specter of the sexual exploitation of women reappeared in the late twentieth century, but this time in an industrialized and internationalized form (Barry 1995; Jeffreys 1999; Raymond et al. 2002; Richard 1999). In short, the "white slave trade" was transformed into "trafficking in women," with the focus this time being on third world and non-Western women. The stereotypical victim is still the innocent young girl who is seduced or kidnapped and forced into sexual slavery. Those analysts, for whom the sex trade is in itself a form of bondage, of violence against women, advocate a vigorous struggle against this new form of victimization of women.

Trafficking in persons is not only a peril to the individual, but to entire communities that come across themselves at risk, because of poor socioeconomic factors. Additionally, in transition societies, trafficking in persons also constitutes a threat to the system of law and order, which is *per se* a threat to the essential components of the state, since by evading the law and corrupting state officials the traffickers threaten citizens' larger interests of security and protection. Trafficking in persons is a human rights violation and is so "damaging to its victims, which it has become a cause of human insecurity" (Bales 1999).

First, trafficking in persons represent a threat to the individuals and their inherent basic human right and freedom. Regardless of the form of exploitation, vulnerable people around the world end up in the webs of traffickers for whom each represents a continuous source of profit, as victims are sold time and again, unlike the one-time trade in drug and arms. Paradoxically, they are at the same time highly expendable, easily replaceable assets (Miller 2006), because victims are considered by the criminals to be disposable goods, it makes the former' situation extremely dangerous and uncertain. In the case of external trafficking, the victims are in a particularly vulnerable situation because of their illegal status of residence.

The involvement of organized criminal networks is equally damaging to the fabric of a community and eventually the general society. The presence and power of organized crime networks can influence the community behavior in two ways that are each equally perilous to the principle and practice of democracy. First, because they locally provide "jobs" and a sort of social safety net, people tend to view them sympathetically and support their activities instead of fighting them. Second, because they succeed in corrupting officials and weakening the enforcement system, many citizens lose the trust in their country's government and more severely in the rule of law. Moreover, because they have a stake in maintaining a country unstable and lawless, they have an incentive to oppose return to normality in post-conflict societies. Consequently, this is not only just a form of forced labor and a violation of the human rights of the people, but it is also a crime that weakens the socioeconomic and legislative bases of the state (Woodward 2005). Increasingly, due to the fact that restrictive migration policies and immigration controls imply much more sophistication than the individual operators and the small gangs can provide, large transnational organized crime networks have been claiming a monopoly over smuggling and cross-border trafficking in human beings. Furthermore, the "low risk high profit" characteristics of trafficking are highly attractive for organized criminal networks who use the money thus obtained to finance other criminal activities like extortion, racketeering, money laundering, drug and arms trade, loan sharking, and the bribery of state functionaries. Thus, traffickers are threatening the state and undermining its authority and legitimacy, and they do so by using its powers, and by corrupting officials and law enforcement officers (Väyrynen 2005).

Among the most quoted figures are the United Nations estimates that four million people in a year are traded against their will to work in some form of slavery, many of them are children and believes that in the last thirty years, trafficking in women and children for sexual exploitation in Asia alone has victimized more than thirty million people. Asia is mainly an origin region as well as a destination for trafficking in persons. Asian victims are reported to be trafficked from Asia to Asian countries, in particular to Thailand, Japan, India, Taiwan, and Pakistan (United Nations 2006). The US Department of State estimates that 600,000 to 800,000 (of which around 250,000 in Europe) women and children are trafficked for sexual purposes across international borders each year, of which approximately 80 percent are women and 50 percent are minors. This does not include the International Labour Organization (ILO) estimated 12.3 million people trafficked worldwide for labor annually (US Department of State 2006).

Being a complex phenomenon, problem of trafficking is profoundly entrenched in the socioeconomic, political, and cultural reality of the context in which it occurs, although this may not be its immediate cause. The perpetrators are the traffickers about them relatively little are known. This gap has to be urgently addressed, along with the demand factors, which drive trafficking. It is a fundamental violation of the rights of human beings and shows a manifest disrespect for the dignity of a person (Sarkar 2011a). The scale of the phenomenon of trafficking is difficult to judge. It is very difficult to collect data on trafficking because of the clandestine nature of the operations. The trade is secretive, the women are silenced, the traffickers are perilous and not many agencies are counting (Hughes 2000).

CURRENT SITUATION OF TRAFFICKING
IN INDIA AND THE UK

Sixty-six years after independence, India has the dubious distinction of being home to half the number of modern-day slaves in the world. The first Global Slavery Index has estimated that 13.3 to 14.7 million people live like slaves in the country—roughly equal to the population of Kolkata. The index, published by the Australia-based Walk Free Foundation, ranked 162 countries based on three factors that include estimated prevalence of modern slavery, a measure of child marriage and a measure of human trafficking in and out of a country (The Times of India 2013). States with the highest levels of poverty are where the largest numbers of victims of trafficking originates include Orissa, Bihar, Jharkhand, Chhattisgarh, and West Bengal. Delhi and Goa on the other hand have both a low percentage of people below the poverty line in addition to relatively high literacy rates among both men and women due to positive economic growth resulting from globalization. Consequently these two states are basically reported as destination rather than source locations. For small number victims that originate in these areas, traffickers must use very different strategies in comparison with those employed in source and transit states (Hameed 2010).

India is located in golden triangle which is most vulnerable region for the trafficking of women and children for flesh trade (Westwood 1998). Literature on trafficking in India is completely dominated by the issue of commercial sexual exploitation, so much so that trafficking as a distinct separate crime does not get highlighted. At times is almost reduced to insignificance in comparison to commercial sexual exploitation. Even though there seems to be considerable information available, one is unable to form a picture which reflects the reality of trafficking in women and children in India. India's sex industry includes some two million sex workers, 20 percent of whom are under age 16 and considered children though different laws use different age limits (Sen and Nair 2004). The trafficking definition legally explains exploitation, the exploiter and the exploited for the first time in India's Independent history. Exploitation is defined as forced labor or services, slavery or practices similar to slavery, servitude, the forced removal of organs and prostitution or other forms of sexual exploitation. Calculations of trafficked people are generally made with reference to commercial sex exploitation. In India, the stigma attached to prostitution and the clandestine nature of operations makes it difficult to arrive at authentic numbers (Gupta 2003). Increasing incidence of trafficking has threatened the social fabric of the country. Girls under eighteen are being lured from Nepal, Bangladesh to Indian metropolitan cities. In India, traffickers also lure girls and young women from Assam, West Bengal, Bihar, Rajasthan, Jharkhand, Madhya Pradesh, Chhattisgarh, and Uttar Pradesh. The counterfeit promises of jobs and better living standards push these girls and young women into prostitution (Sarkar 2011a).

Bangladesh is a major country of origin and transit for trafficking in persons in India, especially forced labor and forced prostitution. There is internal trafficking within the country, but a large proportion of trafficking is cross border. Often such transactions are carried out with ease. There are many enclaves between the border of India and Bangladesh. There are 111 Indian enclaves in Bangladesh and 51 enclaves in Bangladesh in India. Traffickers often use these enclaves as recruitment and collection sites. Many border areas are frequently used as land routes for trafficking. A large proportion of cross-border trafficking of women and children in Bangladesh is due to illegal migration in search of better employment to India. Recruiting agencies acting as middlemen in such cases often charge exorbitantly, and there have been a number of cases of recruitment fraud where such female migrants are misled about terms of employment including payment. They find themselves being forced to work in prostitution.

The political conflicts, followed by an economic instability in Nepal, compel people to migrate to bigger cities. This urge contributes to an increased risk of trafficking. Nepali women and girls are easily lured by local agents, neighbour or relatives promising a better life elsewhere. Although, the borders between India and Nepal have entry posts, the Indian and Nepalese citizens are allowed to cross the border without valid documents or any other formalities. The Indo-Nepal Treaty of Peace and Friendship, 1950 was the official beginning of the peaceful relationship between the two countries. Nonetheless, the Indo-Nepal relationship has been passing through several ups and downs. As there are no immigration laws between Nepal and India and as the borders are open and porous, illegal migration, smuggling and human trafficking are very rampant. Migration of its workforce is very common due to its stagnant economy and shortage of local wage opportunities. The caste-based discrimination, gender inequality, social explosion and breaking down the community support system also lead to trafficking from Nepal. For the purpose of trafficking for exploi-tation, this includes exploiting for prostitution of other sexual exploitation, forced labor, slavery or similar practices or removal of organs (Sarkar 2011b).

Besides, during 2011, 946 potential victims of human trafficking in the UK were referred to the National Referral Mechanism (NRM). Of these, 634 were females and 312 were males, 712 were adults and 234 were children. The majority of potential child victims were reported to be in the 16–17-year-old age category (UK Home Office 2012a). The most prevalent source countries for potential victims who were referred into the NRM were Nigeria, China, Vietnam, Romania, and Slovakia. The most prevalent exploitation type recorded through the NRM, for adults, was sexual exploitation however it is recognized that the incidence of labor exploitation and criminal exploitation is increasing. The most prevalent type of exploitation reported for children was labor exploitation. The recently published Serious Organized Crime Agency (SOCA 2013) Intelligence Assessment report suggests that there are 2,250 potential victims of human trafficking were encountered during 2012 in the UK, which represents an increase of 178 (9 percent) compared to those reported in 2011. Of the 2255 potential victims 1246 (55 percent) were female, 910 (40 percent) were male and the gender of 95 (5 percent) of potential victims was unknown. 1607 (71 percent) of all potential victims were adults, 549 (24 percent) were children and the age of 99 (5 percent) of potential victims was unknown. Potential victims were from 78 different countries of origin. Where identified, the most frequently recorded countries of origin were Romania 272 (12 percent), Poland 240 (11 percent), Nigeria 209 (9 percent), Vietnam 133 (6 percent), Hungary 125 (6 percent), Albania 107 (5 percent), Slovakia 103 (5 percent), UK 86 (4 percent), Lithuania 77 (3 percent) and the Philippines 53 (2 percent). The country of origin of 333 (15 percent) potential victims was unknown. Sexual exploitation (35 percent) and labor exploitation (23 percent) were the two most prevalent exploitation types as assessed by SOCA (SOCA 2013).

Because of the covert nature of human trafficking, the crime is difficult to detect. Organized criminals are involved in the exploitation of people for profit with the largest number of Organized Crime Groups (OCGs) reported to be from Romania. The UK uses a range of intelligence tools to understand the threat of human trafficking and deploys a range of tactics to deter and disrupt trafficking activity. Understanding the recruitment methods used by traffickers is important in mitigating the risk to individuals, and closing down identified trafficking routes and practices. Risk profiles are also used by Border Force to help facilitate the identification of more potential trafficking victims and assist in carefully targeted operational activities against trafficking.

The UK Government published its Human Trafficking Strategy in 2011 which aims to take a comprehensive approach by focusing on preventing trafficking activity and maintaining effective care for victims. Actions have been taken forward to improve the awareness of frontline professionals so that they can better identify, support, and protect victims. Effective adult care arrangements for human trafficking victims are in place across the UK.

Increased international engagement is helping the UK to gain a better understanding of the human trafficking landscape, to raise awareness, and to assist in strengthening law enforcement and justice systems in priority source countries. Concentrated efforts have been made by a range of agencies to work together to share information and maximize capabilities to provide an effective response at the border. Law enforcement agencies across the UK also work collaboratively and with their counterparts in other countries to share intelligence and collectively target traffickers (Sarkar 2014). Raising public awareness of human trafficking, working in partnership with NGOs, and tackling the demand for cheap services and goods are also key aspects of the UK's strategy.

Tackling human trafficking in all its forms is vital and the UK is committed to continually shaping and tailoring its response to mitigate the threat. Although the UK has already achieved significant progress in the fight against trafficking, it recognizes that any response must be able to quickly adapt and evolve to keep pace with the traffickers. Three key areas have been identified where further concerted effort is needed to improve and strengthen the UK's approach—data capture and intelligence sharing, training and awareness raising for frontline professionals, and coordinating prevention activities. The UK is not complacent about the efforts required to stop people from being trafficked for exploitation or punishing the perpetrators and will continue to work collaboratively with stakeholders and key agencies as well as supporting source countries in tackling the issues that fuel the demand for human trafficking. Human trafficking is an abhorrent crime which affects communities throughout the world. The international nature of human trafficking means that it knows no boundaries. The UK Government recognizes the importance of working collaboratively with partners both in the UK and overseas, and of using all the available tools in the fight against organized criminals who seek to exploit others.

However, harsh legislation in itself is not the answer. To rely solely on prosecuting and convicting the perpetrators means that a failure to tackle the core issue, protecting the vulnerable people who are susceptible to traffickers in the first place. Stopping traffickers by deterring and disrupting their activities will help to protect the men, women, and children who may fall prey to these despicable acts.

The UK already works with international partners to ensure that, where possible, the threat of trafficking is reduced. Law enforcement agencies in the UK work with their counterparts in other countries to pool resources to tackle trafficking and to bring the perpetrators of this terrible crime to justice, often through joint investigations. It is this kind of collaborative action that will certainly perk up national and international response to human trafficking. From 2013, the new National Crime Agency is also playing a key role in the fight against traffickers through its enhanced intelligence capabilities and its coordination and tasking functions (UK Home Office 2012b).

For Indian government to respond more effectively and carry out the counter-network and counter-market strategy, they need to set up a system that looks remarkably similar to the one they are trying to destroy. It looks initially at the limits of governance, both in general and specifically in relation to combating human trafficking. It then suggests that the networks involved in human trafficking are agile and difficult to combat, especially because they operate within a dynamic market characterized not only by a high demand for forced labor and commercial sex but also a ready supply of trafficking victims. In short, human trafficking poses enormous challenges to governance and law enforcement, and, at times, these challenges seem to be overwhelming. Even if it is something, which is unlikely to be eliminated, however, more effective steps can be taken to contain or even reduce the scope of the problem. This, in turn, has to be manifest in more effective laws against human trafficking. Many countries continue to have inadequate laws, enforcement is often both problematic and misguided (e.g., treating women who have been trafficked for commercial sex as criminals rather than victims, or simply failing to provide adequate levels of protection and assistance), and on those occasions when penalties are enforced they are often ridiculously low. The fact is that too many states continue to provide safe havens for traffickers and trafficking further reduces the effectiveness of the modest efforts at international law enforcement cooperation, which are currently in place. These issues can only be overcome by a concerted effort to raise the priority of combating human trafficking and by both exerting pressure on and enhancing capacity in country like India, which still lack legal instruments and serious anti-trafficking activities.

METHOD

This study seeks to explore a comparative scenario to understand the growing concern about the degree of human security vis-à-vis engendering sex trafficking in India and the UK. Despite structural differences, data heterogeneity and lack of official data sources reliability, this study seems to grasp the existing gap in the light of demonstrating the structural and functional mechanism on that count which reproduces and reinforces the processes and, perpetuating the phenomenon considering trafficking not as discrete events that are unconnected, but to examine them within the wider framework of human insecurity such as poverty, coercion, and violence as structurally dogged. The human security approach involves giving primacy to human beings, understanding security in terms of real-life, everyday experience of humanity embedded within global social and economic structures. In particular, human security takes into account structures that lead to poverty, unequal gender relations and other inequalities (Broadhead 2000; Ruth et al. 2000).

Since this study was designed, executed, and recorded over a six-month period starting from June 2013 to November 2013, its nature was necessarily limited and exploratory, and its findings should be taken at best as suggestive rather than decisive. The study involved both qualitative and quantitative methods. Semi-structured interviews with the exploiters of trafficking survivors were conducted in India and the UK. Data were analyzed using Stata—data analysis and statistical software version 10.0. Recruiting a sample for research on the demand for commercial sex workers presented great methodological challenges. There was no sampling frame listing everyone who used sex trafficking and it was, therefore, impossible to obtain a random or probability sample of these particular population groups. Accessing clients or pimps who broke the law or engaged in practices regarded as socially undesirable (for instance, buying sexual services where it is illegal to do so, or who contravene legislation regulating the employment of sex workers after they have been trafficked) was even more difficult. It took time to find people willing to be interviewed about personal and sensitive topics and since we had very little time, we recognized that it would be realistic to aim for at least hundred-fifty individual interviews in each country. This meant that the interview research was not, nor could have been, undertaken with a representative cross-section of either. Because we were keen to generate comparable, cross-national data, the research design included the exploring demand for commercial sex to be undertaken in each country. Ultimately, it proved impossible to standardize the sampling techniques used in each country in the time available. Though the survey on trafficking for sexual servitude produced some very interesting data, unfortunately they were not fully comparable. The survey comprised total of 283 trafficked women and girls with 147 from India and 136 from the UK. A standardized questionnaire was used for both the countries. The multistage stratified sampling technique was undertaken. The survey covered rural, semi-urban and urban areas in each of the sample countries. In each area, interviews were proportionally distributed according to the size of settlement. Within each group, settlements were randomly selected applying probabilities proportional to size.

RESULTS AND DISCUSSION

The vast majority of the trafficking victims interviewed in this study (about 56 percent) were Nepali (destination India); Romanian and Nigerian (destination UK). The 39 percent came from countries such as Bangladesh (destination India); China, Poland, Vietnam, Hungary, Albania, Slovakia, Lithuania, and the Philippines (destination UK), and remaining 5 percent was either native Indian or British.

Poverty and gender imbalances in the availability of gainful employment opportunities for women, gender violence, and limited access to resources have created a pool of vulnerable people, which has heightened cross-border trafficking activities (Sarkar 2011a). Although existing research easily identifies the vital role of economics in human trafficking, it has failed to probe the complex relationship between poverty, discrimination, and other sociocultural factors such as deprivation status. Consequently, there is a distinct lack of research relating to traditionally disadvantaged groups and systemic discrimination within the human trafficking literature. Although evidence within the extant literature is suggestive of a link between disadvantaged populations and susceptibility to trafficking, this correlation has been insufficiently investigated. Indeed, it is surprising how little research has been done to explore human trafficking through the lens of minority discrimination. Before policymakers can produce sustainable prevention and development policies, research must identify the strongest indicators of trafficking experienced by marginalized groups. This includes expanding the current ideology on minority groups in order to encompass the endemic bias and the resulting consequences they experience. The study shows that economic depression or poverty was the main reason behind trafficking of women and girls to India (82 percent) and the UK (76 percent) followed by better living conditions with high wages in the destination countries (India 43 percent and UK 64 percent). The interviews reveal that women and girls migrated independently to seek better job opportunity in urban areas and it was after this process that they were sex trafficked (India 24 percent and UK 49 percent). A Bangladeshi girl described that she was sold to India by her father in order to afford medical treatment of her younger brother. Extreme poverty, combined with the low social status of women, often resulted in parents handing over their children to strangers for what they believed was employment or marriage. In some instances, parents received payments or the promise that their children would send wages back home. A Lithuania woman explained: "When I was only 16 then trafficked from *Seta*. A friend offered a job in London and I decided to join her. On arrival I was taken to *Soho*, where a man sold me to a pimp for £2,500. I tried to escape but did not succeed."

The study exposes that many victims suffered rape and violence at the hands of their traffickers or criminal gang in the first instance, often repeatedly until they were sold out to a brothel keeper. After being raped by traffickers all day long, many victims are raped by the associates of the trafficker at night. A Nepali woman narrated "how she raged the shriek on so-called human trafficker after arriving in India with him, she was raped by four men concurrently and dumped semi-naked in the street." She claimed that she was taken to a flat in Kolkata which housed three other Nepali and four Bangladeshi women worked as dancers in a nightclub and I was asked to work as a dancer. She added: "I told that I didn't know how to dance and moreover I have burn marks on my body. He asked me to work as a cleaner in the flat and later I was sold to a brothel in *Sonagachi*." A Romanian woman described that she was traveling to London for better life and prospect. In the way she met with a person who was also traveling to London from Brussels in the same train who recognized himself as an owner of a hotel in central London. She added: "He offered me pineapple juice, I drank and the next thing I knew I was in a hotel in city of London where three men came in the night and raped me until next morning."

The study reveals that 24 percent of the victims were first raped before age 14 while 18 percent were raped between the ages of 16–18. Interestingly, the mean age at first sexual intercourse was similar to the respondents from both the countries studied but the gap between the first sexual intercourse and that in exchange for money was less to Indian respondents. The proportion of survivors having a gap of more than five years between sexual intercourse and that in exchange for money was higher among the non-brothel based victim in comparison with the brothel based.

The percentage of victims in Indian sample who reported experiencing a completed rape was 3 times smaller than the percentage in the UK (7.5 percent compared with 22.5 percent, odds ratio [OR]=1.55; 95 percent confidence interval [CI]=1.2–2.5 for the UK). The Indian respondents attempted rape estimate was 2.5 times smaller than the UK respondents attempted rape estimate (4 percent compared to 10 percent, OR=1.23; 95 percent CI=0.91–1.26 for the UK). A similar pattern was evident for threats of rape—Indian sample estimate was 2 times smaller than the UK sample estimate (2 percent compared to 4 percent, OR=0.69; 95 percent CI=0.43–0.53 for the UK). Comparing the completed rape proportions from data of the two countries sample respondents resulted in a Z = 212.34. Because the test statistic 212.34 exceeds the critical value of 1.96 (α= 0.05), there is a statistically significant difference between the two completed rape proportions of the trafficking survivors.

In this study sexual coercion of the trafficking survivors was measured with two variables, "client insistence" and "client gets angry." "Client insistence" assessed the prevalence of the customer insistence to have sex when the woman did not want to, and was measured in the entire sample. "Client gets angry" assessed customer reaction in the subset of women who reported ever-refusing to have sex with him. Experiences of physical violence by the employer were also assessed in the study. The moderate physical violence included slapping or throwing, pushing, pulling, and hitting with fist while severe physical violence included kicking or dragging and trying to burn. The study shows that sexual coercion and physical violence from the client and pimp had serious short- and long-term physical, mental, sexual, and reproductive health problems for trafficking survivors. A Nigerian survivor described: "I was absolutely terrified when one client forced me to have sex repeatedly. When I refused he pulled my hair and hit me, and finally threw me onto the floor to have sex several times. He tore my clothes off and stayed on top of me for I don't know how long, it felt like it would never end. I didn't scream or even try to hit him because it was hurting a lot it felt like it was burning inside me. I just closed my eyes and wanted it to go away." A teenage girl from Nepal told "every girl remembers her first client; I shall never forget the terrible moments as long as I live. I saw a lot of girls being beaten badly and heard screaming of my co-worker for help when the client is not fully satisfied."

Among the 283 women who reported ever-refusing to have sex with client, 68 percent respondents from India and 62 percent from the UK said that their clients would get crazy in response to their refusal. For physical violence in the couple, of the total sample, 28 percent (India) and 21 percent (UK) said that their employer dragged them. Five percent (India) and 6 percent (UK) also reported that they had beaten their clients while 11 percent (India) and 9 percent (UK) stated that they had been either slapped or hit with fist by the employer. Specifically, 2 percent (India) and 1 percent (UK) reported that their employers had tried to burn or strangle them if they sometime denied working, and 12 women from India and 7 from the UK reported these experiences to burn with a cigarette from clients. Sexual coercion and physical violence were significantly associated. Women who reported client insistence were more likely to also report being beaten (OR =1.62; 95 percent CI =1.2–2.3). All 7 women from India and 8 from the UK who said they had beaten their client also reported being beaten by him. Of the women who had ever refused to have sex with client, those who said that their client reacted furiously were more likely to also report client insistence (OR =4.33; 95 percent CI= 2.9–7.3) and being beaten by their employer (OR= 2.18; 95 percent CI =1.8–3.6), compared to the women who reported other reactions from their clients such as, pushed, pulled, or held on. Of the 283 women, 132 (71 from India and 61 from UK) women were suffering from either type of sexually transmitted infections (OR=1.43; 95 percent CI=1.64–5.89). Twenty-six percent (India) and 32 percent (UK) women were with known sexually transmitted infections (STIs). The susceptibility of a trafficked woman to STIs is certainly higher than that of a person who engages in sex work out of choice because of being exposed to forced and unsafe sex with multiple partners, victims may be injected with drugs to increase their compliance, or they may choose to inject drugs as a coping mechanism. They tend to have less money at their disposal and cannot afford medical care. The clandestine status of trafficking victims makes them invisible and further reduces their access to health services.

Further, descriptive data and multivariate analysis are used to explore the prevalence and patterns of sexual coercion by the clients. Two different models are developed, one for client insistence to have sex (table 4.1) and one for client reaction in refusal to have sex by the victim (table 4.2). For each model, the demographic and behavior variables are entered in a stepwise logistic regression to examine independent predictors of sexual coercion. The independent variables identified were then entered with female current status of STIs in a second logistic regression model. The univariate and multivariate odds ratios for the demographic, the behavioral, and the serostatus variables are presented in table 4.1 and table 4.2.

Woman suffering from STIs remained independently associated to client's insistence to have sex, when adjusting for all the other variables in the model (OR= 1.99; 95 percent CI =1.55–2.82). The strongest independent predictor of client's insistence was women's refusal to have sex. Women who reported frequent sexual contacts with same client, women who attempted to convince their client to use condom, and women who had been somehow in relationship with client were also more likely to report client's insistence. The association with client's insistence approached significance for having a client who drank alcohol. Among the subset of women who ever refused to have sexual intercourse, female STIs positivity remained marginally associated to client's angry reaction, when controlling for the other variables in the model (OR= 1.62; 95 percent CI= 0.89–2.33). The strongest independent predictors of client's angry reaction were condom negotiation. A client who drank alcohol was also independently associated with his angry reaction. We carried out exploratory analysis of possible interactions between female STIs positivity, and condom negotiation in the two multivariate models of sexual coercion. For client's insistence, none of the interactions were significant. In the model of client's angry reaction, all STIs positive women were at elevated risk for client reacting angrily to their refusal to have sex.

The process used to construct the multivariate model of physical violence perpetrated client was identical to that described for the models of sexual coercion, and the univariate and multivariate odds ratios for the demographic, the behavioral, and STIs status variables are shown in table 4.3. Female STIs positivity did not remain significantly associated to physical violence perpetrated by client when controlling for other variables in the model, although a trend was identified. Female who said that client drank alcohol and who were in the relationship longer were significantly more likely to report being beaten by their client. The associations between physical violence perpetrated by client and predictor of condom use approached significance. We carried out exploratory analysis of possible interactions between female STIs positivity and condom negotiation in the multivariate model of client physical violence. Despite a negligible numbers, we found a strong independent association between physical violence and women having STIs positive who negotiated condom, compared to women having STIs negative (OR 11.3; 95 percent CI 2.56–71.45).

CONCLUSION

The study identifies that poverty is among the root causes of sexual violence and has a daily presence in the lives of many trafficking victims and survivors. Poverty is directly linked to be a major cause of trafficking for the victims. The dire need to meet economic demands and escape poverty drives women and girls may compel then to seek solace in trafficking especially in the area of sex work and prostitution. This study also shows a definite link between poverty, sexual coercion, and violence. Sexual violence jeopardizes social and economic security of the victims, often leading to physical and mental health, and other daily stressors and struggles. In turn, living without one's basic needs met can increase a person's risk for sexual victimization (Greco and Dawgert 2007). Poverty is a risk factor for perpetration of sexual violence. Risk factors for perpetration at community and society levels include poverty, lack of employment opportunities, lack of institutional support from administrative system, and a high tolerance for crime and other forms of violence. While these factors exist in all income levels, they are especially prevalent in economically unprivileged communities. Sexual violence is perpetuated by a sexual molestation or rape culture—a system of attitudes, inequities, and acts that support sexual aggression and violence. The study shows that the victims were raped either by the traffickers or boyfriends in the first instance and recognizes many victims had been suffering from post-traumatic stress disorder, substance use disorder, major depression, and generalized anxiety disorder in the consequence of rape. The risk for these disorders was higher for survivors who experienced a sexual assault at a younger age.

The survivors' sexual susceptibility because of larger social and economic factors may be compounded by the possibility of sexual and physical violence. The prevalence of sexual coercion and physical violence reported in this study was very high. We found that men were more violent in relationships than women, and that all women who beat their clients were also beaten by their clients, may be for self-defense or as reactions to exploitation. Abusive behaviors often cluster, and women who experienced sexual coercion were also more likely to have been beaten by their client. We found direct and indirect associations between sexual coercion, physical violence perpetrated by clients, and STIs positivity. The similarities in the factors associated with sexual coercion and physical violence suggest a common pathway, that is, gender influence differentials. Furthermore, it appears that gender inequality coupled with women's sexual resistance (e.g., refusal to have sex) or their assertiveness (e.g., negotiating condom) may be associated with sexual coercion and physical violence. Client's insistence to have sex was most strongly associated with female's refusal to have sex. Although it is true that forcing one to have sex can only take place against some expression of resistance. Condom negotiation and client drinking alcohol were associated with sexual coercion and physical violence. The association between client alcohol drinking, sexual coercion, and physical violence is also consistent with the cross-cultural literature, although alcohol is believed to exacerbate rather than cause violent behavior. The study also shows that there were some differences in the factors predicting sexual coercion and those predicting physical violence. Current female STIs positivity was directly associated with sexual coercion, but not with physical violence. Though there is not necessarily a direct causal correlation between trafficking and STIs always and everywhere, once a person is trafficked they generally face a new and powerless position in an unfamiliar surroundings which increases their STIs vulnerability. The causality pathways between predictors and outcomes could not be determined because of the cross-sectional nature of the data. In addition, it is likely that many of these variables are associated with each other by multiple causal pathways.

REFERENCES

Bales, K. 1999. *Disposable People: New Slavery in the Global Economy*. Berkeley and Los Angeles, CA: University of California Press.

Barry, K. 1995. *The Prostitution of Sexuality: The Global Exploitation of Women.* New York: New York University Press.

Bertone, A. M. 2000. "Sexual Trafficking in Women: International Political Economy and the Politics of Sex." *Gender Issues* 18(1): 4–22.

Broadhead, L. 2000. "Re-packaging Notions of Security: A Sceptical Feminist Response to Recent Efforts." In *States of Conflict, in Sates of Conflict: Gender, Violence and Resistance*, edited by Jacobs Susan et al. New York: Zed Books.

Chuang, J. 1998. "Redirecting the Debate over Trafficking in Women: Definitions, Paradigms and Contexts." *Harvard Human Rights Journal* 11: 65–107.

Corbin, A. 1990. *Women for Hire: Prostitution and Sexuality in France after 1850.* Cambridge, MA: Harvard University Press.

Derks, A. 2000. *Combating Trafficking in South Asia: A Review of Policy and Programme Responses*. Geneva: International Organization for Migration.

Doezema, J. 2000. "Loose Women or Lost Women." *Gender Issues* 18(1): 23–50.

Greco, D. and Dawgert, S. 2007. *Poverty and Sexual Violence: Building Prevention and Intervention Responses*. Enola, PA: Pennsylvania Coalition against Rape.

Gupta, G. R. 2003. *Review of Literature for Action Research on Trafficking in Women and Children*. New Delhi: Institute of Social Sciences.

Guy, D. J. 1992. "White Slavery, Citizenship and Nationality in Argentina." In *Nationalisms and Sexualities*, edited by A. Parker et al. London: Routledge.

Hameed, S. et al. 2010. *Human Trafficking in India: Dynamics, Current Efforts, and Intervention Opportunities for the Asia Foundation*. Ford Dorsey Program in International Policy Studies. California: Stanford University.

Hughes, D. 2000. "The 'Natasha' Trade: The Transnational Shadow Market of Trafficking in Women." *Journal of International Affairs* 53(2): 1–18.

Jeffreys, S. 1999. "Globalizing Sexual Exploitation: Sex Tourism and the Traffic in Women." *Leisure Studies* 18(3): 179–196.

Miller, J. R. 2006. "Slave Trade: Combating Human Trafficking." *Harvard International Review* 27(4): 70–73.

Raymond, Janice G. et al. 2002. *A Comparative Study of Women Trafficked in the Migration Process*. New York: Coalition against Trafficking in Women.

Richard, Amy O'Neill. 1999. *International* Trafficking in Women to the United States: A Contemporary Manifestation of Slavery and Organized Crime. Washington, DC: Center for the Study of Intelligence.

Rosen, J. 1982. *The* Lost Sisterhood: Prostitution in America, *1900–1918.* London: John Hopkins University Press.

Ruth, J. et al. 2000. "Introduction." In *States of Conflict, in Sates of Conflict: Gender, Violence and Resistance,* edited by Jacobs Susan et al. New York: Zed Books.

Sarkar, S. 2011a. "Trafficking in Women and Children to India and Thailand: Characteristics, Trends and Policy Issues." *International Journal of Afro-Asian Studies* 2(1): 57–73.

Sarkar, S. 2011b. "Engendering Trafficking and Human Security: A Comparative Study of India and Hungary." *International Journal of Development Research and Quantitative Techniques* 1(2): 25–42.

Sarkar, S. 2014. "Trans-border Sex Trafficking: Identifying Cases and Victims in the UK." *Migration and Development* 3(1): 95–107.

Sen, S. and Nair, P. M. 2004. *A Report on Trafficking in Women and Children in India 2002–2003.* Volume I, NHRC - UNIFEM - ISS Project. New Delhi: National Human Rights Commission.

Shelley, L. 2010. *Human Trafficking: A Global Perspective.* New York: Cambridge University Press.

SOCA. 2013. *UKHTC: A Strategic Assessment on the Nature and Scale of Human Trafficking in 2012.* Intelligence Assessment Report, London.

The Times of India. 2013. "India has Half the World's Modern Slaves: Study." *The Times of India,* October 18.

UK Home Office. 2012a. *First Annual Report of the Inter-departmental Ministerial Group on Human Trafficking.* London: UK Home Office.

UK Home Office. 2012b. *Report on the Internal Review of Human Trafficking Legislation.* Policy Paper. London: UK Home Office.

United Nations. 2006. *Trafficking in Persons: Global Patterns.* New York: United Nations.

US Department of State. 2006. *Trafficking in Persons Report.* Washington, DC: US Department of State.

Väyrynen, R. 2005. "Illegal Immigration, Human Trafficking and Organized Crime." In *Poverty, International Migration and Asylum,* edited by George J. Borjas and Jeff Crisp. New York: Palgrave Macmillan.

Walkowitz, J. 1982. *Prostitution and Victorian Society: Women, Class, and the State.* Cambridge: Cambridge University Press.

Westwood, D. 1998. *Child Trafficking in Asia.* World Vision Briefing Paper No. 4, World Vision International.

Woodward, S. L. 2005. "Enhancing Cooperation against Trans-border Crime in Southeast Europe: Is there an Emerging Epistemic Community?" In *Fighting Organized Crime in Southeast Europe,* edited by E. Athanassopoulou. Oxon: Routledge.

APPENDIX

Table 4.1 Correlates of Sexual Coercion (Client Insists to have Sex when Woman does not want to): Univariate and Multivariate Logistic Regressions

Independent variables	Category	Univariate analysis Unadjusted odds ratio (N=283)			Multivariate analysis Adjusted odds ratio (N=283)		
		Odds ratio	95 percent confidence interval	P	Odds ratio	95 percent confidence interval	P
Age group	<25 years	1.29	0.67–2.36				
	25–29	1.03	0.71–1.48				
	30–34	1.13	0.87–1.86				
	≥35 years	–	–				
Sexual frequency with clients (per week)	≤4	1.22	0.77–1.65	*	1.74	1.33–2.65	0.015
	5–7	1.45	1.16–2.21				
	8–10	1.37	1.72–3.21				
	≥11	1.86	0.89–1.48				
Woman drinks alcohol with client		1.86	0.91–1.57	*	2.23	1.31–3.16	0.06
Client gets drunk		1.89	1.42–3.65	***	1.67	1.36–3.78	0.053
Woman ever negotiated condom		2.87	2.06–4.07	***	2.61	1.71–4.02	0.002
Women ever used condom with client		1.55	1.23–1.99	**			
Woman ever refused to have sex		29.45	17.94–68.56	***	42.11	18.43–77.76	0.001
Woman suffered from STIs	Positive	2.33	1.77–3.53	***	1.62	0.89–2.33	0.003

Note: Overall model $p < .0001$; goodness-of-fit Hosmer-Lemeshow chi-square test $p = .5$. ***$p \leq .001$; **$p \leq .01$; *$p \leq .05$.

Table 4.2 Correlates of Sexual Coercion (Client's Angry Reaction to Woman who Refused to have Sex): Univariate and Multivariate Logistic Regressions

Independent variables	Category	Univariate analysis Unadjusted odds ratio (N=283)			Multivariate analysis Adjusted odds ratio (N=283)		
		Odds ratio	95 percent confidence interval	P	Odds ratio	95 percent confidence interval	P
Age group	<25 years	1.54	0.78–3.59				
	25–29	1.07	0.62–1.67				
	30–34	1.36	0.79–2.49				
	≥35 years	–	–				
Sexual frequency with clients (per week)	≤4	1.32	0.63–1.15	*	1.64	1.67–2.89	0.012
	5–7	1.18	1.23–2.49				
	8–10	1.47	1.44–2.72				
	≥11	1.65	0.99–3.36				
Woman drinks alcohol with client		1.62	1.83–2.05	*	1.53	1.65–2.18	0.009
Client gets drunk		2.77	1.23–4.09	***	2.67	1.96–4.78	0.013
Woman ever negotiated condom		2.56	1.23–4.34		2.43	1.66–3.74	0.000
Women ever used condom with client		2.22	1.11–2.76	**			
Woman suffered from STIs	Positive	2.65	1.36–3.35	***	1.58	0.97–2.53	0.099

Note: Overall model $p < .0001$; goodness-of-fit Hosmer-Lemeshow chi-square test $p = .5$. ***$p \leq .001$; **$p \leq .01$; *$p \leq .05$.

Table 4.3　Correlates of Physical Violence Perpetrated by Client: Univariate and Multivariate Logistic Regressions

Independent variables	Category	Univariate analysis Unadjusted odds ratio (N=283)			Multivariate analysis Adjusted odds ratio (N=283)		
		Odds ratio	95 percent confidence interval	P	Odds ratio	95 percent confidence interval	P
Age group	<25 years	1.51	0.73–2.42				
	25–29	0.78	0.51–1.39				
	30–34	1.17	0.67–1.83				
	≥35 years	—	—				
Sexual frequency with clients (per week)	≤4	1.03	0.66–1.47	*	1.56	1.08–2.44	0.074
	5–7	1.11	1.16–2.21				
	8–10	1.43	1.72–3.21				
	≥11	1.65	0.89–1.48				
Woman drinks alcohol with client		1.41	1.09–1.86	*	1.77	1.53–2.98	0.066
Client gets drunk		3.45	2.56–6.13	***	3.58	1.76–6.55	0.001
Woman ever negotiated condom		1.84	1.33–2.66	**	1.56	0.91–2.30	0.068
Women ever used condom with client		1.11	0.64–1.48	*			
Woman ever refused to have sex		1.52	1.21–2.19	*			
Woman suffered from STIs	Positive	1.43	0.76–1.47		0.67	0.39–1.22	0.13

Note: Overall model $p < .0001$; goodness-of-fit Hosmer-Lemeshow chi-square test $p = .5$. ***$p \leq .001$; **$p \leq .01$; *$p \leq .05$.

Chapter 5

Securitization in India and Hungary

Trafficking of human beings, especially of women and children, is an organized crime that violates basic human rights. As per the UN Protocol to prevent, suppress, and punish trafficking in persons, especially women and children, supplementing the UN Convention against Transnational Organized Crime, trafficking is defined as any activity leading to recruitment, transportation, harboring or receipt of persons by means of threat or use of force or a position of vulnerability. Human trafficking has been identified as the third largest source of profit for organized crime, following arms and drug trafficking, generating billions of dollars annually at the global level. Trafficking takes places for various purposes such as labor, prostitution, organ trade, drug couriers, arms smuggling, and so on. However, these cannot be seen in isolation as they have a crosscutting nexus and linkage, which compounds the constraints faced in tackling the problem. It is also seen that while the methods used for trafficking such as coercion, duping, luring, abducting, kidnapping, and so on are commonly cited, it is the social and economic constraints of the victims that make them most vulnerable.

With growing globalization and liberalization, the possibilities and potential for trafficking have also grown. People tend to migrate in search of better opportunities. Though this is a positive trend, it has also led to the emergence of other complex issues such as smuggling of people across borders and unsafe migration by unscrupulous touts and agents. While trafficking has severe implications on the psycho-social and economic well-being of the victim, highly adverse ramifications are also seen on the society and the nation. By denying the victims their basic rights to good health, nutrition, education, and economic independence, the country loses a large number of women and children as victims to this crime, who otherwise would have contributed productively to its growth. A growing concern is that trafficking has an adverse impact on the problem of HIV/AIDS too. Some studies have revealed that the longer the confinement in brothels, the greater is the probability of the victims contracting HIV/AIDS due to poor negotiation for safe sex methods. The country has to incur huge costs for health and rehabilitation as well as for law enforcement.

Being a complex phenomenon, problem of trafficking is profoundly entrenched in the socioeconomic, political, and cultural reality of the context in which it occurs, although this may not be its immediate cause. The perpetrators are the traffickers about whom relatively little is known. This gap has to be urgently addressed, along with the demand factors, which drive trafficking. It is a fundamental violation of the rights of human beings and shows a blatant disregard for the dignity of a person (Sarkar 2011).

The scale of the phenomenon is difficult to judge. It is very difficult to collect data on trafficking because of the clandestine nature of the operations. The trade is secretive, the women are silenced, the traffickers are dangerous and not many agencies are counting (Hughes 2000).

Among the most quoted figures are the United Nations estimates that four million people in a year are traded against their will to work in some form of slavery, many of them are children and believes that in the last 30 years, trafficking in women and children for sexual exploitation in Asia alone has victimized more than 30 million people. Asia is mainly an origin region as well as a destination for trafficking in persons. Asian victims are reported to be trafficked from Asia to Asian countries, in particular to Thailand, Japan, India, Taiwan, and Pakistan (United Nations 2006). The US Department of State estimates that 600,000 to 800,000 (of which around 250,000 in Europe) women and children are trafficked for sexual purposes across international borders each year, of which approximately 80 percent are women and 50 percent are minors. This does not include the International Labour Organization (ILO) estimated 12.3 million people trafficked worldwide for labor annually (US Department of State 2006a).

India is located in golden triangle, which is most vulnerable region for the trafficking of women and children for flesh trade (Westwood 2008). Literature on trafficking in India is completely dominated by the issue of commercial sexual exploitation, so much so that trafficking, as a distinct separate crime does not get highlighted. At times is almost reduced to insignificance in comparison to commercial sexual exploitation. Even though there seems to be considerable information available, one is unable to form a picture, which reflects the reality of trafficking in women and children in India (Sen and Nair 2004).

Calculations of trafficked people are generally made with reference to commercial sex exploitation. In India, the stigma attached to prostitution and the clandestine nature of operations makes it doubly difficult to arrive at authentic numbers (Gupta 2003). Increasing incidence of trafficking has threatened the social fabric of the country. Girls under 18 are being lured from Nepal and Bangladesh to Indian metropolitan cities. In India traffickers also lure girls and young women from Assam, West Bengal, Bihar, Rajasthan, Jharkhand, Madhya Pradesh, Chhattisgarh, and Uttar Pradesh. The counterfeit promises of jobs and better living standards push these girls and young women into prostitution.

There are many reasons of human trafficking. But the traffickers look for most lucrative purpose through which they can be more benefited. Because of this, most of the women and children from rural Nepal and Bangladesh are more innocent and attractive and they become the target of traffickers in this sense. Sexual trafficking is highly profitable and low penalty nature business than others in India. There is a huge demand for women and female children in the sex industries in India, Pakistan, and Middle East. The demand for women and female children is undoubtedly more compared to males in sex industries in South Asian countries. A special target of traders are female children because, among customers of commercial sex establishment, there is a perception that female children are virgins and are less likely to be infected with HIV. Moreover, there is a common myth that sex with a virgin, specially a child, cures a person of STDs. There is no scientific explanation to this belief, but it exists and adds to child prostitution. According to the information received from different GOs and NGOs in India the traffickers prefer Bangladeshi and Nepali women and children, as they are more easily accessible and also easy to take to India.

Moreover, women and female children are generally less productive than males; they are easier to abuse, easily forced, less assertive, and less able to claim their rights. Accordingly, they can be made to work for longer hours with little food, poor accommodation, and no benefits, which also attracts the traffickers to traffic women and female children more rather than males.

The most important reason behind trafficking women and female children massively from Bangladesh and Nepal is as the Bangladeshi and Nepali girls are relatively free from the deadly disease AIDS and HIV virus that is why they have high demand to the customers of the brothels. And this is the reason, which compels the traffickers to traffic women and female children massively from Bangladesh and Nepal to India.

At present, Hungary is both a transit and a destination country for migration trafficking. Not only are citizens of the neighboring countries trafficking, but there are growing numbers originating from more distant countries. The future of Hungary as a destination or a transit country for them will depend mainly on the further European policy developments. Western countries have introduced more and more restrictions on the flow of trafficking. Arrival in Hungary, whether it is legal or not, does not provide for the legal possibility of progressing further into Europe in the majority of cases. As a consequence, many of them will try to cross the borders illegally, often with the help of human traffickers.

Located along a corridor between Eastern and Western Europe, Hungary has become a key transit country for various intra-regional transactions, both legitimate and illicit. In particular, it has become a gateway to Western Europe for persons trafficked from Eurasia. With its accession to the European Union (EU), Hungary now forms the eastern edge of the EU; its importance in this area will increase as it assumes responsibility for monitoring those who enter and exit the EU. In 2007, Hungary will officially become subject to the Schengen Agreement, which applies to countries within the European Union and enables citizens of participating states to cross-shared borders without checks. With fewer border checks between EU states, those along the perimeter will be tasked with controlling entry into the EU. Consequently, Hungary will serve as a first line of defense against trafficking for the EU.

According to US Department of State (2006) report Hungary is a source, transit, and destination country for women and girls trafficked from Ukraine, Moldova, Poland, the Balkans, and the PRC to Austria, Germany, Spain, the Netherlands, Italy, France, Switzerland, Japan, the United States, the UK, and several countries in Scandinavia and Central America for the purpose of sexual exploitation (US Department of State 2006b).

Limited employment opportunities for women and discrimination against women in the labor market in Hungary, specifically young women and women with young children make Hungary a country of origin. Unemployment is a greater problem in Eastern parts of the country, and therefore, women here are more vulnerable to becoming victims of trafficking.

Hungary currently lacks reliable estimates of the number of people who are trafficked to, from and through the country annually. This is partly due to the fact that no agency has been charged with compiling national data on victims of trafficking. At present, statistics are maintained at the local level. Recent estimates have suggested that "as many as 1,50,000 victims transit through Hungary each year" (US Department of State 2004). However, this figure is believed to be too high, as it conflates smuggling and trafficking (Srivastava and Choudhury 2005).

Prosecution statistics are available, but fail to capture the scope and gravity of Hungary's trafficking problem. Only twenty-two individuals were prosecuted under Hungary's trafficking law in 2004 (United States of America State Department 2004). This low rate of prosecution is due to a number of factors: trafficking victims are often too intimidated to testify against their traffickers; police systematically fail to recognize trafficking victims; border guards lack jurisdiction to investigate suspected trafficking cases; and perverse incentives discourage the police from investigating trafficking cases.

In short, prosecution statistics do not reflect the fact that a large number of trafficking cases are never detected, and those that are detected are rarely prosecuted.

It is also difficult to gauge what forms of trafficking are most prevalent in Hungary. The prosecution data provided by the National Police was not disaggregated to distinguish between sex, labor, and other forms of trafficking. Moreover, any effort to extrapolate based on such a small sample would be inconclusive. The division leader of the Criminal Investigation and Intelligence Department of the Hungarian Border Guards reported that 60 percent of Hungarian trafficking cases were related to forced labor while the other 40 percent were related to other forms of trafficking, such as forced sex labor (Choudhury and Zureick 2005).

The lack of reliable data on trafficking in Hungary poses a serious challenge to the police's anti-trafficking efforts. Many officers said that they could not gauge the gravity of Hungary's trafficking problem because of the absence of data. One officer responded: "I don't have an answer because I don't have any data. You need to ask someone with data who knows about this. I have only heard lectures about it (Srivastava and Tressa Johnson 2005). The victims trafficked through and to Hungary come primarily from the CIS, the Balkans, Poland, and China. The Hungarian victims of trafficking are to a great extent recruited in the eastern part of the country, where the social and economic situation is presently the most difficult. The target area for women trafficked from and through Hungary is the EU (Austria), and to some extent also the United States. Presently, Hungary is estimated to have 10,000 prostitutes, of whom 500 are minors. One-third of the prostitutes are foreigners, mainly Ukrainians, Russians, and Romanians. Trafficking from Hungary has decreased considerably over the last few years, but unfortunately a corresponding positive trend is not seen in trafficking through and to the country (Lehti 2003). The scarcity and inconsistency of statistics, and the fact that prosecution statistics tend to seriously downplay the prevalence of trafficking, give the impression that trafficking is not a major problem in Hungary. This creates a vicious cycle—law enforcement officials fail to investigate trafficking because they perceive it to be a minor problem; yet, their failure to investigate further exacerbates the deficiency of data on the crime.

TRAFFICKING PATTERNS AND
TRENDS IN ASIA AND EUROPE

Traffickers lure victims from their homes with false promises of economic opportunities and better lives. Naturally, less developed countries with high rates of poverty, violence, and corruption constitute their best recruiting bases. South and South East Asia, South East Europe, and Latin America are the largest source of trafficking victims.

In East and Southeast Asia the main countries of origin for trafficking are Thailand, China, the Philippines, Myanmar, Vietnam, and Cambodia, while the major countries of transit and destination are assumed to be Thailand, Malaysia, and Japan. Myanmar is regarded as both a country from which persons are trafficked into Thailand and as a transit country for the trafficking of Chinese women and girls from Yunnan province into Thailand (Caouette 1998).

In Cambodia, trafficking has become an issue since the early 1990s. In response to the growing sex industry in the country most trafficking of girls and young women within Cambodia is for the purpose of commercial sexual services. Cambodia is known as a destination for trafficked persons from Vietnam. It is also regarded as a country of origin and transit for Cambodians and Vietnamese sent to Thailand and elsewhere in Asia (IOM Project Outline 2000–2002).

Trafficking in Indonesia is generally assumed to take place in the context of labor migration to the Middle East and East and Southeast Asian countries, though the issue has so far not received much attention. Due to the economic crisis, Indonesian women have reportedly become more exposed to illegal forms of migration.

The eight Lao provinces bordering on Thailand are known to be areas from where large numbers of people go to Thailand to work, the majority illegally. Little is known about how they cross the border and their whereabouts in Thailand.

More than two decades of labor shortage in Malaysia have resulted in a high level of immigration of professionals as well as unskilled labor, which in the case of women mostly means domestic work. For this reason women from countries like Indonesia, the Philippines, Thailand, China, and also from India and Sri Lanka, go to Malaysia. According to the IOM some of them have been trafficked. Malaysian women are also victims of trafficking for prostitution and other purposes within as well as outside the region. However, since the issue has mainly been addressed within the context of illegal migration there are no reliable estimates of the number of persons trafficked to and from Malaysia (IOM 2000).

Japan is regarded to have the largest sex industry in Asia, recruiting women and girls mainly from Thailand and the Philippines and also from for instance Russia and Ukraine but most trafficking in China occurs within the country especially from poor rural areas of Yunnan, Sichuan, and Guizhou.

In the 1990s female Filipino migrants outnumbered Filipino male migrants, especially with respect to domestic work, entertainment and commercial sex service, but also more qualified work. Within the context of large-scale labor migration, trafficking processes have developed through specialized agencies or informal networks. The victims include girls who are promised high-paying jobs, but end up as prostitutes; girls who leave as tourists, but end up as maids, dancers or bar girls; and girls forced into the mail-order bride trade. The trafficking of young children is arranged mainly through adoption, which subsequently leads to commercial or other exploitation, abduction or purchase and sale for the purposes of exploitation in prostitution or pornography. Women and girls from the Philippines who are victims of trafficking are found in Japan, Singapore, Brunei, Malaysia, and the Middle East (ARIAT 2000).

In the 1980s women and girls were recruited from the poorer provinces in the North and Northeast of Thailand for commercial sex services in the urban areas. This traffic consisted mostly of 12–16-year-old girls from the hill tribes of the North and Northeast. This pattern was to some extent replaced in the 1990s by the trafficking of women and children, primarily from Myanmar, but also from Lao PDR, Cambodia, and Yunnan province in China. Today, Thailand is considered a major transit and destination country for trafficked women and children from countries in the Greater Mekong sub-region. Thailand receives from neighboring countries considerable number of children trafficked for different forms of labor and begging. Many of them subsequently end up in the sex industry. Sometimes women from Russia, Yugoslavia, Poland, and the Czech and Slovak Republics end up in Thailand (ILO 2000). Thai women and girls are trafficked out of the country by advanced networks, in particular to Japan, Australia, India, Malaysia, and the Middle East, as well as to Europe.

Vietnamese women and girls are trafficked from Northern Vietnam to China, mainly for marriage, but also for labor and household work or to be sold as prostitutes. Women and girls from Ho Chi Minh City are lured to Hong Kong, Macao and Taiwan under the guise of marriages between Vietnamese and foreigners. Women and girls from the Southern provinces of Vietnam are trafficked into Cambodia and further abroad.

In South Asia, Bangladesh and Nepal are the main countries of origin for trafficking, while India and Pakistan are considered countries of destination, and Kolkata in India is regarded as a major transit point for other destinations.

Extensive internal trafficking of minors seems to occur in Bangladesh. Bangladesh is also a supplier of young women and girls, and some boys, to the sex industry in India and Pakistan. In addition several thousands of young Bangladeshi women and girls are taken across the border to India each year for marriage. Many of these girls, who mainly originate from western Bangladesh close to the Indian border, end up in brothels in Kolkata, Mumbai and Goa or are sold several times.

India is not only the main country of destination for traffickers, but also a country of origin for women and girls trafficked in the region. Most of the trafficking in India occurs within its borders, from rural to urban areas and from poorer states like Bihar to wealthier states like Maharashtra.

Thousands of children in Nepal live apart from their families. Some of them have migrated voluntarily, for example, to Kathmandu, to work in manufacturing, sweatshops, hotels, or as domestic workers. Many of these children then become victims of the cross-border trafficking to India.

Pakistan is regarded a major destination for trafficked women and children in South Asia. Every year, thousands of women and children are trafficked from Bangladesh across India into Pakistan. They are forced into prostitution, sold or auctioned for marriage, or employed as bonded labor. The typical trafficking scenario in Pakistan is one of the women arrive in the country as migrant worker and then end up sexually abused.

Reports indicate that tribal children from the hills are trafficked to the big cities, or to the coast in the South and Southwest of the country. Sri Lanka is one of the favored destinations of pedophile sex tourists from Europe and the United States. In Sri Lanka, unlike other countries in South Asia, the majority of the child prostitutes are boys. These boys are often referred to as "beach boys" since they live and work on the beach. Other prospects that trafficked children from Sri Lanka may face are domestic work and illegal adoption. A large number of adult women go to the Middle East, primarily with the intention of working as maids.

Information from across the region suggests that a growing number of women and girls are being trafficked for the purpose of sexual exploitation within and into Europe. The data and information are unpredictable and there are few reports on the trafficking situation. However, the focal destinations in Europe are the countries in Western Europe, while the countries in Central, Eastern, and Southeastern Europe provide the women and girls. Women are also coming into Europe from Southeast Asia, mainly the Philippines and Thailand, from Africa, mainly Ghana, Nigeria, and Morocco and from Latin America, mainly Brazil, Colombia, and the Dominican Republic.

The former Soviet Union and Central and Eastern Europe have replaced Asia as the main source of trafficked women to Western Europe. Victims come from Russia, Ukraine, and other Eastern European countries. After the breakup of the Soviet Union, trafficking from the region has escalated from a minor problem before 1991 into a major issue. As criminal organizations have grown, especially in Russia, they have gravitated to this lucrative business. Russian organizations now play a dominant role not just in the trafficking of Russian women but also women from throughout Eastern Europe. Russian organized crime groups and others including Albanian, Estonian, Czech, Serb, and Italian groups are involved in human trafficking in Europe.

Furthermore, Russian organized crime is starting to take over the sex industry in a number of European countries.

In the countries of Central and Eastern Europe, including the Balkans and in Central Asia, the increase in demand and supply for trafficking has led to the growth of the trafficking in women and girls for sexual exploitation. Many of the Central and Eastern European countries have particular difficulty in dealing with the problem, because of their weakened social control system and the high degree of ineffectiveness of their formal criminal justice systems.

In the region, the rise of small, middle-size, and complex organized criminal networks whose main interests are in human trafficking coincides with the growth of the shadow economy and the high levels of unemployment among the female population. According to official estimates, in the last decade alone at least 400,000 women have been trafficked from the Ukraine (UNICRI 1999). In 1995, it was estimated that the money generated by the informal (and illegal) economy accounted for 50 percent the gross national product, furthermore unemployment mostly affects women, constituting 64 percent of the total unemployed (Hughes 2001). The huge availability of illegal services greatly facilitates trafficking, for example, there is evidence that traffickers can obtain a forged passport for young girls under 18, for about $800 (OSCE 1999).

Recent estimates on trafficking show that a quarter of trafficking flows worldwide originates from Central and Eastern Europe, region which presents the most impressive increase in trafficking activities on a global level. Despite the increasing magnitude of the internal sex markets, the main flows of the traffic are still directed outside of the region. The region now rivals "traditional" trafficking source regions such as Asia, Africa, and the Caribbean. Generally women and girls are normally younger than those trafficked from developing countries. In Germany, where nine out of ten victims of trafficking are from Central and Eastern European countries, the percentage of girls aged between 15 and 18 is estimated to be as high as 20 percent. However, few data have been collected, within Europe, on the percentage of girls among the trafficked population.

As regards figures, according to OSCE calculations, in 1997, some 175,000 women and girls were trafficked from the eastern countries of the OSCE region to Central and Western Europe. The transfer of trafficked women and girls flows from the Eastern countries to the Western countries and to a less visible extent from the Southern countries (Romania, Bulgaria, and Albania) to the Northern countries (Poland, Hungary, Czech Republic, Lithuania). Cities such as Budapest, Prague, and even Belgrade, as well as major towns and cities situated along border areas are used as transit points. The geography of trafficking is changing fast. At the beginning of the 1990s, Central European countries like Poland, the Czech Republic, Hungary, and Lithuania were mainly origin countries for trafficking of women and girls to the Western countries. Nowadays they are important *origin, transit, and even destination* countries. Most of the women trafficked into Czech Republic and Poland—a country where 15,000 arrivals are estimated each year—are nationals of the former Soviet Republics. In fact, although new origin areas emerge, trafficking of nationals from Russia and Ukraine persists. Eastern countries such as the Ukraine, Belarus, Moldova, Romania, and Bulgaria are now origin and transit areas for the trafficking of women. Even Belarus has become a strategic *origin and transit* state, used on the way to the Western European countries through the Ukraine and Poland, and to Scandinavia through the Baltic states.

Former Soviet Republics of Central Asia are now booming as *recruitment areas*. Even if information on the scope or extent of the phenomenon is still very limited, local NGOs report a growing number of trafficking cases from Armenia, Georgia, Azerbaijan, and Kazakhstan. According to IOM about 4,000 women have been trafficked in 1999 from Kyrgyzstan, with different destinations: one-third of them were traveling to or through Central Europe, two-thirds were traveling to China, the Middle East, and the West European countries. The major push factors for trafficking in Central Asia are the presence of strong organized criminal groups, a high rate of female unemployment (80 percent), along with high levels of poverty, weak institutions, and open borders (Redo 2000). The Balkan region is acquiring increasing importance not only as a ground for recruitment practices, but even for the transit and final exploitation of trafficked women and girls. In Macedonia local authorities recorded (UNICRI 1999) a sharp rise in the number of trafficked women and girls (but mainly young girls), citizens of Russia, Ukraine, Belarus, Moldova, Bulgaria, Romania, and Albania during 1998. In Macedonia traffickers are said to be well organized, with regional connections and a good level of technology. The same is true of Bosnia-Herzegovina, where the problem has reached alarming proportions. Bosnia has become a final destination for hundreds of women as the presence of 20,000 foreign peacekeepers has provided a ready market for brothel keepers. According to IOM survey (IOM 1997), one-third of the women working as prostitutes declared to have been lured, and trafficked into the country. They come mostly from Moldova, Romania, and the Ukraine, or other parts of the former Soviet Union and 5 percent of them are minors. Often recruited by acquaintances or friends, they have been transported to Belgrade, where they have been sold to traffickers and provided with false documents, before being introduced in Bosnia-Herzegovina.

The business of trafficking from and within Central and Eastern Europe is increasingly controlled by Russian and Ukrainian middle-size and transnational criminal organizations. Ukrainian and Russian networks especially provide call girl or escort system services worldwide. Some of them, at any given time, can control over 100 girls and women, mainly nationals of Russia and the Ukraine, as well as other CIS countries. Equipped with modern means of communication, and well introduced in the sex market structures abroad, they often run all the phases—recruitment, travel, and exploitation of the business. Sometimes they are involved only in the recruitment and transport phases of trafficking, "selling" women on the foreign sex markets. The reputation of Russian and Ukrainian traffickers is widespread and, depending on their area of action, they are able to cooperate with the main organized criminal groups involved in human trafficking worldwide, such as Turkish and ex Yugoslavian networks, as well as Chinese triads or yakuza.

It is worth noting the huge extension of the routes of such traffic: women are circulated among different countries, by air and land. Important flows controlled by Russian and Ukrainian groups end up in the United States, where it seems that 4,000 women from Eastern and Central Europe arrive each year to work on prostitution. They also end up in some Asian megalopolis, including Bangkok, Hong Kong, Beijing and Singapore, as well as in Japan, the Middle East, Israel, and Turkey. In some parts of the world, such as Turkey and Israel, the presence of women from Russia and other former Soviet republics is so prevalent that prostitutes are called *Natasha* (Hugues 2001). Generally, routes directed to the neighboring countries are less demanding from the organizational point of view. For that reason too, in Finland, Russian criminal organizations closely control the "carousel" system (ECPAT 2001), while in Greece over half of the trafficked women are estimated to be from Russia and Ukraine. Ukrainian and Russian organized crime groups also control the main part of street prostitution and clandestine brothels in localities in Poland and the Czech Republic situated close to the border area with Germany and Austria. In this border area since 90 percent of clients come from the Western countries, high profits are assured. The most attractive women and girls, once trained, are selected and moved on to other Western European countries. Otherwise in the Baltic states, especially in the strategic border areas, trafficked women working on the streets are mainly nationals of Russia, Ukraine, and Belarus, which have been "exported" mainly by Russian and Ukrainian groups.

Similarly to what happens in the Czech Republic and Poland, two recent trends have been noted in the border areas—first, the arrival of trafficked women from the Eastern countries and secondly, the arrival of sexual tourists from richer countries visiting the local sex markets, because of the low prices. The main trafficking flows out of the Baltic States go from Lithuania, a country of origin of strong criminal groups which are able to coordinate their activities with Russian and Ukrainian groups.

With respect to their victims, the methods used by Russian and Ukrainian groups, as well as Lithuanians, Polish, and other criminal networks from Central European countries, are the same. Even those women who voluntarily engage in prostitution are blackmailed and become prey to their exploiters. There is evidence that organizers of trafficking sexually abuse the newcomers and then collect pornographic materials of this abuse. They threaten them, saying that they will show videos of them to their families if they attempt to report to the police or escape. Other menaces usually concern the eventual killing or torture of family members. Their passports are confiscated, and in some cases women are locked up, beaten and even tortured. Patterns of sexual exploitation may vary depending on local sex-work structures, however a strict and permanent control of the organized crime emissaries on the victims is held. Even if the women are compelled to work for "external" exploiters, they have enormous debts to pay back to the organization, generally on a weekly rate.

Organized criminal groups from Albania are also involved in trafficking in women and girls all over Europe. They are different from the Russian and Ukrainian groups in the routes they use, the kind of markets they supply, and the type of girls they exploit. As regards routes, they operate exclusively within Europe. Albanian gangs initially began to traffic girls from their country into Italy. Recently, Albania has also become a transit country for trafficking originating in the former Soviet Republics. Women entering Albania are "bought" before being transported to Bosnia, Macedonia, and Kosovo. Italy is still one of the main countries of transit and destination, for trafficked girls and women of Albania and the Eastern countries. Traffickers also pass through Italy, or through the eastern countries, such as Slovenia, to enter the Schengen area and reach the North-Western European countries, especially the Netherlands, Belgium, and France. In Western European countries the Albanian organized criminal groups supply the lowest level of prostitution markets. While women from the former Soviet Republics who are exploited by Russian and Ukrainian groups are often well educated, and better trained, it seems that women exploited by the Albanian rings are mostly uneducated.

MIGRATION, SEX EXPLOITATION, AND SECURITIZATION

The scholarly literature on trafficking can be broadly divided into two approaches—first, the "sexual violence" approaches linking trafficking to sexual exploitation (Barry 1995; Hughes 2003; Raymond 1998), and secondly, the "migration" approaches linking trafficking to the widespread occurrence of irregular migration (Skeldon 2000). The first approach can be further subdivided into two "camps" representing fundamentally opposing views of the legitimacy of the sex industry. This is a somewhat broader (and older) debate. In view of much migration taking place under irregular conditions, the second approach in theory also includes men as potential victims of trafficking. These two strands—trafficking for sexual exploitation and irregular migration, however, rarely engages with each other. In this sense, the conceptual debate on trafficking has reached an impasse.

Keeping with the sex trafficking approach, within the geographical context of India as well as Hungary has undergone unprecedented scrutiny of its sex industry and hence the trafficking of women into it. Indian and Hungarian prostitutions cannot be discussed without recognition that certain US pressure groups (anti-prostitution feminist coalition and the Christian right) have joined forces with the US Government to argue that any country that does not aggressively deal with its own sex industry, are promoting sex trafficking thereby, a security threat. Moreover, the trafficking issue cannot be divorced from the practice of migration—domestically as well as trans-nationally. Illegal migration, which also includes trafficking, is historically not new to India and Hungary. It was only after the introduction of compulsory passports did, migration, therefore become a form of controlling peoples' movements by governments to protect their national sovereignty, security, and identity. Migration discourse, in all its forms, focuses on issues such as poverty, violence, and push-pull factors; the exploitation and victimization of the migrants is often central to the analysis. Inevitably exploitation exists but when the issues of trafficking and migration are brought together, conditions that make up the many reasons for which women migrate are given very little attention and the concept that women do make decisions based on choice (albeit constrained) is typically ignored. It needs to be further investigated as to whether all women, trafficked or prostituted, are incapable of choice and, therefore, are never able to exercise agency—which is not to deny the structural changes that are part of the push/pull factor (Agustin 2003).

Hence, it is with these points in mind, that make questions such as whether or not the sex industry in India and Hungary is being securitized, and if so, by whom, why, and how. The analytical framework that we will take as a preparatory point is the security and securitization, and more specifically the societal sector. By showing that securitization is occurring we will suggest that an alternative perspective could be a valid option: human security. This approach could then advance the debate on trafficking for sexual exploitation versus irregular migration and yield important policy recommendations that address the root causes of trafficking—a crucial aspect previously neglected. Linked to addressing root causes are issues to do with socioeconomic development. Our contribution to this debate is by taking a sociological perspective, that is, to look at this subject as a "bottom up" process in which nongovernmental actors/agents try to achieve social change. We shall discuss certain civil society groups and their approaches to various security aspects of trafficking such as sex work and human rights issue. We approach human security as socially driven, therefore, highlighting the importance of social action and activism in the efforts to find countermeasures to trafficking.

DATA, APPROACH, AND METHOD

This study on engendering trafficking and human security in India and Hungary is pioneering and exploratory. It is not surprising that reliability and authenticity of existing data is a matter of concern. The aim of this research is to gain an overview of human trafficking on migration patterns in India and Hungary. It will attempt to identify the main types of trafficking and their dimensions through the experience of different governmental agencies, other institutional actors, NGOs dealing with migrants, as well as the people directly involved in trafficking. This last group consists primarily of migrants but includes some traffickers. We carried out the pilot project in India first and subsequent analysis of data before visiting Hungary and also continued to expand the network of interested parties and disseminate results from review and expert consultations to NGOs networks. There are some basic prerequisites to achieving results from the study. These comprise of—(a) the cooperation of all parties involved including collaborating institutions, government ministries, local authorities, and participating communities in India as well as Hungary in project implementation and in monitoring and evaluation; (b) useful documents should be prepared so the activity can be replicated by relevant grassroots NGOs and extension agencies working with women's groups. The research team engaging in field survey found useful a wide variety of data-gathering tools and methods, with the most important being policy and institutional analysis, the use of both qualitative and quantitative data.

Trafficking is a complex, multidimensional phenomenon, with a variety of—often interrelated—aspects covering large geographic spaces. It is not possible to address all the areas simultaneously. Broadly, the study focuses on: the crime of trafficking and the responses engaged in preventing and countering it. The role played by the demand factor in trafficking for different purposes, which has received scant attention earlier, may also be studied explicitly. This may be primarily examined from the "client" angle of the commercial sexual exploitation "sector." The sources and scale of profitability from this "sector" are also examined to find out the motivations behind the demand—the causal mechanism that reproduces the system.

The lack of reliable information is characteristic on all aspects of human trafficking. Not only are information and practices scarce concerning such issues as the effects of trafficking on migration patterns, the scale and extent of operations, structure and working principles of the trafficking organizations, but even information on the trafficked migrants, their personal characteristics, reasons for using the services of the traffickers, remains incomplete. Although there are some indicators connecting human trafficking with other criminal activities, the real scale and depth of this relationship are unclear. Typologies of how the migrant trafficking business is organized, and the functions performed thereby, are quite simplistic and heuristic. The elaboration of effective strategies and potential actions against trafficking is not possible without a detailed knowledge of the different aspects of the phenomenon.

The analysis of the study is based on household survey from India and Hungary carried out during October and November 2011. The survey comprises total of 534 individuals from India and Hungary. At least 200 individuals per country were interviewed, with 327 from three-districts of West Bengal, India and 207 from three-districts of Budapest, Hungary. A standardized questionnaire was used in both the countries. The multistage stratified sampling technique was undertaken. The survey covers both urban and rural areas and sampled households in all regions in the sample countries. In each region, interviews were proportionally distributed according to the size of settlement. Within each group, settlements were randomly selected applying probabilities proportional to size.

Interviews were structured in order to acquire information on the structure and functioning of trafficking networks, financial arrangements, specific methods in use, and how these relate to each type of migrant. Through the findings of individual cases, we aim to understand the process from mobilization through transition to destination. This includes recruitment in the place of origin, methods of border crossing, etc. Most of the interviews with migrants were conducted in detention or holding centers and in refugee camps. Others were conducted in railway stations, restaurants, places where trafficking is organized, police cars, and through personal contacts. Some other interviews were done in a "panel" format involving small groups of migrants familiar with the smuggling experience. The number of migrants interviewed varied between one and ten at one time in one location. The length of the interview varied between couples of minutes to two hours, depending on the circumstances, the willingness to cooperate and on the value of information the migrant could provide. Most interviews were at least partly taped. Some interviews were carried out with people who acted as human smugglers or assisted in the smuggling process. We arranged site visits at five different detention centers and various refugee camps in India and Hungary. We also managed to visit border communities and relevant interior sites in both the countries where smuggling is organized and experienced. In certain cases we were able to follow some parts of the trafficking process. Field observations took place in India around the Indo-Nepal and Indo-Bangladesh border areas and in Budapest around the central railway station. Further observations in Budapest took place in a town near the Austrian border known as a major "transit-waiting" center for migrants mainly from Kosovo. More interviews were conducted with NGOs and migrants who planned to cross the border, some of whom had been readmitted several times. During the research we enjoyed the support of governmental agencies, especially the Border Security Force or Guard. Most officials were not only willing to share official statements, but were helpful and open about their personal experiences. Meetings with migrants were arranged and upon our insistence provisions were made to speak with them without surveillance. The project team was selected on the basis of their previous experience; language knowledge and communication skills. Some had to deal with virtually all types of respondents; others contacted just very specific categories. Besides language knowledge familiarity with the circumstances in the place of origin of the migrants, the sex or the citizenship of the interviewer played an important role in establishing contact and receiving relevant and reliable information from migrants.

To estimate the determinants of human trafficking on the household level, we use binary response models. A potential problem in this regard is that human trafficking, although affecting millions of people, is a relatively rare event on the household level, so that standard procedures such as probit and logit models might yield inaccurate estimates. As baseline method, we, therefore, rely on the rare events logit model suggested by King and Zeng (2001). Our dependent variable is a dummy denoting whether the interviewed person reported a victim of human trafficking among close family members. Given the relatively small number of individuals with trafficking in their close family, we combine sexual exploitation and other forms of exploitation. More specifically, the dummy takes the value of one if a close friends and relatives had traveled abroad and experienced one of the situations—"was offered a domestic or nursing job, but was locked and forced to work for no pay" or, "was offered a job at an enterprise, on a construction site, or in agriculture, but was locked and forced to work for no or little pay" or, "was offered employment, but the passport was taken away upon arrival to the destination country and was forced to work in the sex industry."

It is to be noted that the data are likely to suffer from some degree of reporting bias. Victims of human trafficking and their friends and relatives might be unwilling to share their experiences, being anxious of stigmatization or problems with authorities at home or abroad. Overall, seventy-eight individuals indicated a victim of human trafficking in their close friends and relatives. Out of these, there are fifty-six reported cases of members being forced to work in the commercial sex market, while twenty-two cases were associated with nonsexual forms of exploitation. This is especially true for the case of sexual exploitation, which is a highly sensitive and husky issue (Laczko 2005). The survey did look into on marginal social groups, among whom trafficking predominance rates could be higher. Despite these concerns, we believe that the potential reporting bias will not nullify our results. The main problem here is that the number of victims may actually be too low, that is, a problem of underreporting. To minimize the degree of underreporting, the survey instrument used various ways of reducing the stigma associated with human trafficking. First, instead of asking directly whether a family member had been "trafficked," the survey instrument rather referred to typical situations of coerced labor. Second, the respondent did not have to reveal the identity of a trafficked family member. Third, if there was a case of sexual exploitation in the family, the interviewed person could still "bury" this experience in a more general answer category of exploitation. However, there is no reason to assume that there are systematic regional differences in reporting behavior. Moreover, we would certainly have a more serious problem if the bias were upward, that is, if there was a potential problem of over-reporting. Taken together, and despite the unavoidable drawbacks, we suppose that the dataset at hand is well suitable for the purpose of our analysis.

Looking at the explanatory variables used in our analysis, we consider a set of household and regional characteristics. We also include age, gender, marital status, and educational level of the respondents, which should manage for systematic reporting biases along these dimensions.

On the household level, we use household size, the number of children aged 14 or below, a dummy for households living in rural areas and another dummy indicating whether households live in urban or semi-urban areas around their respective city or town. In addition, a household's living standard is surrogated by subjective measures of its perceived financial status. To capture access to public information and news, we also code a dummy for households that use the television, as opposed to other media and social contacts, to get informed about social and political issues. With a view to the empirical literature on the determinants of migration in South Asia and Central Europe, we suppose household size, the number of children and poverty to enhance the likelihood of human trafficking. In contrast, television use can be seen as a source of relatively objective and high-quality information and is anticipated to raise awareness of trafficking risks, thus lowering the trafficking likelihood.

Our main proxy of migration pressure, the key variable of interest, is the migration prevalence ratio on the regional level. This variable allows us to identify "hot spots" of migration, where individuals had a significantly higher propensity to migrate compared to other regions. Areas with high out-migration are also likely to witness strong herd and network effects, which have been shown to be a main driver of migration in South Asia and Central Europe. To strengthen our argument, we use a second proxy for migration pressure, namely the share of individuals in the region who stated that they could not imagine to ever working abroad.

To proxy the degree of information asymmetries, we include a risk aware-ness measure, which corresponds to the regional share of respondents who assured that they had heard of the phenomenon of human trafficking before. We try to most closely resemble a migrant's knowledge status before depar-ture and reduce potential endogeneity by excluding respondents who knew a victim of human trafficking or lived in a migrant household in computing this share. We suppose that a person who is aware of the risk of being trafficked would be more alert in dealing with people during the migration process and perhaps even disregard the possibility of migration. Hence, we expect the regional risk awareness to reduce the likelihood of having a trafficked family member.

We also use a regional measure for the prevalence of illegal migration. It is defined as the share of households in each region that reported to have had a member working abroad illegally. On the one hand, this variable aims to capture the fact that their notorious vulnerability makes illegal migrants more prone to be trafficked than legal migrants at any stage of the migration process. On the other hand, shadow migration sectors, which might act as a breeding ground for trafficking networks, are presumably more present in areas with high levels of illegal migration. Consequently, we predict that the risk of being trafficked should rise with the extent of illegal migration.

RESULT AND DISCUSSION

Before thrashing out the econometric results, it is worthwhile to look at the summary statistics (table 5.1 in the appendix). A simple mean suggests that overall, 14.7 percent is of a victim of human trafficking in their close sur-roundings while human trafficking in household is 1.8 percent. The average regional prevalence of migration is about 20.1 percent. The internet user in the region is 11 percent while cell phone user is 75.6 percent. Regional wage gap to capital is 30.1 percent while regional crime rate is about 174.7 per 12,000 inhabitants. The table also shows that regional prevalence of migration is 20.1 percent where as regional awareness of human traffick-ing is 67.4 percent. The share of families which uses the television to get informed about socioeconomic issues and knows about the phenomenon of human trafficking is noticeably higher as 95.4 percent. Among the dwellers prevalence of poor financial condition is significant (51.4 percent). Regional prevalence of legal migration is 20.7 percent and illegal migration is 12.9 percent but share of illegal migrants among all migrants is significantly higher (44.3 percent).

Table 5.2 in the appendix shows key estimation results. Migration pressure, as measured by migration prevalence, turns out to be a vigorous and highly significant predictor of human trafficking both within the household and among close friends and relatives. This is true for different specifications and subsamples. The migration prevalence ratio also has a sizable marginal effect compared to other explanatory factors. Interestingly, we find a (weakly) significant link between risk perception and trafficking. In regions where more people are aware of the phenomenon of human trafficking, the likelihood of human trafficking is lower. This finding, although not fully robust, underlines the potential benefit of awareness campaigns to combat human trafficking. A further interesting finding is that the role of illegal migration plays a significant role. In areas where a larger share among the emigrants worked abroad illegally, trafficking risks are higher. This is very much in line with common belief and confirms the intuition of existing theoretical models that close connections to people acting in the illegal sector increases the risk of exploitation. Converse to what we expected, weak rule of law in the home region (as surrogated by high crime rates) does not emerge to amplify the likelihood of trafficking abroad. The variable of regional crime rates has a negative sign and is only feebly significant for some specifications. A similarly surprising finding is that the dispersion of information technology as measured by the share of internet users in the region does not lower the risk of trafficking. On the contrary, internet use on the regional level appears to significantly increase its likelihood. Use of cell phone also appears to matter much more for trafficking risks. Access to television news, however, seems to lower trafficking risks, although this finding is not very robust.

Generally, remoteness and low socioeconomic development do not appear to matter much for trafficking risks. A lower quality of public services as measured by low density of physicians and high infant mortality rates, the household's locality (rural or urban), and low wages compared to the capital town do not increase the likelihood of trafficking in a certain region. Likewise, the share of the rural population, although positively related to trafficking, is only significant in some cases.

On the household level, the number of children appears to increase the risk of trafficking, while household size does not matter. As we are not able to control for household composition in more detail, the interpretation of this effect warrants caution. The number of children is a good proxy for the presence of prime-age individuals, who are most likely to migrate. Age also appears to be an explanatory factor, which is very much in line with the stylized facts. In households with a young respondent, the risk of trafficking is much higher. While we do not have any information on the age of the trafficked friend or relative, it is reasonable to assume that young respondents know more people of their own age. Hence, one can infer that being young increases the likelihood that you know a trafficking victim, because trafficking mostly happens to young people. Apparently, poorer households are not exposed to higher risks of trafficking than wealthier ones. It should be kept in mind, however, that the survey does not report any premigration assessments of living standards. Hence, no strong conclusions should be drawn from this result. Lastly, it is worth comparing the determinants of migration to the determinants of trafficking. As shown in table 5.2, there is surprisingly little difference between the estimation results. The fact that the same factors appear to influence migration and trafficking prevalence strengthens our argument and exemplifies the close causal link between the two phenomena. In particular, we find that regional migration prevalence is the main predictor of migration on the household level, although the marginal effect is much higher than the effect for trafficking. Moreover, one should underline that the migration probability seems to be lower in regions where more people are aware of human trafficking.

CONCLUSION

This study analyzes the determinants of human trafficking on a micro level. The results strongly underline our main argument: migration pressure is the key driver of human trafficking. Moreover, the determinants of migration do not differ much from the determinants of trafficking. Our estimation results for India and Hungary suggest that it is difficult to identify other socioeconomic drivers of human trafficking other than migration prevalence. Victims of human trafficking appear to be a relatively heterogeneous group coming from both urban and rural areas that can be rich or poor. We find that poverty on the household level; regional crime levels and several other regional development and remoteness indicators do not play a significant role. What appears to matter, however, are risk perceptions and the relative role of illegal migration. In regions where less people are aware of human trafficking risks and in areas where migration is predominantly illegal, the probability of trafficking is significantly higher. Moreover, families with many children and younger individuals appear to face a higher likelihood of being trafficked. Several conclusions can be drawn from our findings. First, policy measures to counter human trafficking and related awareness campaigns should mainly be targeted to those areas where migration rates are high or on the rise. Second, it seems quite probable that the market of human trafficking and the number of victims will continue to grow as long as migration pressure remains high.

REFERENCES

Agustin, L. M. 2003. "Forget Victimization: Granting Agency to Migrants, Thematic Section." *Society for International Development* 46(3): 30–36.

ARIAT. 2000. *Philippine Country Paper and a National Plan of Action to Combat Trafficking in Women and Children.* Manila: Asian Regional Initiative against Trafficking in Women and Children.

Barry, K. 1995. *The Prostitution of Sexuality.* New York: New York University Press.

Caouette, T. 1998. *Needs Assessment on Cross-border Trafficking in Women and Children: The Mekong Sub-region.* Draft Prepared for the UN Working Group on Trafficking in the Mekong Sub-region, Bangkok.

Choudhury, N. and Zureick, A. 2005. *Interview with Zoltan Boross.* National Headquarters of Hungarian Border Guards, 17 March. Budapest: Division Leader of Criminal Investigation and Intelligence Department.

Gupta, G. R. 2003. *Review of Literature for Action Research on Trafficking in Women and Children.* New Delhi: Institute of Social Sciences.

Hughes, D. M. 2000. "The 'Natasha' Trade: The Transnational Shadow Market of Trafficking in Women." *Journal of International Affairs* 53(2): 625–651.

Hughes, D. M. 2001. "The 'Natasha' Trade: Transnational Sex Trafficking." *National Institute of Justice Journal* 246: 8–15.

Hughes, D. M. 2003. "The Driving Force of Sex Trafficking." *Vital Speeches of the Day* 69(6): 182–184.

ILO. 2000. *Trafficking in Children and Women: A Regional Overview.* Background Paper No. 4, ILO/Japan Asian Regional High-Level Meeting on Child Labour, 8–10 March, Jakarta.

IOM. 1997. *The Baltic Route: The Trafficking of Migrants through Lithuania.* Geneva: International Organisation for Migration.

IOM. 2000. *Combating Trafficking in South-east Asia: A Review of Policy and Programme Responses.* Migration Research Series 2/2000, Geneva.

IOM Project Outline. 2000–2002. *Return and Reintegration of Trafficked and Other Vulnerable Women and Children between Selected Countries in the Mekong Region (2000–2002).* Bangkok.

King, G. and Zeng, L. 2001. "Logistic Regression in Rare Events Data." *Political Analysis* 9(2): 137–163.

Laczko, F. 2005. "Data and Research on Human Trafficking." *International Migration* 43: 5–16.

Lehti, M. 2003. *Trafficking in Women and Children in Europe.* Helsinki: The European Institute for Crime Prevention and Control.

OSCE. 1999. *Trafficking in Human Beings: Implications for the OSCE.* ODIHR Background Paper 1999/3, Organization for Security and Co-operation in Europe.

Raymond, J. G. 1998. "Prostitution as Violence against Women: NGOs Stonewalling in Beijing and Elsewhere." *Women's Studies International Forum* 21(1): 1–9.

Redo, S. 2000. *Migrant Trafficking and Organized Crime, United Nations Office for Drug Control and Crime Prevention (UNDCP)*. Tashkent, Uzbekistan: Centre for International Crime Prevention (CICP), Regional Bureau for Central Asia.

Sarkar, S. 2011. "Trafficking in Women and Children to India and Thailand: Characteristics, Trends and Policy Issues." *International Journal of Afro-Asian Studies* 2(1): 57–73.

Sen, S. and Nair, P. M. 2004. *A Report on Trafficking in Women and Children in India 2002–2003*. Volume I, NHRC - NIFEM - ISS Project. New Delhi: National Human Rights Commission.

Skeldon, R. 2000. "Trafficking: A Perspective from Asia." *International Migration* 1: 7–30.

Srivastava, K. and Choudhury, N. 2005. *Interview with Jozef Poltl*. National Police Headquarters of Hungary, National Bureau of Investigation, Organized Crime Department, Division of Trafficking in Human Beings, March 19, Budapest.

Srivastava, K. and Tressa Johnson, T. 2005. *Interview with Captain at Rail Station*. March 16, Miskolc.

UNICRI. 1999. *Proceedings of the Conference "New Frontiers of Crime: Trafficking in Human Beings and New Forms of Slavery."* October 26–29, Verona.

United Nations. 2006. *Trafficking in Persons: Global Patterns*. New York.

US Department of State. 2004. *Trafficking in Persons Report*. Washington, DC.

US Department of State. 2006a. *Trafficking in Persons Report*. Washington, DC.

US Department of State. 2006b. *Hungary 2005 Country Report on Human Rights Practices*. http//www.state.gov/g/drl/rls/hrrpt/2005/61652.htm.

Westwood, D. 1998. *Child Trafficking in Asia*. World Vision Briefing Paper No. 4, World Vision International.

APPENDIX

Table 5.1 Summary Statistics

Variable	Mean	Standard Deviation	Minimum	Maximum
Neighboring Human trafficking	0.146	0.596	0	1
Human trafficking in household	0.018	0.127	0	1
Age	0.228	0.385	0	1
Male	37.532	14.761	15	80
Female	33.491	13.564	14	86
Primary education or lower	0.297	0.432	0	1
Secondary education	0.475	0.495	0	1
Employed	0.509	0.532	0	1
Television user	0.954	0.453	0	1
Cell phone user	0.756	0.546	0	1
Number of children (0–14)	0.431	0.699	0	6
Rural	0.378	0.422	0	1
Rural population in region (percent)	56.311	41.870	0.000	84.344
Regional wage gap to capital (percent)	0.301	0.267	0.000	0.611
Physicians per 12,000 in region	22.276	9.763	0.000	.496
Regional crime rate (per 12,000 inhabitants)	174.743	123.305	37.890	367.652
Internet users in region (percent)	0.110	0.089	0.011	0.356
Regional prevalence of migration (percent)	0.201	0.137	0	1
Regional awareness of human trafficking (percent)	0.674	0.098	0.218	1.000
India	0.392	0.503	0	1
Hungary	0.199	0.376	0	1
Share of illegal migrants among all migrants (percent per region)	0.443	0.178	0	1
Poor financial status	0.514	0.549	0	1
Moderate financial status	0.413	0.527	0	1
Household size	3.306	1.432	1.000	13.000
Regional share of people not willing to migrate (percent)	0.612	0.231	0.000	0.105
Regional prevalence of migration, census-based (percent)	0.093	0.043	0.028	0.098
Regional prevalence of legal migration (percent)	0.207	0.127	0.000	0.812
Regional prevalence of illegal migration (percent)	0.129	0.102	0.000	0.685

Table 5.2   Key Statistics

Variable	Human trafficking in close Surrounding			Human trafficking in household			Migration in household	
	Basic	with financial status and household	with role of illegal migration	Basic	with financial status and household	with role of illegal migration	Basic	with financial status and household
Age	-0.008**	-0.010**	-0.008***	-0.006	-0.005	-0.005	-0.010***	-0.009***
	(0.005)	(0.004)	(0.004)	(0.005)	(0.008)	(0.007)	(0.003)	(0.002)
Male	0.038	0.071	0.037	0.167	0.251**	0.175	0.049	0.169*
	(0.129)	(0.139)	(0.131)	(0.152)	(0.124)	(0.167)	(0.159)	(0.089)
Female	0.028	0.064	0.031	0.154	0.234**	0.164	0.038	0.152*
	(0.121)	(0.126)	(0.112)	(0.146)	(0.119)	(0.154)	(0.141)	(0.077)
Primary education or lower	-0.076	0.114	-0.066	-0.236	-0.011	-0.253	-0.298***	-0.332***
	(0.168)	(0.209)	(0.163)	(0.226)	(0.284)	(0.248)	(0.067)	(0.101)
Secondary education	0.158	0.256	0.167	-0.007	0.181	0.001	-0.054	-0.102
	(0.181)	(0.246)	(0.182)	(0.258)	(0.266)	(0.245)	(0.059)	(0.078)
Employed	0.332***	0.423***	0.332***	0.276	0.513**	0.276	-0.177**	-0.246**
	(0.116)	(0.103)	(0.115)	(0.211)	(0.205)	(0.219)	(0.083)	(0.107)
Television user	-0.322*	-0.276	-0.298*	-0.309	-0.338	-0.323	0.106	0.287**
	(0.176)	(0.167)	(0.154)	(0.204)	(0.240)	(0.227)	(0.108)	(0.137)
Cell phone user	-0.272*	-0.255	-0.278*	-0.309	-0.338	-0.323	0.106	0.287**
	(0.142)	(0.147)	(0.154)	(0.204)	(0.240)	(0.227)	(0.108)	(0.137)
Number of children (0–14)	0.136**	0.174*	0.137**	0.121	-0.070	0.122	0.127***	0.163**
	(0.054)	(0.097)	(0.055)	(0.084)	(0.137)	(0.082)	(0.037)	(0.068)
Rural	0.164	0.221	0.165	0.203	0.209	0.202	0.234	0.115
	(0.252)	(0. 267)	(0.222)	(0.378)	(0.432)	(0.368)	(0.142)	(0.143)
Rural population in region (percent)	0.034*	0.037	0.026*	0.028*	0.018	0.031	0.003	-0.002
	(0.015)	(0.019)	(0.017)	(0.019)	(0.014)	(0.016)	(0.006)	(0.003)

Regional wage gap to capital (percent)	-3.023* (1.543)	-2.256 (2.207)	-3.131* (1.657)	-4.456** (2.210)	-4.543 (3.624)	-4.573** (2.342)	0.107 (0.426)	0.364 (0.526)
Physicians per 12,000 in region	0.004 (0.012)	0.013 (0.020)	0.002 (0.009)	-0.005 (0.020)	-0.004 (0.023)	-0.002 (0.011)	-0.001 (0.002)	-0.000 (0.001)
Regional crime rate (per 12,000 inhabitants)	-0.003 (0.002)	-0.002* (0.001)	-0.002** (0.001)	-0.001 (0.002)	-0.002 (0.002)	-0.001 (0.002)	-0.001** (0.001)	-0.001** (0.001)
Internet users in region (percent)	3.677** (1.452)	6.435 (4.647)	4.765** (1.897)	3.879** (1.763)	1.865 (4.111)	4.324* (2.113)	0.018 (0.235)	-0.163 (0.456)
Regional prevalence of migration (percent)	4.867*** (1.203)	4.176** (1.647)	4.789*** (1.035)	4.187*** (1.453)	4.465 (3.003)	3.634*** (1.465)	2.876*** (0.321)	3.656*** (0.437)
Regional awareness of human trafficking (percent)	-1.124* (0.621)	-1.654* (0.876)	-0.689 (0.467)	-1.376* (0.756)	-1.578** (0.668)	-1.121 (0.785)	-0.103 (0.143)	-0.243** (0.154)
India	-1.423*** (0.285)		-1.521*** (0.274)	-1.511*** (0.399)		-1.672*** (0.487)	-0.012 (0.109)	
Hungary	0.687 (0.421)		0.843** (0.400)	0.865 (0.723)		0.909 (0.637)	-0.278** (0.114)	
Poor financial status		-0.190 (0.327)			-0.032 (0.381)			-0.176 (0.112)
Moderate financial status		-0.203 (0.221)			-0.265 (0.407)			-0.263** (0.104)
Household size		0.013 (0.056)			0.178** (0.081)			-0.063 (0.053)
Share of illegal migrants among all migrants (percent per region)			1.188** (0.589)			0.602 (0.780)		
Constant	-3.958*** (1.120)	-4.084*** (1.407)	-4.581*** (1.140)	-3.830*** (1.326)	-3.610** (1.494)	-4.073*** (1.450)	-1.107*** (0.338)	-0.930** (0.424)
Number of observations	523	467	509	523	467	509	523	467

Note: Standard errors in parentheses; *** p<0.01, ** p<0.05, * p<0.1.

Chapter 6

Trafficking Survivors in India

Trafficking in persons implies their illicit movement or acquisition by improper means, such as force, fraud, or deception with an intention of exploiting them. At least 20.9 million adults and children are bought and sold worldwide into commercial sexual servitude, forced labor and bonded labor (ILO 2012). About two million children are exploited every year in the global commercial sex trade (UNICEF 2005). Selling of young women is one of the fastest growing organized crime and most lucrative criminal activity in the world (Shelley 2010). This, undoubtedly, is a crime against humanity. Almost every country in the world is affected by such organized crime.

The scale and extent of trafficking in persons remains little explored in the Indian context. Trafficking in human beings, especially in women and children, has become a matter of serious concern in India (Gupta 2003; Sen and Nair 2004; Sarkar 2011; Uddin 2014). Trafficking is an organized crime which thrives on human dejection. Despite strong steps taken by the Government of India, the trafficking rackets and gangs have become more organized and expanded into newer forms of trafficking. The crime has prolonged in such a way that today almost every Indian state is affected with this social and criminal nuisance. Although trafficking for commercial sexual exploitation continues to be an area of concern, of late, there has been an increasing trend of migration and trafficking of children for forced labor, bondage, and slavery (UNODC 2013).

Bonded and sex labor comprise the vast majority of human trafficking in India, though child soldiering, forced begging and organ harvesting have also been identified (Huda 2006; DuPont 2009). Compelled by the socioeconomic conditions, a large number of women and children are trafficking from economically backward areas to big cities for work. They are forced to work under highly exploitative situations such as very long working hours, petty wages, unhygienic, and most difficult working conditions. Such women and children mostly work in industries like *zari* making (gold thread work), jewelry units, domestic help, *dhabas* (highway motels), tea stalls, and so on. Very often, they are kept within the confines of the work places and, therefore lack any kind of freedom they become vulnerable to abuse. There are instances of migration or trafficking of women and children for labor from neighboring countries like Nepal and Bangladesh. So far away from their families, these children are highly vulnerable to all kinds of exploitation, including physical and sexual abuse. There has been an increasing trend of children being trafficked from the states of Jharkhand, Chhattisgarh, Odisha, Assam, West Bengal, and Madhya Pradesh for the purpose of domestic labor (Sen and Nair 2004; Sarkar 2011). The trafficking of children is being undertaken by illegal placement agencies. Many of these placement agencies are operating from Delhi and the National Capital Region. These placement agencies are earning huge profits by bringing in children from these states (UNODC 2013).

The movement of persons from one city to another and from one country to another for the purpose of involving them in criminal activities, keeping them in brothels, or using them as slaves is a criminal offense against humanity and a violation of civil rights of individuals. It is reported that India is the main recipient of an estimated 150,000 women and girls trafficked into India from South Asia to feed the commercial sex industry (Silverman et al. 2007). Moreover, India is also a source and transit country for the sex trafficking of women and children from and for the Middle East (Consulate General of the United States 2008). More than two million women and children are tapped in commercial sex work in the red-light districts in India. The Indian government estimates that the vast majority of the 500,000 children in the sex industry are girls (Centre for Development and Population Activities 1997). In addition, Nepalese and Bangladeshi girls are trafficked into India to work in brothels and so-called "cage sex workers." A little over 50 percent of the total commercial sex workers in India are from Nepal and Bangladesh (Shamim 2001). Prevalence of girl sex workers from Nepal and Bangladesh can be attributed to prevailing abject poverty and ignorance in both these countries compared to India.

CONCEPT, CAUSES, AND MODUS OPERANDI

Definition

The term trafficking can be applied to any kind of commodities being traded; however, it also has sinister and illicit implications. The concept of trafficking in persons refers to the criminal practice of exploitation of human beings where they are treated as commodities for monetary gain and after being trafficked are subjected to long-term abuse. In a general sense, trafficking in human beings is a process of transportation of persons from one place to another, facilitated by agents seeking commercial benefit for purposes of exploitation.

The Protocol to Prevent, Suppress and Punish Trafficking in Persons, especially women and children, supplementing the United Nations Convention against Transnational Organized Crime (Trafficking Protocol) that was adopted in the year 2000 and came into force in December 2003, has perhaps brought the much needed and widespread consensus on a working definition of trafficking at the global level. Article 3 of the Protocol defines trafficking as follows (United Nations 2000):

(a) "Trafficking in persons" shall mean the recruitment, transportation, transfer, harboring, or receipt of persons, by means of the threat or use of force or other forms of coercion, of abduction, of fraud, of deception, of the abuse of power, or of a position of vulnerability or of the giving or receiving of payments or benefits to achieve the consent of a person having control over another person, for the purpose of exploitation. Exploitation shall include, at a minimum, the exploitation of the prostitution of others or other forms of sexual exploitation, forced labor or services, slavery or practices similar to slavery, servitude or the removal of organs;
(b) The consent of a victim of trafficking in persons to the intended exploitation set forth in subparagraph (a) of this article shall be irrelevant where any of the means set forth in subparagraph (a) have been used;
(c) The recruitment, transportation, transfer, harboring or receipt of a child for the purpose of exploitation shall be considered "trafficking in persons" even if this does not involve any of the means set forth in subparagraph (a) of this article;
(d) "Child" shall mean any person less than 18 years of age.

The above definition clearly spells out that trafficking covers not only the transportation of a person from one place to another, but also their recruitment and receiving so that anyone involved in the movement of another person for their exploitation is part of the trafficking process. It further articulates that trafficking is not limited to sexual exploitation only for it could occur also for forced labor and other slavery-like practices. This means that people who migrate for work in agriculture, construction or domestic work, but are deceived or coerced into working in conditions they do not agree to, be also defined as trafficked people. Known as the Palermo Protocol, the Protocol to Prevent, Suppress and Punish Trafficking in Persons, Especially Women and Children, supplementing the United Nations Convention against

Transnational Organized Crime, was adopted by a UN resolution in 2000 and signed by India on December 12, 2002. The Protocol is significant because it gave the first comprehensive definition of human trafficking, and required countries to criminalize the practice, and to adopt legislation to translate the Protocol's obligations into national law. After a long delay India finally ratified the UN protocol on human trafficking on May 5, 2011, along with conventions against internationally organized crime and corruption. Year-on-year, the annual Trafficking in Persons Report has highlighted that India had failed to ratify the Protocol (UNODC 2011). Ratification of this convention means that it is now binding upon India to develop a law that conforms to the International Convention and its provisions. Often, the criminal gangs involved in large-scale kidnappings, abductions and forced labor of children go scot-free as the laws in the country are more biased toward prosecuting the employers or pimps in case of prostitution. However, traffickers of forced labor now come within the purview of the law in the country. The concern has been that India lacked a comprehensive definition of human trafficking to provide a common platform for the different Indian states to use in legislation and enforcement. Nevertheless trafficking has not been regarded as an organized crime in India, so provisions relevant to such crime are not utilized in enforcement. Also, legislation and enforcement has often failed to distinguish between the traffickers and the victims, so survivors are often punished rather than perpetrators.

The Route Causes

In India, commercial sexual exploitation is mostly associated with poverty and lack of education. Children and girls in particular are forced into prostitution in order to support their family income. Women and children (particularly girls) tend to be the most frequent trafficking victims (Sarkar 2011). Poverty is the root cause of many *Dalit* and *Tribal* being vulnerable to human trafficking and other forms of modern slavery. The pressure of making wealth to survive, the need to repay debts, illiteracy and the lack of education are the driving forces.

The *Devadasi* system is still prevalent in some states in India, particularly in the South, including in Karnataka, Tamil Nadu, Andhra Pradesh, and Maharashtra (Black 2007). *Devadasis* are dedicated to a goddess from as young as five years old. When they reach puberty, they are forced into a lifetime of ritual sex slavery. It is a form of prostitution sanctioned by religious practice—in effect, ritualized. It is sometimes known as temple prostitution, but this is misleading. Different names are used in different areas, including "*Jogini*" and "*Mathamma*." All these practices are outlawed, but they still go on. Almost all those trapped in ritual sex slavery are *Dalits*. After she reaches puberty the girl is given to an elder in the village—a priest, rich man, or land-owner. She will become the concubine of that elder until he is fed up with her—whether that is after one night or several years. The girl then becomes the property of the village to be used and abused by any man. Sometimes they will be trafficked to a brothel where they are "broken in." The poverty and superstition that forced the parents to dedicate their child also play a powerful part in keeping the girl in ritual sex slavery. Since the goddess brings good fortune, many believe that becoming a *Devadasi* or *Jogini* will bring good luck not just to the girl, but to her family and village. Women will tell their husbands to use a *Devadasi* or *Jogini* to bring good luck to their own mar-riage and family. Certain communities like the *Rajnat* of Rajasthan, the *Bedia* of Madhya Pradesh and the *Bachada* of the Rajasthan—Madhya Pradesh border also have some socially sanctioned practices enabling trafficking and commercial sexual exploitation.

Begging is witnessed as a major social disease in India whereas it is con-sidered as a lucrative business without investment at the dark side of the world using children as products. Hundreds of thousands of children in India are being forced to beg, often by unscrupulous mafia-style gangs. Many of the children are trafficked into gangs, some are kidnapped, others may have been handed over by their family out of desperation or because they have been duped. Every year some 43,000 Indian children fall into the clutches of the gangs (Arogya Wellbeing 2014). Many child beggars are addicted to solvents, alcohol and *charras* (a powerfully narcotic and intoxicating gum resin of Indian hemp). Even where children are taken off the streets and put in government shelters, many are re-trafficked back into begging.

Those most at risk of being trafficked for the organ harvesting are the poor and the desperate. If one is living in extreme poverty and there seems no way out, then he will be very tempted by the offer of a large amount of money for one of his kidneys, especially when this is accompanied by promises of life-time care. In January 2008, police discovered a kidney trafficking ring of four doctors and forty support staff thought to have supplied 400 to 500 kidneys for "transplant tourists" (Gentleman 2008). The severe shortage of organs for transplant in India is a reflection of the international imbalance in supply and demand. Inevitably, there are people who see the potential for making a lot of money; hence, there is a flourishing black market in organs in India.

Mode of Operation

The traffickers adopt various methods of trafficking of women and children. Usually, the ingenuity of the trafficker, coupled with the vulnerability of the victim, determine the modus operandi that is used. The available literature (Sen and Nair 2004; Sarkar 2011; Mishra 2013; Ghosh 2014) shows that the following methods have been commonly employed for trafficking in women and children in India—(a) offering them jobs as domestic servants; (b) promising jobs in the film world; (c) dangling before them jobs in factories; (d) offering money; (e) luring them with "pleasure trips"; (f) making false promises of marriage; (g) befriending them by giving goodies (girls who have run away from home or are street children are highly vulnerable to the traffickers); (h) offering to take them on pilgrimages; (i) making other kinds of false promises and, (j) coercion and so on.

The vulnerable situation in which the woman finds herself is a contributory factor in trafficking. The economic dependence of most women and their low social status leaves them with a relatively narrow range of options for eking out a livelihood. Women with no assets and hardly any alternatives have been easy targets of traffickers, who are able to persuade them to give in to commercial sexual exploitation in order to support themselves and their dependents. The traffickers modulate their strategy according to the specific situation. The more vulnerable the victims are, the easier it is for the traffickers to lure them. Traffickers lure victims and their families with promises of better employment and high earnings in the city (Sen and Nair 2005).

There is a trend of girls from the North East being brought to Haryana for forced marriage. The districts of Karnal, Mewat, Rewari, Kurukshetra, Jind, Yamuna Nagar, and Hisar in Haryana are known to be a destination for girls trafficked from the North Eastern states. Bride trafficking is particularly evident in Haryana due to its dismal sex ratio (The Times of India 2012a). Traffickers who set out with the purpose of providing a bride for a client will use one of several methods, or a combination. They may take a girl forcibly, or they may entice the girl with promises of a good job or an attractive lifestyle. They may groom the girl by developing a relationship with them, making them feel exceptional, so that the offer to take them to a big city and where they can be married is very attractive, but eventually they are then sold on. India's National Crime Records Bureau says that half of the nearly 45,000 kidnapping cases reported in 2012 were for the purpose of marriage. But that doesn't include unreported cases, or girls who are sold or persuaded to leave home. Human rights groups estimate that as many as 100,000 women are trafficked as part of the bride buying trade every year (Kelkar 2014).

The accessibility of the trafficker to the prospective victim is an important factor in trafficking. The method adopted is usually influenced by the proximity or otherwise of the trafficker to the victim. The modus operandi of the placement agencies is to recruit children from remote tribal villages in India by luring them with the promise of getting jobs. Once these children reach the capital, they are traded off to prospective employers who pay an advance of ₹30,000 to ₹45,000 in addition to ₹10,000 to ₹15,000 as placement agency charges (UNODC 2013). The Nepali girls and women who were interviewed by Human Rights Watch were forcibly trafficked into India. They did not work as prostitutes voluntarily but were held in conditions tantamount to slavery. Promises of jobs and marriage are common techniques by which recruiters entice their victims to leave home. But other, more overtly coercive tactics such as kidnapping are also reported. Girls who are already in debt bondage in other industries, particularly carpet factories, are more vulnerable (Human Rights Watch 1995).

NATURE, EXTENT, AND IDENTIFICATION OF TRAFFICKING VICTIMS

Internal Trafficking

The trafficking of persons can be broadly classified as sexual exploitation and nonsexual exploitation. It is possible that the former may contain elements of the latter and *vice versa*. India is a source, destination, and transit country for persons subjected to forced labor and sex trafficking. The forced labor of an estimated 20 to 65 million people comprise India's largest trafficking problem (US Department of State 2014); men, women, and children in debt bondage—sometimes inherited from previous generations—are forced to work in industries such as brick kilns, rice mills, agriculture, and embroidery factories. Children are subjected to forced labor as factory workers, beggars, agricultural workers, and, in some rural areas of Northern India, as carpet weavers. India's hand-made carpet sector accounted for 2,612 cases of forced labor and 2,010 cases of bonded labor of adults and children in nine Northern Indian states, including entire villages subjected to debt bondage in Uttar Pradesh and Madhya Pradesh (US Department of State 2014).

In June 2013, seventeen police officers, including two superintendents, were suspended in Kerala for their involvement in a sex trafficking network run through two airports. In July 2013, disciplinary action was taken against three Kerala police officers for facilitating the transport of trafficking victims to Dubai. In August 2013, two New Delhi police officers were arrested for running an alleged prostitution and extortion racket (US Department of State 2014). Police also reportedly accepted bribes in the form of money and sexual services in exchange for ignoring or failing to pursue trafficking charges, sexually abused trafficking victims, tipped suspected traffickers off to raids, released suspected traffickers after their arrests, and helped suspected traffickers destroy evidence (US Department of State 2014).

The problem of trafficking of women and children has assumed alarming proportions in Andhra Pradesh and it is one of the highest prone source areas in India. Trafficking is prevalent at various levels—local, interdistrict, interstate, and cross-border. Commercial sexual exploitation of women and children takes place in various forms including brothel-based prostitution, sex tourism, entertainment industry, and pornography in print and electronic media. Data indicates that nearly 50 percent of the victims belong to Scheduled Caste and up to 30 percent belong to the other backward classes (Government of Andhra Pradesh 2003).

Offences related to sex trafficking is also on the rise. In 2012, 525 minor girls, who were allegedly forced to dance naked at a theatre in a rural fair near the Indo-Nepal border in Bihar's Araria district, were rescued and 44 people were arrested under human trafficking charges. The rescued minor girls belonged to neighboring areas and from Nepal. Investigations proved that all the girls were minors and the arrested people were from Haryana, Uttar Pradesh, Nepal, and other parts of Bihar (Indo-Asia News Service 2012).

According to a former Chief Minister of Chhattisgarh, during last couple of years about 20,000 girls belonging to tribal region of Chhattisgarh have been trafficked in cities like Delhi, Mumbai, Bangalore, and Chennai. These girls mainly belonged to Jashpur, Surguja, and Raigarh districts and were taken away by the traffickers in the name of better opportunities and trainings (Jogi 2013).

In 2010, eleven girls from the North East were rescued in Goa. They were lured to Goa with a promise to teach them skills in order to get a job. They had been brought by agents and traffickers and forced into the sex trade. Of the eleven victims, six belonged to Nagaland, three from Mizoram and the rest from Belgaum. In a similar incident, Mizoram police had rescued ten girls and arrested thirteen people, who wanted to send them to Goa (Surahmar 2010).

Raids in Maharashtra, Madhya Pradesh, and Uttar Pradesh have reported an increasing trend of victims from Gujarat. Police officials in Maharashtra have reported that Gujarat and Rajasthan are emerging as new source areas in trafficking. The trend is supported by the missing children and women data of Gujarat which reports a sizable number of missing women and children (The Times of India 2012b).

The number of women and child trafficking cases in Karnataka has been on the increase in the last five years, with a total of 3,234 such offences being reported during the period. In the last five years, there had been as many as 3,234 cases of women and child trafficking reported in the state. In 2007, there were 440 cases which rose to 488 the next year and to 534 in 2009. While in 2010 and 2011, there were 697 and 672 cases reported respectively, as many as 403 cases had been reported till June 2012 (Press Trust of India 2012).

Children are trafficked from Bihar, Uttar Pradesh, Madhya Pradesh, and Chhattisgarh to work in the "Bt cotton fields" in Rajasthan. In order to curb trafficking to provide labor for "Bt cotton fields," the Rajasthan Government started a child tracking system to trace missing children with the help of the education department. Every year, a large number of children from districts including Udaipur, Dungarpur, and Banswara are trafficked to Gujarat to work in "Bt cotton fields." Despite concerted efforts of the district administration and the police, the illegal practice continues (The Times of India 2012c).

In West Bengal, almost all districts are vulnerable to trafficking. Jalpaiguri, Darjeeling, North and South Dinajpur, Cooch Behar, and Malda are trafficking prone districts in North Bengal. These districts have international borders with Bangladesh, Nepal, and Bhutan and have reported rampant trafficking from the tribal areas, tea estates, and border areas. The districts of North and South 24 Parganas are other vulnerable areas prone to trafficking. The villages here are far flung as the districts are located in the Sunderban area. In the year 2011, 14,000 adults and children have disappeared from West Bengal. Most of them are believed to have been swallowed up by the huge trafficking trade that is accustomed to treating West Bengal as its catchment area (Bhattacharjee 2012).

Trans-border Trafficking

India has a common border with Bangladesh, Nepal, Bhutan, Myanmar, China, and Pakistan. India is not only a country of destination within the region, but a transit country as well. Bangladesh and Nepal, on the other hand, may be characterized as sending countries or countries of origin, whereas Pakistan is both a country of destination as well as transit. It has been observed over the years that trafficking of South Asian persons occurs not only within and across countries of the region but to other regions and continents as well. There is an increase in the trafficking of persons alongside an increase in illegal and undocumented migration within the region (Sanghera 1999).

India shares 4,222 kilometer border with Bangladesh (Shamim 2001), a large part of which is flat terrain and has only twenty official checkpoints manned by the Border Security Force along this border. Being few and widely dispersed, often they are ineffective in maintaining strict vigil and illegal entries by traffickers are very common. There are many enclaves between the border of India and Bangladesh. There are 111 Indian enclaves in Bangladesh and 51 enclaves in Bangladesh in India. Traffickers often use these enclaves as recruitment and collection sites. Many boarder areas are frequently used as land routes for trafficking. A large proportion of cross-border trafficking of women and children in Bangladesh is due to illegal migration in search of better employment to India. A number of illicit migration businesses have developed to facilitate this cross-border movement from Bangladesh to India which may charge up to rupees fifty per person for each

Table 6.1   Indo-Bangladesh Border Crossings Used by the Traffickers

Districts	Trafficking Route from Bangladesh to India	Destination Point in India
Brahmanbaria, Comilla	Gopinathpur, Chouara	Agartala
Dinajpur	Hilli, Biral, Hakimpur, Amtoli, Komolpur	Hilli, Balurghat, Radikapur
Jessore	Shalkuna, Benapole ,Goga, Bahadurpur	Bongaon, Kurulia, Kalini, Bonabari
Jhenaidah	Jadabpur, Talsar, Samkur	Krishnanagar, Shantipur, Ranaghat
Khustia	Pragpur, Dhotarpara	Baharampur
Lalmonirhat	Mogholhat Burimari, Hatibandha	South Gitaldaha, Shitalkhuchi
Nawabganj	Shibganj	New Farakka
Nilphamari	Chatna, Chilahati, Thakugonj	Jalpaiguri
Panchagarh	Tetulia, Banglabandha, Baroshashi	Islampur, Fulbari, Manikganj, Haldibari

Source: Shamim 2001.

trip (Asian Development Bank and International Organisation for Migration 2009). Recruiting agencies acting as middlemen in such cases often charge exorbitantly, and there have been a number of cases of recruitment fraud where such female migrants are misled about terms of employment including payment. They find themselves being forced to work in prostitution. Table 6.1 shows bordering districts in Bangladesh with trafficking routes from Bangladesh to India and Indian transit point.

Movement of persons from Nepal to India is quite easy considering the long border it has with India. India has 1,740 mile-long open border with fourteen legal entry points (Asian Development Bank 2002), but illegal cross-border movement without documents often takes place since India has an open border policy with Nepal. Nepalese have free access to enter India, and, therefore, trafficking becomes difficult to identify. Under the 1950 Treaty between India and Nepal there is no immigration control for Nepalese traveling or migrating to India, which makes it easier for the traffickers to cross undetected. The Asian Development Bank (2002) study on Nepal lists the districts through which this movement takes place and identifies the entry and exit points as well as the major border regions used by traffickers between Nepal and India. Traffickers use different routes including unofficial border points, and some traffickers also use truck to change girls from one truck to another. They finally move to mainly Kolkata, Delhi and Mumbai by train or bus traveling from areas throughout the five regions of Nepal (table 6.2).

It is estimated that every year between 5,000 to 10,000 Nepali women and girls are trafficked to India for the purposes of commercial sexual exploitation and work in brothels in various cities in India. However, 90 percent of

Table 6.2   Indo-Nepal Border Crossings Used by the Traffickers

Regions	Indo-Nepal Border Crossings
Eastern Border	Kakarbhitta (Nepal) to Panitanki-New Jalpaiguri
	Trains from New Jalpaiguri connect major cities of India
	Biratnagar (Nepal) to Jogbani-Katihar (Bihar)
	Trains from Katihar connect major cities in India
Central Border	Birgunj (Nepal) to Raxual-Muzffarpur
	Muzzafarpur is a major junction connecting east-west and south bound trains
Western Border	Bhairahawa (Nepal) to Sunauli-Gorakhpur
	Direct bus to Delhi via major cities in Uttar Pradesh State available from Sunauli
	Trains from Gorakhpur connect to Delhi, Mumbai, Bangalore, and other major cities
Midwestern Border	Nepalgunj (Nepal) to Rupadiya-Baraich-Lucknow
	Buses available from Gaurifanta to Lucknow via Baraich.
	Trains from Baraich and Lucknow connect Mumbai, Delhi and other major cities
Far Western Border	Dhangadi (Nepal) to Gaurifanta-Baraich-Lucknow
	Direct buses to Delhi and train connections available from Baraich.
	Mahendranagar-Gaddachowki (Nepal) to Banbasa-Tanakpur-Nainital-Haridwar (Uttarakhand State, India)
	Direct bus connections to Delhi and trains to other Indian cities

Source: The Asia Foundation 2013.

India's sex trafficking is internal with victims of trafficking mostly being used for forced labor. Trafficking from neighboring countries accounts for the remaining 10 percent. Of this 10 percent about 2.17 percent is from Bangladesh and 2.6 percent from Nepal (UNODC 2006). Internal conflicts in Nepal and Bangladesh have been a boon for traffickers. While adverse human security conditions in this part of South Asia have contributed to the process of forced migration and thereby created opportunities for trafficking, traffickers have also used the ongoing conflict to their advantage. Since border controls and normal policing are reduced at the time of turmoil, it becomes easier for the traffickers to move victims across borders. A study conducted by the UNDP (2000) shows that the average age of trafficked girls from Nepal to India fell from 14–16 years in the 1980s to 10–14 years in 1994. Citing the data collected by *Sanlaap*, a leading Kolkata based NGO working for the rescue and rehabilitation of trafficked girls in West Bengal, the Asian Development Bank report indicates that about 10,000 women have been found in Kolkata brothels, of which 70 percent are from Bangladesh (Asian Development Bank 2002). Some Bangladeshi people are subjected to forced labor in India through recruitment fraud and debt bondage. Boys from Nepal and Bangladesh continue to be subjected to forced labor in coal mines in the state of Meghalaya. Trafficking victims—primarily girls—continue to be recruited from Bangladesh and Nepal and brought to different states in India. An increasing number of foreign women, mostly from Central Asia and Bangladesh, were rescued from debt bondage within Hyderabad; labor trafficking, including bonded labor, reportedly continues in Odisha (US Department of State 2014).

CONCLUSION

There has been a rising inclination of women and children being trafficked from the states of Jharkhand, Chhattisgarh, Orissa, Assam, West Bengal and Madhya Pradesh for the purpose of labor. Trafficking for commercial sexual exploitation is on the increase. West Bengal, Andhra Pradesh, Karnataka, Maharashtra, and Orissa continue to be the high source areas in India for the purpose of trafficking to the red-light areas across India. Child soldiering and organ harvesting are also forms of trafficking that occur in India, though on a much lesser scale than forced labor and sexual exploitation. Due to the skewed sex ratio resulting from female foeticide there has been an increasing demand for marriageable age girls in the states of Northern India including Haryana, Western Uttar Pradesh, Punjab and Rajasthan. This has led to a trend of trafficking of girls and women from states like West Bengal, Assam, Orissa, and Jharkhand. Children are subjected to forced labor as factory workers, beggars, agricultural workers, and, in some rural areas of Northern India, as carpet weavers. Millions of women and children are victims of sex trafficking in India. Children continue to be subjected to sex trafficking in religious pilgrimage centers and tourist destinations. A large number of Nepali, Afghan, and Bangladeshi females—the majority of whom are children aged nine to fourteen years old—and women and girls from China, Russia, Uzbekistan, Azerbaijan, the Philippines, and Uganda are also subjected to sex trafficking in India (US Department of State 2014). West Bengal continues to be a source for trafficking victims, with girls more frequently subjected to sex trafficking in small hotels, vehicles, huts, and private residences than conventional red-light districts. Trafficking victims—primarily girls and children—continue to be recruited from Bangladesh and Nepal and brought to metropolitan cities in India.

Therefore, human trafficking and illegal migration, which works through social network in India, is a very complex and multidimensional phenomenon. Trafficking involves deep-rooted process of gender discrimination, lack of female education, ignorance of rural folk, poverty and lack of economic opportunities. Woman's lack of empowerment or lack of information about what may happen if they migrate—these factors can be assumed to increase vulnerability to trafficking. Hence economics of illegal female migration can be linked with economics of trafficking. Human trafficking has all the characteristics of multifaceted dimensions, characterized by emergent behavior, network relationships, high degrees of resilience, and a remarkable degree of adaptability in response to law enforcement efforts to interfere with the business. For Indian government to respond more effectively and carry out the counter-network and counter-market strategy, they need to create a system that looks remarkably similar to the one they are trying to destroy. It looks initially at the limits of governance, both in general and specifically in relation to combating human trafficking. It then suggests that the networks involved in human trafficking are agile and difficult to combat, especially because they operate within a dynamic market characterized not only by a high demand for forced labor and commercial sex but also a ready supply of trafficking victims. In short, human trafficking poses enormous challenges to governance and law enforcement, and, at times, these challenges seem to be overwhelming. Even if it is something, which is unlikely to be eliminated, however, more effective steps can be taken to contain or even reduce the scope of the problem.

REFERENCES

Arogya Wellbeing. 2014. *Trafficking: Women and Children.* http://www.arogyawel lbeing.com/uncategorized/sex-trafficking-girls-women/.

Asian Development Bank. 2002. *Combating Trafficking of Women and Children in South Asia.* Country Paper Bangladesh, Manila: Asian Development Bank.

Asian Development Bank and International Organisation for Migration. 2009. *Review of the SAARC Convention and the Current Status of Implementation in Bangladesh.* Dhaka: Asian Development Bank and International Organisation for Migration.

Bhattacharjee, K. 2012. *A Trip to a Part of Bengal Where Humans Are Bought and Sold Every Day.* http://www.ndtv.com/article/india/a-trip-to-a-part-of-bengal-wher e-humans-are-bought-and-sold-everyday-193667.

Black, M. 2007. *Ritual Slavery Practices in India: Devadasi, Jogini and Mathamma.* http://www.antislavery.org/includes/documents/cm_docs/2008/r/ritual_slavery _briefing_paper_1_august_2007.pdf.

Centre for Development and Population Activities. 1997. *Girls' Right: Society's Responsibility, Taking Action against Sexual Exploitation and Trafficking.* Facts on Asia and Country Profiles. Washington, DC: Centre for Development and Population Activities.

Consulate General of the United States. 2008. *India's Country Narrative for the Trafficking in Persons Report 2008.* http://kolkata.usconsulate.gov/usgovtreportst ipind.html.

DuPont, K. L. 2009. *Global Issues: Human Trafficking.* New York: Facts on File.

Gentleman, A. 2008. *Kidney Thefts Shock India.* http://www.nytimes.com/2008/01/30/world/asia/30kidney.html.

Ghosh, B. 2014. "Vulnerability, Forced Migration and Trafficking in Children and Women: A Field View from the Plantation Industry in West Bengal." *Economic & Political Weekly* XLIX(26–27): 58–65.

Government of Andhra Pradesh. 2003. *GO Notification on Rehabilitation Policy 2003.* http://nlrd.org/wp-content/uploads/2012/01/ANDHRA-PRADESH-POLICY-TO-COMBATTRAFFICKING-.pdf.

Gupta, G. R. 2003. *Review of Literature for Action Research on Trafficking in Women and Children.* New Delhi: Institute of Social Sciences.

Huda, S. 2006. "Sex Trafficking in South Asia." *International Journal of Gynaecology and Obstetrics* 94: 374–381.

Human Rights Watch. 1995. *Rape for Profit: Trafficking of Nepali Girls and Women to India's Brothels.* New Delhi: Human Rights Watch.

Indo-Asia News Service. 2012. *Police Rescue 25 Minor Girls from Bihar Fair.* http://www.ndtv.com/article/cities/police-rescue-25-minor-girls-from-bihar-fair-176008.

International Labor Organization. 2012. *ILO Global Estimate of Forced Labor: Results and Methodology.* Geneva: International Labor Organization.

Jogi, A. 2013. *20,000 Chhattisgarh Girls Sold.* http://www.bharatwaves.in/news/20,000-Chhattisgarh-girls-sold:-Jogi-26118.html.

Kelkar, K. 2014. *Bride Buying: India's Darkest Secret.* http://www.vocativ.com/culture/society/bride-buying-indias-darkest-secret/.

Mishra, E. 2013. "Combating Human Trafficking: A Legal Perspective with Special Reference to India." *Sociology and Anthropology* 1(4): 172–179.

Press Trust of India. 2012. *Women, Children Trafficking on Increase in Karnataka.* http://www.ndtv.com/article/south/women-children-trafficking-on-increase-in-karnataka-249247.

Sanghera, J. 1999. *Trafficking of Women and Children in South Asia—Taking Stock and Moving Ahead: A Broad Assessment of Anti-trafficking Initiatives in Nepal, Bangladesh and India.* New Delhi: UNICEF Regional Office and Save the Children Alliance.

Sarkar, S. 2011. "Trafficking in Women and Children to India and Thailand: Characteristics, Trends and Policy Issues." *International Journal of Afro-Asian Studies* 2(1): 57–73.

Sen, S. and Nair, P. M. 2004. *A Report on Trafficking in Women and Children in India.* Volume I, NHRC- UNIFEM-ISS Project. New Delhi: National Human Rights Commission.

Sen, S. and Nair, P. M. 2005. *Trafficking in Women and Children in India.* New Delhi: Orient Longman.

Shamim, I. 2001. *Mapping of Missing, Kidnapped and Trafficked Children and Women: Bangladesh Perspective.* Bangladesh: International Organization in Migration.

Shelley, L. 2010. *Human Trafficking: A Global Perspective.* New York: Cambridge University Press.

Silverman, J. G. et al. 2007. "HIV Prevalence and Predictors of Infection in Sex-trafficked Nepalese Girls and Women." *Journal of the American Medical Association* 298(5): 536–542.

Surahmar. 2010. *Nagaland Cops Arrive in Goa to Probe Trafficking.* http://surahmar .wordpress.com/2010/10/20/nagaland-cops-arrive-in-goa-to-probe-trafficking/.

The Asia Foundation. 2013. *Labor Migration Trends and Patterns: Bangladesh, India, and Nepal 2013.* Kathmandu: The Asia Foundation.

The Times of India. 2012a. *Northeast Girls being Trafficked to Haryana for Marriage.* http://articles.timesofindia.indiatimes.com/2012-01-19/india/30642582_ 1_trafficking-home-ministry-ahtus.

The Times of India. 2012b. *11 Minor Girls Rescued from Red-light Area.* http:// articles.timesofindia.indiatimes.com/2012-07-20/nagpur/32763445_1_minor-girls-brothel-owners-red-light-area.

The Times of India. 2012c. *Child Tracking System to Curb Trafficking to Cotton Fields in Gujarat.* http://articles.timesofindia.indiatimes.com/2012-06-18/jaipu r/32298212_1_cotton-fields-child-trafficking-udaipur-and-dungarpur.

Uddin, M. B. 2014. "Human Trafficking in South Asia: Issues of Corruption and Human Security." *International Journal of Social Work and Human Services Practice* 2(1): 18–27.

UNDP. 2000. *SADC Region Human Development Report 2000.* New York: UNDP.

UNICEF. 2005. *Children out of Sight, out of Mind, out of Reach; Abused and Neglected, Millions of Children have become Virtually Invisible.* London: UNICEF.

United Nations. 2000. *United Nations Protocol to Prevent, Suppress and Punish Trafficking in Persons, Especially Women and Children.* New York: United Nations.

UNODC. 2006. *Trafficking in Persons: Global Patterns.* Vienna: UNODC.

UNODC. 2011. *Responses to Human Trafficking in Bangladesh, India, Nepal and Sri Lanka.* New Delhi: UNODC.

UNODC. 2013. *Current Status of Victim Service Providers and Criminal Justice Actors in India on Anti-Human Trafficking.* New Delhi: UNODC.

US Department of State. 2014. *Trafficking in Persons Report.* Washington, DC: US Department of State.

Chapter 7

Evidence from India and Thailand

Trafficking of human beings, especially of women and children, is one of the fastest growing trades, generating unaccountable profits annually. The reasons for the increase in this global phenomenon are multiple and complex, affecting rich and poor countries alike. India and Thailand is no exception to this. The source areas or points of origin are often the more deprived places, regions or countries, and the points of destination are often—although not always—urban conglomerates within or across borders. For all those who view trafficking in economic terms, it is the real or perceived differential between the economic status of source and destination areas that is important. In practice, however, human beings may be and are trafficked from one poor area to another poor area as well for reasons best known to the traffickers, a fact that has been corroborated by research studies and documentation across the world. The fact is that the process of trafficking is designed and manipulated by traffickers for their own ends for which they employ all kinds of means. Therefore, the assumption that human beings are always trafficked from undeveloped to more developed places is untenable.

There is a strong indication from the available information that women and children are becoming vulnerable to trafficking, as they are unable to survive with dignity because of lack of livelihood options. In the absence of awareness of human rights, the economically and socially underprivileged people at the grassroots have become easy prey to the trafficking trade. Migrating populations have become most vulnerable to exploitation by traffickers. The fact that notwithstanding this stark reality, such gross violations of human rights continued to be a low priority area with law enforcement agencies, made it imperative that this area be investigated.

Being a complex phenomenon, problem of trafficking is profoundly entrenched in the socioeconomic, political, and cultural reality of the context in which it occurs, although this may not be its immediate cause. The perpetrators are the traffickers about whom relatively little is known. This gap has to be urgently addressed, along with the demand factors, which drive trafficking. It is a fundamental violation of the rights of human beings and shows a blatant disregard for the dignity of a person.

The scale of the phenomenon is difficult to judge. It is very difficult to collect data on trafficking because of the clandestine nature of the operations. The trade is secretive, the women are silenced, the traffickers are dangerous and not many agencies are counting (Hughes 2000).

Among the most quoted figures are the United Nations estimates that four million people in a year are traded against their will to work in some form of slavery, many of them are children and believes that in the last thirty years, trafficking in women and children for sexual exploitation in Asia alone has victimized more than thirty million people. Asia is mainly an origin region as well as a destination for trafficking in persons. Asian victims are reported to be trafficked from Asia to Asian countries, in particular to Thailand, Japan, India, Taiwan, and Pakistan (United Nations 2006).

India is located in golden triangle, which is most vulnerable region for the trafficking of women and children for flesh trade (Westwood 1998). Literature on trafficking in India is completely dominated by the issue of commercial sexual exploitation, so much so that trafficking, as a distinct separate crime does not get highlighted. At times is almost reduced to insignificance in comparison to commercial sexual exploitation. Even though there seems to be considerable information available, one is unable to form a picture, which reflects the reality of trafficking in women and children in India (Sen and Nair 2004).

Calculations of trafficked people are generally made with reference to commercial sex exploitation. In India, the stigma attached to prostitution and the clandestine nature of operations makes it doubly difficult to arrive at authentic numbers (Gupta 2004). Increasing incidence of trafficking has threatened the social fabric of the country. Girls under 18 are being lured from Nepal, Bangladesh to Indian metropolitan cities. In India traffickers also lure girls and young women from Assam, West Bengal, Bihar, Rajasthan, Jharkhand, Madhya Pradesh, Chhattisgarh, and Uttar Pradesh. The counterfeit promises of jobs and better living standards push these girls and young women into prostitution.

Thailand has one of the most serious human trafficking problems in Asia and is a primary source, transit point, and final destination for untold numbers of women and children (US Department of State 2005a). Because of its relative affluence, Thailand is the biggest recipient of labor migration, both legal and illegal, in the Greater Mekong sub-region, which includes Cambodia, Laos, China's Yunnan Province, Myanmar, and Vietnam. While there are no official government statistics on numbers trafficked into and out of Thailand, it is widely accepted that a significant number of illegal migrant workers are actually victims of trafficking.

International Labour Organization (ILO) report estimated that 200,000 to 300,000 women and children are trafficked into Thailand each year for the purpose of prostitution (ILO/IRPC 2005). According to the US-based research institute "Protection Project," estimates of the number of child victims of prostitution living in Thailand ranges from 12,000 to the hundreds of thousands (ECPAT International 2003). The Government, university researchers, and NGOs estimated that there are as many as 30,000 to 40,000 prostitutes less than 18 years of age, not including foreign migrants (US Department of State 2005b). A government estimate reveals that five percent of child prostitutes were found to be boys (UNICEF 2004). Thailand's Health System Research Institute reports that children in prostitution make up 40 percent of sex workers in Thailand. At the other end of this debate many NGOs estimate the number of CSEC victims to be in the hundreds of thousands. Other reports estimate the number of child victims of prostitution to be at least 80,000 but likely to be in the hundreds of thousands (The Protection Project 2002).

In the 1980s women and girls were recruited from the poorer provinces in the North and Northeast of Thailand for commercial sex services in the urban areas. This traffic consisted mostly of 12–16 year old girls from the hill tribes of the North and Northeast. This pattern was to some extent replaced in the 1990s by the trafficking of women and children, primarily from Burma and Myanmar, but also from Lao PDR, Cambodia, and Yunnan province in China. Today, Thailand is considered a major transit and destination country for trafficked women and children from countries in the Greater Mekong sub-region. In addition to exploitation in commercial sex services, persons have been trafficked to Thailand to work as maids or in construction, agriculture, or factories. The disparity in economic development between neighboring countries in the Mekong sub-region has been one catalyst of cross-border migration into Thailand. The opening of borders, increased mobility between countries, corruption and the high profits generated by the sex industry are some of the indirect incentives for trafficking. Thailand receives from neighboring countries considerable number of children trafficked for different forms of labor and begging. Many of them subsequently end up in the sex industry (ILO 2000).

The estimates found in various reports vary over time and across regions, primarily because human trafficking is an extremely difficult activity to investigate. There are also differences in focus and in methodologies. As the evidence base is shaky, and easy to challenge, it is important to consider how knowledge on this issue can be improved, in order to properly inform efforts to prevent and reduce trafficking.

Table 7.1   Trafficking Routes from South and Southeast Asian Countries

Source	Intermediate	End Point
Nepal	→	India
	→ India →	Middle East
India	→	Middle East
Bangladesh	→	India
	→ India →	Pakistan
	→ India →	Middle East
	→ India → Pakistan →	Middle East
Pakistan	→	Middle East
China	→ Chiang Mai (North Thailand) →	Bangkok (Central Thailand)
Myanmar	→ Chiang Mai (North Thailand) →	Bangkok (Central Thailand)
Lao PDR	→ North East Thailand →	Bangkok (Central Thailand)
Vietnam	→ North East Thailand →	Bangkok (Central Thailand)
Cambodia	→	Bangkok (Central Thailand)
Thailand	→	Australia, South Africa, Japan, Bahrain, Taiwan, Europe and North America

TRAFFICKING ROUTES: SOUTH AND SOUTHEAST ASIA

South and Southeast Asia is considered the most vulnerable region for trafficking because of its large population, large-scale rural-urban migration, large populations living in conditions of chronic poverty, and recurrent natural disasters. India and Thailand has one of the most serious human trafficking problems in Asia and is a primary source, transit point, and final destination for untold numbers of women and children. Women and children are sold, traded, exchanged for sexual slavery and prostitution, and bonded labor across borders, such as from Bangladesh to India, Pakistan, and the Middle East, from Nepal to India, from Myanmar, China, Cambodia, Lao PDR and Vietnam to Thailand and from Thailand to Australia, South Africa, Japan, Bahrain, Taiwan, Europe, and North America. Following figure shows distribution of Asian countries between which trafficking takes place (table 7.1).

PUSH AND PULL FACTORS

The circumstances and situations that influence migration are usually examined in terms of push and pull factors. Push factors are associated with sending regions and pull, with receiving regions.

These factors are interdependent, and are classified as economic, political, sociocultural, or environmental in nature. The push factors include: growing inequalities in wealth between and within countries; economic decline; lack of economic opportunities and underdevelopment of an area, characterized by poverty, underemployment, landlessness and impoverishment among rural populations; discrimination; population pressure; harsh economic policies; limited access to resources; lack of opportunities for local employment that would allow women to explore better jobs, or acquire greater skills to obtain a more secure future; and lack of basic subsistence.

The pull factors are listed as—real or perceived differences in wages; more and better employment opportunities in destination areas; demand for female migrant workers in more developed regions; an economic boom in destination areas; a growing number of women and men in destinations who relegate domestic work to hired help; and the increasing acceptance of the practice of prostitution.

TREND

Economic and social inequalities and political conflicts have led to the movement of persons within each country and across the borders in South Asia. South Asia is witnessing an alarming trend of increasingly younger girls being trafficked into the sex trade. The majority of trafficking in India, both trans-border and in-country, happens for the purpose of sex work. In South Asia, the link between sex trafficking and HIV is emerging stronger than ever before. The nexus between poverty, HIV, and the trafficking of women and children within and across borders is creating ever-widening circles of insecurity that disproportionately threaten the lives of the victims and further impoverish the poor through sickness, loss of livelihood and rejection by society. Moving beyond the narrow epidemiological profile of the HIV/AIDS epidemic within the region and examining the broader socio-economic and development causes, an integral connection is evident between HIV/AIDS, gender and sex trafficking through the nexus of vulnerability and sexual violence.

It is thus crucial to adopt rights protective strategies in combating the crime of sex trafficking, reducing vulnerabilities of victims including stigmatization, which results in multiple burdens for HIV-positive survivors. It is important to mainstream sex trafficking and HIV/AIDS with a multisectoral approach maximizing linkages and coordination between national and regional programs related to trafficking of women and girls and HIV/AIDS. Special attention is needed on legal, social, physical and psychological protection of people who are affected by, or exposed to, sex trafficking and HIV/AIDS.

In the recent years, various initiatives and programs in the countries of South Asia have begun addressing the problem of human trafficking, especially in

Table 7.2   Number of Trafficked Victims in Prostitution in India

State/Union Territories	Total Average
Andhra Pradesh	240018
Arunachal Pradesh	2062
Assam	39468
Bihar	120990
Chhattisgarh	9375
Goa	40312
Gujarat	110212
Haryana	11625
Himachal Pradesh	4031
Jharkhand	15000
Jammu & Kashmir	11625
Karnataka	150525
Kerala	51562
Madhya Pradesh	108253
Maharashtra	300975
Manipur	3556
Meghalaya	3187
Nagaland	4500
Orissa	33799
Punjab	33750
Rajasthan	125478
Sikkim	318
Tamil Nadu	227812
Tripura	1031
Uttar Pradesh	203901
Uttarakhand	6093
West Bengal	275293
Chandigarh	8062
Delhi	12588
Pondicherry	105
Daman & Diu	369
Total	2120620

Source: New Delhi: Various Report of Government of India.

women and children. Governments are becoming active, although most programs are carried out by non-governmental organizations with a focus on local communities. Concerted efforts have also been undertaken at the subregional level to combat human trafficking in South Asia.

In India, the estimates of trafficked victims (women and girls) who are in prostitution number around 2.12 million in India. Most of the women and girls are reported in the state of Maharashtra, West Bengal, Rajasthan, Andhra Pradesh, and Karnataka (table 7.2).

A large number of female adults and children are reported missing in India. Out of them a large chunk of such population is reported in the metropolitan cities. As per police records, the number of female adults and children are

Table 7.3   Number of Female and Children Reporting Missing in India

State	Average Number of Female Adults Reporting Missing in a Year	Average Number of Children Reporting Missing in a Year
Andhra Pradesh	771	2007
Arunachal Pradesh	22	63
Assam	365	785
Chandigarh	54	30
Chhattisgarh	106	164
Delhi	2043	6227
Goa	290	219
Gujarat	932	1624
Haryana	105	251
Himachal Pradesh	199	155
Karnataka	1678	3660
Kerala	861	707
Madhya Pradesh	2950	4915
Maharashtra	8103	16656
Meghalaya	3	17
Nagaland	1	6
Orissa	255	591
Rajasthan	882	2356
Tamil Nadu	2094	5541
Tripura	56	54
Uttaranchal	139	369
Uttar Pradesh	361	2124
West Bengal	186	591
Total	22980	493

Source: New Delhi: Various Report of Government of India.

reported missing is increasing at a high alarming rate in the metropolitan cities (table 7.3).

Minister of State for Women and Child Development, Government of India addressed that trafficking of children, including minor girls; saw a rise in India's North Eastern region over the period of 2008–2009. According to the National Crime Records Bureau (NCRB), six such cases were reported in the region until September 2010. As per the NCRB data, the number of cases registered under the Immoral Traffic (Prevention) Act, 1956, in the North Eastern region increased from 32 in 2008 to 43 in 2009. As per the data, Assam saw the biggest rise, from 27 cases in 2008 to 37 cases in 2009. Funds have been released for establishing eighteen antihuman trafficking units (ATHUs) in the North Eastern States. National Crime Records Bureau (NCRB) data, the number of cases registered under the Immoral Traffic (Prevention) Act, 1956 in the North Eastern Region increased from 32 in 2008 to 43 in 2009. The state-wise details are given in table 7.4.

In Thailand, commercial sexual exploitation is mostly associated with poverty and a lack of education. Children and girls in particular are forced

Table 7.4   Child Trafficking in Northeast India

State	2008	2009*	2010* Up to the month of
Arunachal Pradesh	0	0	0 (June)
Assam	27	37	1 (March)
Manipur	0	0	2 (September)
Meghalaya	3	1	2 (August)
Mizoram	1	1	0 (August)
Nagaland	1	3	0 (July)
Sikkim	0	1	1 (August)
Tripura	0	0	0 (August)
Total	32	43	6

*Provisional Data.

into prostitution in order to help subsidize their family's income. Women and children (particularly girls) tend to be the most frequent trafficking victims. Gender is an issue in trafficking on both the supply and demand sides of equation. Girls are often seen as expendable, and laws and law enforcement, as well as some cultural and traditional contexts, provide them unequal protection. Girls are in many societies expected to sacrifice education and security and take on responsibilities toward parents, siblings, and even their children. Women are forced to migrate to enter urban employment, in which they are easily vulnerable to exploitation and in which remuneration rates are low. The poor income-earning opportunities for women with low levels of education, the desire to provide substantial support for their families and a relatively tolerant attitude toward prostitution in some segments of Thai society help to ensure that some of this labor supply will be directed toward the sex industry.

Studies show that the majority of girls in prostitution are from Northern Thailand. This is particularly true of children from Northern Thailand's hill tribes. Most vulnerable are women and children from ethnic minority groups, such as the Akha, Lahu, Lisu, Thai Yai, Thai Leu, and Luwa. These children are denied Thai citizenship and are viewed as having a lower cultural status than lowland Thais. Being under privileged, having little education and little understanding of the dangers of leaving home, and with no alternative viable means of income, children from tribal groups often leave for or are lured to "work" in urban areas and fall victim to prostitution. The situation is so desperate for some living in hill tribes it has been reported in some cases that women and children from tribal groups succumb to the pressure of prostitution in an attempt to feel more "valuable" and become "accepted" by Thai society.

Thailand is seen as the primary destination country for migrants in the Greater Mekong sub-region, with most coming from Myanmar, Laos, and

Table 7.5   Number of Trafficked Cases in Thailand

Type of Case	2008	2009	2010	Total
Prostitution	19	56	49	124
Sexual Exploitation	0	1	0	1
Forced Begging	8	6	2	16
Removal of Organs	0	0	0	0
Pornography	0	0	0	0
Slavery	0	4	0	4
Forced Labor or Service	13	27	9	49
Forced Extortion	0	1	0	1
Total	40	95	60	195

Source: Bangkok: Antihuman Trafficking Division.

Cambodia. Workers particular from these three countries, often tend to migrant without valid documents, fleeing condition of poverty, or political conflict in search of greater opportunities and a place where they can live without anxiety. Industrial growth related to global capitalism has been one of the major factors that have triggered migration. The Thai economy is relatively prosperous in the region and there is a great demand of cheap foreign unskilled laborers to sustain its growth.

In table 7.5 the number of trafficked cases in Thailand during 2008–2010 is shown. It reveals that the number of victims in prostitution is high followed by forced labor or service and forced begging. A total of 129 such cases have been recorded in Antihuman Trafficking Division of Thailand, out of which 27 cases have been resolved up to September 2010.

Thai Ministry of Social Development and Human Security has set its strategies on prevention and protection of foreign trafficking victims at different levels, namely, serving as the center of welfare protection and assistance victims of human trafficking and domestic violence. The Department of Social and Welfare Development under Ministry of Social Development and Human Security provides protection service and shelter to the foreign victims who suffer from all kinds of social problems such as sexual exploitation and other domestic violence. Table 7.6 shows that foreign trafficked and vulnerable victims who are receiving assistance in different shelters under the Department of Social and Welfare Development and in table 7.7 number of the foreign victims protected in each center is shown.

Trafficking in women and children, due to root cause and manifestation of poverty and human deprivation, is a major challenge to all stakeholders in Thailand. Thai women and children are trafficked to Australia, South Africa, Japan, Bahrain, Taiwan, Europe, and North America for sexual exploitation. Internal trafficking also occurs in Thailand, involving victims from Northern Thailand. The most common trafficking routes within Thailand are from

Table 7.6   Number of Foreign Trafficked and Vulnerable Victims in Thailand

Nationality	2001	2002	2003	2004	2005	2006	2007	2008	2009	2010	Total
Cambodia	134	134	128	152	177	102	80	45	57	75	1084
Myanmar	81	113	220	66	64	201	69	252	260	128	1454
Laotian	62	66	74	159	170	334	209	214	195	198	1681
Chinese	1	11	11	2	3	1	3	0	2	0	34
Vietnamese	0	2	0	6	5	8	0	3	11	2	37
Other	0	1	2	6	0	1	1	6	0	0	17
Unidentified	1	1	0	0	0	0	1	0	5	0	8
Total	279	328	435	391	419	647	363	520	530	403	4315

Source: Bangkok: Department of Social and Welfare Development.

Table 7.7   Number of Foreign Victims Protected in Different Shelters in 2010

Nationality *Shelter/Home*	*Cambodia*	*Laotian*	*Myanmar*	*Chinese*	*Vietnamese*	*Other*	*Unidentified*	*Total*
Bann Kredtrekarn	9	95	16	0	0	0	0	120
Bann Nareesawad	0	14	0	0	0	0	0	14
Bann Songkhwae	1	4	4	0	0	0	0	9
Bann Srisurat	0	4	4	1	0	0	0	9
Pakkred Reception Home for Boys	10	6	13	0	0	0	0	29
Pathumathani Home for Men	6	0	21	0	0	0	0	27
Chaing Rai Home for Men	0	1	11	0	0	0	0	12
Rangon Home for Men	0	0	8	0	0	0	0	8
Songkhala Home for Men	2	0	7	1	0	0	0	9
Total	28	124	84		0	0	0	237

Source: Bangkok: Department of Social and Welfare Development.

North to South and from rural areas to Bangkok. The trafficked people are usually the rural poor and are often from ethnic minorities. The internal traffic of Thai girls consists mostly of 12–16-year-old from hill tribes of the North/Northeast. Girls from the Northern hill tribes of Thailand are often trafficked to Thai cities for prostitution some local officials, immigration officers, and police reportedly either are involved in trafficking directly or take bribes to ignore it. Police personnel are poorly paid and are accustomed to taking bribes to supplement their income. Official corruption facilitating the worst forms of trafficking in persons is generally at the lower and middle levels. There is no evidence that high-level officials benefit from or protect the practice. Compromised local police protect brothels and other sex venues from surprise raids. Corrupt immigration officials assisted (both indirectly and directly) the movement of women and girls from Myanmar, Laos, and China into the country, and of Chinese victims out of the country to the United States and other destinations.

RESEARCH DESIGN

This study on trafficking in women and children to India and Thailand is pioneering and exploratory. It is not surprising that reliability and authenticity of existing data is a matter of concern. The broad objectives of our study follow from this major concern. These are:

(a) To understand the trends and patterns of trafficking, and the structural and functional mechanism that reproduces and reinforces the processes that perpetuate the phenomenon
(b) To analyze the roles and functions of the formal and voluntary agencies that are involved in containing and combating this phenomenon
(c) To prepare a comprehensive database

In this study both primary and desk review of literature is undertaken. Primary data was collected by use of questionnaires administered on key informants in government and nongovernment organizations both law enforcement authority and service provider and group of academic researchers in the field. A total of fifteen organizations responded to the survey comprising five from India and ten from Thailand and eight action individual researchers/activists in the field from India and seven from Thailand have been interviewed. Judgment and purposive sampling methods were employed to select the sample due to the nature of the problem under investigation and scanty possible sources of information.

FINDINGS

Poverty and gender imbalances in the availability of gainful employment opportunities for women, gender violence, and lack of educational opportunities in most parts of India and Thailand have created a pool of vulnerable workers, which has heightened international trafficking activities to the countries. The high incidences of poverty amplify in dependency levels especially due to the effects of HIV/AIDS, and moral decay has all contributed to a worsening trafficking situation in India and Thailand.

Our survey shows that there is a general awareness of the existence of trafficking in persons in India and Thailand from all the respondents. However, there was no tangible or documented evidence of the extent of the vice. The problem of lack of secondary data is compounded by limited knowledge on the vice, which means that not much may be gathered through primary surveys. Even in government and support institutions, which would be expected to have data on human trafficking, there was a lacuna on the same. This might make it difficult to come up with programs and policies to control trafficking in persons in India and Thailand.

About 75 percent of the people interviewed from India and 65 percent from Thailand defined human trafficking as the transporting of human beings from one place to another illegally while 10 percent and 15 percent respectively defined it as illegal migration or human trade. The rest, 15 percent (India) and 20 percent (Thailand) defined human trafficking to involve forcing, defrauding, and coercing into labor or sexual exploitation. The definitions from the survey concur with the usual definition of human trafficking by the UN Transnational Organized Crime Protocol. About 70 percent (India) and 75 percent (Thailand) of the respondents described the activities that would portray human trafficking as dealings in child prostitution, religious sects that trafficked victims through fake promises of miracles, foreigners pretending to adopt children from poor families and removal of organs. Other activities identified by 30 percent (India) and 25 percent (Thailand) of the respondents included fake job advertisements through the Internet and newspapers by employment agencies promising jobs, attractive salaries and many benefits.

The most dominant *forms of human trafficking* identified from our survey include women and child trafficking and prostitution (95 percent from India and 80 percent from Thailand of the respondents). Children fall victims of illegal adoption or may be adopted legally but become victims of child labor and prostitution. Other forms identified by 15 percent of the respondents were smuggling and abduction of human beings, store ways and slave trade (manifested by forced labor and deception). In deception, victims from Thailand are often eluded with offers to marry foreigners (mostly tourists), however, the promises fall down once they arrive at their destination, and instead they are forced into labor and prostitution. The victims are often molested by their new masters. Another common form of deception is through promises of scholarships for further education, where prospective students take up the scholarship offers only to realize that they have been deceived after they have been turned into prostitutes or domestic workers in the destination countries. The survey further revealed that these forms of trafficking might be carried out at three levels—domestic, cross border, or even international.

Domestic trafficking mostly involves children and young women being trafficked from rural to urban areas for domestic work and prostitution. A combination of poverty, gender inequality, inadequate legislation, and poor law enforcement has made trafficking in girls to thrive in India and Thailand. This has developed slowly from former foster arrangements where parents of poorer rural families would send their children to go live (and work) with wealthier families, often in urban areas. Today, that practice has been exploited by traffickers so that many such children are in fact child domestic workers with no access to education, no freedom of movement and working long hours in poor conditions for little or no pay. All respondents in this survey concur that many children are trafficked internally from rural areas to urban areas into involuntary servitude, including working as street vendor and day labor, and into prostitution. In addition children are trafficked to the Indian's coastal area where they are sexually exploited in the tourism industry serving mainly foreigners. However, children also move to urban areas on their own in order to earn money, and then find themselves living on the streets or in slum areas and are at this stage vulnerable to abuse, especially commercial sexual exploitation.

Cross-border trafficking is similar to domestic trafficking only that the victim moves to a neighboring country. It may be initiated by the victim, the victim's family or trafficking agents. There is significant cross-border movement within South and Southeast Asia for domestic labor (both male and female) and prostitution. Our survey shows that women and children are trafficked from Nepal and Bangladesh to India and from Cambodia, Laos and Myanmar to Thailand for sexual exploitation in the growing sex tourism industry. Others are also engaged in the massage parlors, hotels, restaurants, and domestic services where they are coerced into bonded labor and prostitution for provision of "escort services" in the parlors.

So far as the *international trafficking* is concerned, our survey findings show that victims are trafficked to other countries for various purposes, mostly through employment agencies that deceive victims on the working conditions in destination countries. Our field survey shows that the major destination countries for South and Southeast Asian Countries trafficked victims are India, Middle East, Thailand, Malaysia, and Singapore as cited by almost 90 percent of the respondents from both India and Thailand. The main destinations to the Middle East include Kuwait, Saudi Arabia, United Arab Emirates, Lebanon, and Bahrain. Our field survey also shows that the key source of trafficked victims into India and Thailand include mostly Bangladesh, Nepal, Pakistan, Cambodia, Laos, and Myanmar as cited by 95 percent of our respondents.

Majority of the respondents (90 percent and 85 percent respectively) opined that false promises of marriage and job opportunity were rampant in cross-border human trafficking to India and Thailand. Poor families giving their children to rich relatives were cited by 30 percent (India) and 40 percent (Thailand) of the respondents as the most dominating form of domestic human trafficking.

Most women who are trafficked from neighboring countries of India and Thailand are trafficked through *informal friendly networks* though sometimes highly organized criminal networks are involved. Respondents also said that child trafficking in India and Thailand occurs through personal and familial networks and also through organized international criminal networks, some posing as religious organizations. Most traffickers in persons in India and Thailand that recruit women and girls are mainly women who, in most cases have previously been trafficked or are currently sex workers. Results from the survey also reveal that the most common trafficking agents include wealthy relatives and other well connected people, recruitment and employment agencies, massage parlors, child trafficking syndicates, former trafficking victims, leaders of religious sects, tourists, hospitals and nurses, lawyers who specialize in adoption cases, some NGOs and drug traffickers.

Our survey shows that the main methods used by the *trafficking agents* are outright abducted and purchase from family members to work as child laborers, sex slaves and even domestic laborers (15 percent and 10 percent from India and Thailand respectively), trickery of girls and young women into believing they are being recruited for legitimate education, employment or marriage abroad (80 percent and 75 percent) and deception about conditions of work (5 percent and 15 percent). However, for trafficking of children, deception or coercion is not necessary for trafficking to occur; it is more the facilitated movement of the child into exploitation.

This study found that *gender* plays an important role in influencing whether a migrant ends up as a smuggled migrant or a victim of trafficking. Most trafficked persons are young women or children who end up being victims of coercion, abduction, fraud, deception, abuse of power, or abuse of force. Orphaned girl children in the care of relatives are thought to be especially vulnerable to trafficking. Almost 95 percent of the respondents in our survey from both the countries were in agreement that women and young children, mostly girls are the most vulnerable persons to both international and domestic human trafficking.

Educated people looking for jobs were also cited by 65 percent and 70 percent of the respondents as being vulnerable to international human trafficking. 30 percent and 25 percent of the respondents also noted that illiterate people are also victims of human trafficking both international and domestic. Low-income people hoping to strike it rich in foreign countries or in urban areas were also said to be vulnerable to human trafficking as reported by 25 percent (India) and 30 percent (Thailand) of the respondents. Other vulnerable victims of trafficking as reported by 30 percent and 35 percent of the respondents include economic migrants, political asylum seekers, those rendered homeless or jobless after natural disasters or civil conflict, or individuals looking for a better way of life.

Our survey found that India and Thailand are the source, transit and destination of trafficking victims. In our survey, 95 percent (India) and 90 percent (Thailand) of the respondents identified factors that make the countries to be a source of trafficked victims as poverty, unemployment, tourism, high dropout rates from school, neglect and discrimination of the girl child, orphanhood caused by HIV/AIDS, and illiteracy. In 100 percent of the cases, corruption was said to enhance human trafficking because it makes the office of the registrar of societies register employment bureaus irregularly which end up advertising fake jobs while their real business is to facilitate the trafficking of human beings.

Instability in neighboring countries such as Nepal, Pakistan, Afghanistan, Vietnam, Myanmar, Cambodia, and corruption among police and government immigration officials were reported by 80 percent and 75 percent of the respondents as contributing to India and Thailand serving as a transit for trafficked human beings. Relaxed and weak (porous) borders and tourism make India and Thailand a sex holiday destination and hence a transit for trafficked victims as noted by 40 percent and 30 percent of the respondents respectively. About 90 percent (India) and 80 percent (Thailand) of our survey respondents cited lack of proper enforcement of immigration laws (once people get in, nobody follows to know what they do) and corruption as factors that make India and Thailand a destination for trafficked victims.

CASE STUDIES

Case 1: Punam, 28 years old woman from Nepal, saw her father and mother being murdered due to political conflict. During her trip, she lost touch with her husband and one-year-old child, and ended up in a refugee camp in India. She made contact with an old female friend who had gone to *Darjeeling* many years before. This friend helped her and then forced her to work as a prostitute in a hotel.

Case 2: Nila and Miram, ages 20 and 22, traveled from rural Uzbekistan to India to work for a fashion design company after hearing a friend's stories of lavish parties and unending wealth. But once they arrived, their passports were taken and they were told they would not be designing clothing but instead servicing clients at various luxury hotels. Indian authorities eventually discovered the sex trafficking ring. The women returned to Uzbekistan and received necessary victim care and rehabilitative assistance from a shelter.

Case 3: To help her family, *Laxmi,* age 29, from Indo-Bangladesh border sought work. She was put in touch with a man who proposed to go with her to India, where she would be able to work. It was neither made clear to her what kind of work was involved, nor how much she would earn. She started work as a housekeeper with the men's sister at *Changrabandha* and stayed with the man's family. During the two months she worked there for which she was never paid and she was constantly insulted and beaten. The girl was sexually and physically abused by the man when his sister was out of the house.

Case 4: Lin Lin, 13 years old girl from Myanmar was recruited by an agent for work in Thailand. Her father took about 4,500 Baht from the agent with the understanding that his daughter would pay the loan back out of her earnings. The agent took the girl to Bangkok, and three days later she was taken to the *Ran Dee Prom* brothel. Latter the Crime Suppression Division of the Thai police raided the brothel in which she used to work, and she was taken to a shelter run by a local nongovernmental organization. She was 15 years old, had spent over two years of her young life in compulsory prostitution, and tested positive for the human immunodeficiency virus or HIV.

Case 5: In Cambodia, *Phirun* a 22-year boy worked in the fields growing rice and vegetables. Promised higher wages for factory work in Thailand, Phirun and other men paid a recruiter to smuggle them across the border. But once in Thailand, the recruiter took their passports and locked them in a room. He then sold them to the owner of a fishing boat, on which the men worked all day and night slicing, and gutting fish and repairing torn nets. They were given little food or fresh water, and they rarely saw land. *Phirun* was beaten nearly unconscious and watched the crew beat and shoot other workers and throw their bodies into the sea. Phirun endured this life at sea for two years before he persuaded his traffickers to release him.

Case 6: A teenage girl *Nang* is from the North of Laos in *Luang Namtha* province and was trafficked with two other girls, *Ping* and *Oi* by someone she knew from her village, and forced into prostitution. The girls were taken to *Thachilek* port, a local checkpoint between *Bokeo* province and Thailand, a common transfer point used by traffickers. The girls were then separated and *Nang* was sent to a house where there were about thirty other Lao girls working. Two days later, a man came to the house and took her to a hotel where he raped her every day for about a week until she was forced to start working as a prostitute. Once she began working, she was locked up in a hotel and forced to provide sexual services to clients eight to ten times a day. She never received any money. Nang was able to escape her situation with the help of her friends *Ping* and *Oi*. She later found out that she has been sold out for 30,000 baht. Trafficker did not succeed in selling *Ping* and *Oi* because the former was not deemed attractive enough and the latter was disabled, although they discovered trafficker still had plan of selling them as domestic help. As soon as they got back to *Long* district, *Luang Namtha*, the girls went to the police to report about trafficking. The provincial police eventually arrested the trafficker and fined her six million kip and put her in jail for six months.

CONCLUSION

Trafficking is a problem that today affects virtually every country in the world. Normally the flow of trafficking is from less developed countries to advanced countries. As trafficking is an underground criminal enterprise, there are no precise statistics regarding the magnitude of the problem. Very often estimates are found unreliable. But even by conservative estimates the scope of the problem is enormous. This study is an attempt to fill in this gap for India and Thailand. To achieve the objectives of the study, we rely on desk review and a limited survey of government organizations and supporting institutions.

The results of the survey confirm that human trafficking has been a silent crime and there is limited knowledge and a paucity of documented evidence on the subject. Furthermore, supporting institutions are unwilling to divulge any information on human trafficking. Nevertheless the key findings are that the most dominant forms of human trafficking in India and Thailand are women and child trafficking for forced labor and prostitution. This is done through outright abduction, illegal child adoption and deception (fake marriages and scholarships, nature of the job, etc.). Trafficking is perpetrated by wealthy relatives, employment agencies, trafficking syndicates, former trafficking victims and leaders of religious sects. Most of these agents may be part of well-organized criminal networks operating across countries/continents. The most vulnerable groups for human trafficking are women and children, the poor and the uneducated.

The predisposing factors to human trafficking in India and Thailand were identified as poverty, unemployment, illiteracy, ignorance, HIV/AIDS, better life syndrome, drug peddling, tourism, cultural and ethnic conflicts, famine, high dropout rates from school, discrimination of women and the girl child, corruption and instability in neighboring countries. Corruption and lack of enforcement of immigration laws were cited as the major factors that contribute to both the countries being a source, a transit and a destination of trafficked victims.

Very often, trafficking is equated with prostitution and this is one of the prime reasons why the human rights violation inherent in trafficking is not correctly understood, while the traffickers who are actual criminals go scot-free. In fact, for too many years, trafficking in person was treated as "victimless crime." Therefore, there is a need to demystify the term "trafficking" and understand it trend and dimensions within a human rights paradigm. However, it is important that laws intended to protect trafficking are not themselves so restrictive that they violate such rights. In spite of its overwhelming human rights dimension, trafficking continues to be treated as mainly a "law and order" problem, and that victims of trafficking can suffer from "revictimization" as they are "criminalized and prosecuted as illegal aliens, undocumented workers or irregular migrants rather than as victims of a crime themselves" coupled with coercion, exploitation, deception, violence, and other forms of either physical or psychological abuse. Names and identifying information of trafficked persons and their family members are not disclosed which leads to cycle of trafficking all over again for the victim.

To successfully combat and suppress trafficking, which has been equated with modern-day slavery and constitutes one of the greatest human rights challenges of our time a multipronged strategy is to be evolved. There should be enactment of a proper comprehensive legislation to target the traffickers and provide for proper rescue and rehabilitation programs for the victim survivors. New norms take roots only when there is the power of enforcement behind them. Purposive action by government as well as civil society to empower the vulnerable and restore to the trafficked women and children their dignity and worth as human beings is called for. Prevention activities at source and destination locations include awareness raising campaigns on human trafficking and safe migration, as well as education, capacity building and vocational training. It also involves advocacy on the incorporation of human rights into school curricula, strengthening the capacities of families, communities and community-based organizations, and the creation of child protection networks and poverty alleviation projects through microcredit schemes.

Our findings call for policy options focusing on prevention, protection, and assistance to trafficking victims and prosecution and enforcement against traffickers. In these efforts, there is need for the Government to tap the cooperation of foreign governments in efforts to combat trafficking for both international and cross-border trafficking. In addition, there is dire need for documentation of human trafficking. Toward this end, the government with assistance from NGOs and other stakeholders need to create a database on all cases (involving human trafficking) of complaints and/or testimonies of victims from consular offices/embassies, letters to relatives, newspaper reports and any other sources. The government also needs to address factors enhancing human trafficking by promoting education/vocational training/ scholarship program for vulnerable groups (women and children). The government should also encourage gender sensitive perspective in the training of law enforcement agents, prosecutors, lawyers, and community leaders. There is also need to encourage greater national and regional cooperation for broad-based skills training and economic opportunities for women and youth who are at risk of being trafficked. The government should provide more shelter and economic, psychological, medical, and legal assistance for trafficked persons based on humanitarian and compassionate grounds. It is also important to increase protective services for children found in situations of prostitution. In addition, the safe return of victims, instead of automatic deportation should be ensured for all trafficked victims. The tourism sector must be regulated to prevent sex predators. Other policy options include curbing corruption and enforcement of strict immigration laws as well as effective information technology act.

Given the magnitude of the trafficking problem and its relationship with migration, sometimes there are difficulties in differentiating between and identifying irregular migrants from trafficked persons. A clear understanding of how to identify trafficked persons would improve victim identification, victim protection, and the identification and pursuit of criminals and their prosecution.

- Addressing the demand side of human trafficking, including those who exploit cheap labor, societal sexual and gender norms, institutional attitudes to trafficked persons and perpetrators, law and prosecution, is crucial in approaching counter-trafficking in a holistic way.
- Assessing cases and the processes of victim protection and the prosecution of traffickers is essential to determine the strengths and weaknesses in the victim protection and criminal justice responses under the new law.
- Research on human trafficking in South and South East Asia especially in India and Thailand must be strengthened in sectors other than commercial sex industry, in order to obtain a more accurate picture of human trafficking in both countries. Moreover, better-focused research is needed to further improve and strengthen counter-trafficking approaches and targeting.

REFERENCES

ECPAT International. 2003. *ECPAT Report on the Implementation of the Agenda for Action against the Commercial Sexual Exploitation of Children 2001–2002.* https://www.ecpat.net/eng/Ecpat_inter/projects/monitoring/monitoring.asp.

Gupta, G. R. 2003. *Review of Literature for Action Research on Trafficking in Women and Children.* New Delhi: Institute of Social Sciences.

Hughes, D. M. 2000. "The 'Natasha' Trade: The Transnational Shadow Market of Trafficking in Women." *Journal of International Affairs* 53(2): 625–651.

ILO. 2000. *Trafficking in Children and Women: A Regional Overview.* Background Paper No. 4, ILO/Japan Asian Regional High-Level Meeting on Child Labour, 8–10 March, Jakarta.

ILO/IRPC. 2005. *Combating Trafficking in Children for Labour Exploitation in the Mekong Sub-region.* https://www.ilo.org/public/english/region/asro/bangkok/child/trafficking/wherewework-thailand.htm.

Sen, S. and Nair, P. M. 2004. *A Report on Trafficking in Women and Children in India 2002–2003.* Volume I, NHRC – UNIFEM – ISS Project. New Delhi: National Human Rights Commission.

The Protection Project. 2002. *A Human Rights Report on Trafficking of Persons, Especially Women and Children, Thailand.* https://www.protectionproject.org/main1.htm.

UNICEF. 2004. *At a Glance: Thailand, the Big Picture.* https://www.unicef.org/infobycountry/Thailand.html.

United Nations. 2006. *Trafficking in Persons: Global Patterns.* New York: United Nations.

US Department of State. 2005a. *Trafficking in Persons Report.* https://www.state.gov/g/tip/rls/tiprpt/2005/.

US Department of State. 2005b. *Country Reports on Human Rights Practices, Thailand.* https://www.state.gov/g/drl/rls/hrrpt/2003/27790.htm.

Westwood, D. 1998. *Child Trafficking in Asia.* World Vision Briefing Paper No. 4, World Vision International.

Chapter 8

Cross-Border Movement
from Nepal to India

Trafficking is an illicit and clandestine movement of persons within and across national borders for buying, selling, recruiting, transporting, transferring, harboring, or receipt—by means of threat or the use of violence or other forms of coercion, of abduction, of fraud or deception, of the abuse of authority, or of position of vulnerability, or of giving or receiving of payments or benefits to obtain the consent of a person having control over another person, for the purpose of any kind of exploitation. Exploitation shall include, at a minimum, nonconsensual sex work or exploitation of the prostitution of others or other forms of sexual exploitation, forced or bonded labor, fraud marriage, camel jockeys, slavery or practices similar to slavery, whether for pay or not, servitude or involuntary servitude (domestic, sexual, or reproductive), or the removal of organs, adoption, or other illegal purposes (United Nations 2000). Trafficking can be internal and trans-border for the purpose of sexual exploitation; labor exploitation; trafficking for illicit activities as involvement in pornography, drugs trafficking, forced begging, involuntary servitude or debt bondage or slavery; and trafficking for the purpose of organ removal and trafficking in organs, tissues, and cells. Human trafficking especially trafficking in women and children is an intense form of human rights violation as it denies the fundamental rights of "mobility, freedom, dignity, and integrity of the people" (Sarkar 2014a). Nepal has been an "origin" country from the very beginning but the phenomenon of intra-country trafficking for sexual and labor exploitation has also been apparent. The Government of Nepal (GoN) has recognized human trafficking as a serious crime against humanity as well as the violation of human rights and made its commitments to fight against trafficking with regulatory and policy interventions. For the effective implementation of the government plan of action against trafficking in persons, the GoN has closely been working in collaboration with national and

149

international development partners. The National Human Rights Commission (NHRC 2011) established in 2000 as a statutory body under Human Right Commission Act 1997, was upgraded as a constitutional body by the Interim Constitution of Nepal, 2007. The NHRC is mandated for the protection, promotion, and effective enforcement of human rights in Nepal. The NHRC has been actively working against the trafficking in persons since its inception. The Commission has placed the elimination of trafficking as one of the eight strategic concerns of its Strategic Plan (2004–2008). The Strategic Objectives 4 and 5 were directly relevant for the control and prevention of trafficking in persons. The objective 4 states "to help improve the legislative and regulatory mechanisms for control and cessation of domestic and dowry related violence against women and trafficking of women" while the objective 5 affirms "to help improve legislative, monitoring and enforcing arrangements for the elimination of violence against children in the form of trafficking, abuse, exploitation, and the use of children in conflict." Similarly, the Strategic Plan 2008–2010 of the NHRC has included the protection and promotion of the right of the trafficking vulnerable under the strategic objective—"gender equality, empowerment and combating violence and discrimination."

The Office of the National Rapporteur on Trafficking (ONRT) was established by a memorandum of understanding between the Ministry of Women, Children and Social Welfare and the NHRC in 2002, and it is a part of the NHRC (Ekberg and Manandhar 2005). The Commission has appointed the National Rapporteur on Trafficking under the direct supervision of the Chairperson of the Commission. The ONRT is also mandated to monitor the incidence of trafficking; coordinate national, regional, and international efforts to combat crime of trafficking; and generate high-level commitment to the efforts aimed at improving the human rights situation of women and children. In order to fulfill its mandates, the ONRT has the responsibility of publishing the National Annual Report by critically analyzing the efforts to combat trafficking in Nepal.

Nepal has one of the highest incidences of trafficking of women into sex trade in the South-Asia region (Wilson 1997). Although exact figures are difficult to obtain, the best estimate is that 5,000 to 7,000 Nepali girls and women are trafficked each year, primarily to urban areas in India, and at least 200,000 Nepali girls and women currently work in Indian brothels (Huntington 2002; Pradhan 1994). Given the data available, the problem of trafficking has crossed the geographical regions and social groups in Nepal. Trafficking occurs through a multitude of routes; it takes place mostly in networks of traffickers from village or working places to border and border to the destination for the purpose of sexual exploitation, labor exploitation, and other illegal activities (Sarkar 2011a). Movement of persons from Nepal to India is quite straightforward considering the long border it has with India.

There are fourteen legal entry points, but illegal cross-border movement without documents often takes place since India has an open border policy with Nepal. Nepalese have free access to enter India, and, therefore, trafficking becomes difficult to identify (Sarkar 2014b). Hence female trafficking and illegal migration, which works through social network between Nepal and India, is a very complex and multidimensional phenomenon. Trafficking involves deep-rooted process of gender discrimination, lack of female education, ignorance of rural folk, poverty and lack of economic opportunities. Lack of empowerment or lack of information for women about what may happen if they migrate—these factors can be assumed to increase vulnerability to trafficking (Sarkar 2011b).

The majority of existing studies on trafficking focus on why and how women are victimized in trafficking. The major objectives of such studies are to analyze policy implications and existent situation of trafficking in general. Various studies show that sociocultural structures, gender roles and power differentials, poverty and economic hardships are the major factors contributing to trafficking (Gupta 2010; Mahendra et al. 2001; Pradhan 2004; Scarpa 2008). In addition, many other causes behind the trafficking of Nepali girls and women have been identified and they include lack of vocational skills, migration, growing consumerism, ill-treatment by parents, desertion by spouses, rejection in love, gender discrimination, debt bondage, fenced love or marriage, unemployment (Mukherjee and Mukherjee 2007). In particular, labor migration from Nepal to India results into enhanced vulnerability of many women to sex trafficking across border. Due to loss of traditional jobs in rural Nepal as a result of technological transformation rural unskilled women are pushed especially to migrate for their survival into India and Middle East countries. However, many people in the rural communities of Nepal equate women's migration to India and job to their participation in sex trade.

According to a study by Henrik and Simkhada (2004), in most cases, traffickers get "their victims" through hoaxing, luring by false promises, physical force, feigned love or marriage, isolation and even forced drug abuse. Most of the trafficking victims are lured by the members of their community including their relatives, like uncles, aunts, cousins, brothers, stepfathers. However, Brown (2006) critically explains the causes of trafficking in her study of trafficking in South Asia. She accepts the various purposes and causes of trafficking but argues that prostitution is not just a product of poverty but may be a career option for some individuals. One of the causes of women and girls trafficking to India is considered the open national state borders. Nepalese people can freely visit India without any documents, hence making or creating easy access to the traffickers. Some of the major exit points of Nepal have police check posts and some organizations' vigilance cells but these are not sufficient to check the exits. Moreover, traffickers have changed the actual routes frequently for the fear of being intercepted (Ali 2005). Likewise, some policy documents and studies focus their analysis on the government plans and policies to combat trafficking. Policy document of GoN such as *Human Trafficking (Control) Act, 1986; National Plan of Action to Control Trafficking, 1998; and Trafficking Control Bill, 2002* has presented various preventive measures for the victims akin to awareness and advocacy program, rescue, and rehabilitation. However, it has not explicitly stressed the programs for rehabilitation and reintegration of victims of trafficking, though GoN have established a number of rehabilitation centers, but its priority is lesser.

This study seeks to address a number of research questions which include— Why are Nepali women and girls trafficked to India? What should be a human rights-based approach to trafficking in the context of Nepal? How and to what extent legal instruments are part of domestic law in Nepal follows? What are the demographic and social characteristics of trafficking victims? What are methods of operation followed by the traffickers as well as key experiences faced by the victims? How do traffickers recruit their potential victims? What are the policies and programs required to combat trafficking in person from Nepal to India? In order to answer these questions this study describes a conceptual framework to provide a clear understanding of the causes and context of trafficking for sexual exploitation from Nepal to India. It addresses that how the governments of Nepal and India should approach the problem of trafficking from a human rights perspective, and proposes additional areas of further inquiry for future research.

TRAFFICKING IN NEPAL: CAUSES AND CONTEXT

Nepal is a source country for men, women, and children who are subjected to forced labor and sex trafficking. Nepalese women and girls are subjected to sex trafficking in Nepal, India, the Middle East, and China (US Department of State 2013). In addition, trafficking takes place for the purpose of organ transplant to India; to Korea and Hong Kong for the purpose of marriage and to other Asian countries including Malaysia, Hong Kong, and South Korea (NHRC 2012). The Trafficking in Persons Report 2009 provided an estimate of 10,000 to 15,000 Nepali women and girls are trafficked to India each year (US Department of State 2009). Most of the girls are poor and come from villages where they are lured by false marriages or the promises of employment or education (Ghimire 1994; Paudel and Carryer 2000). Many of them are sold by their families (Ghimire 1997; Paudel and Carryer 2000). The traffickers pull together women and girls from the isolated districts like Sindhupalchok, Makwanpur, Dhading, and Kavre of Nepal where the populations are largely illiterate, poor, and highly infected of HIV (Prasai 2008). They are usually processed through Kathmandu on their way to the Nepal-India border, where they face a very meager checkpoint. They and their traffickers are not required to show a passport, residence permit, or visa as they cross into India. The destinations like Nagpur, Meerut, Allahabad, Kerala, and so on are emerging as new challenges in combating girls trafficking (Maiti Nepal 2012). When they reach their destination at a brothel, they quickly learn of their fate. Consequently, nearly all of these girls are forced to begin having sex with clients within a day of their arrival. Many are gang raped and beaten to be initiated, and they are often held in cages. Their torturous introduction is designed to ensure future compliance (Human Rights Watch 1995; Rao1996).

There is a lack of scientific data on the numbers of trafficked persons, places of origin and destination, and purposes of trafficking in Nepal and, since trafficking involves the clandestine nature of operation, collection of representative data has been also very complicated (O'Dea 1993; Bashford 2006). A study conducted by Central Child Welfare Board (CCWB) and the Save the Children Alliance (2004) provided some indications that child trafficking was happening across the India-Nepal border. The outflow of child migrants to India was significantly higher than inflows. A total of 17,500 children were found crossed the borders from Nepal to India during the three months between October and December, 2004. The same study indicated that armed conflict was the second major causes for child migration from Nepal to India (24 percent) after poverty (36 percent). The children and women are not only trafficked for commercial sexual exploitation from Nepal but also to carpet factories, circus agencies, agricultural projects, and road construction sites in India as well as to forced beggary in the bigger cities like Delhi, Mumbai, and so on (Child Work in Nepal 2002). Poor economic status and gender inequality are underlying factors of trafficking in Nepal (NHRC 2008). Gender inequality prevails in economic activities; education, patriarchal norms, and domestic violence among others are also regarded as other predominant factors leading to women and girls trafficking in Nepal. Moreover, studies have also pointed out the lack of female empowerment and an acute absence of overall awareness the other causes of women and girls trafficking in Nepal (Hennink and Simkhada 2004).

The studies among trafficked women suggest that, as in the case of men (Seddon et al. 2002), trafficking or migration operates through personal connections and social networks. For example, a female returns to the village and takes her childhood friend back to the city with her. It also operates through unregistered brokers who may or may not be strangers to the locality. In terms of trafficking, neither source is "risk free." Women and girls are reportedly attracted by reports of wealth and fun in the city, and are apparently easily "duped" into trusting the mediator. Likewise, some women are deceived into false marriages with the broker and are subsequently sold into the sex industry. It has been suggested that brokers are increasingly operating within organized trafficking networks (Sarkar 2013). The extent of family involvement in trafficking is cause for much controversy in Nepal. In certain communities (such as the *Badi* and the *Deuki*), sex work is a customary practice and continues to this day. In other communities in a few districts, notably Nuwakot and Sindhupalchok, there has likewise been a tradition of sending girls to "service" the ruling classes in Kathmandu that, in time, has changed into involvement in commercial sex. In these communities, female involvement in sex work is common knowledge and an important source of income. In most cases, however, it is suggested that though parents may sanction a daughter's migration and may even accept money in advance for her labor, they do not fully understand her risk of entering the sex trade (or of otherwise being exploited). Likewise, parents may accompany daughters to the carpet factories in Kathmandu but may not be aware of, or involved in, any subsequent trafficking (Evans and Bhattarai 2000).

Nepal is the poorest countries in the world. People are really living a hard life in lack of basic facilities. Poverty is identified as the major cause of girls trafficking in Nepal. Political situation is also one of the motivations for girls trafficking in Nepal. Political situation of Nepal is getting worse day by day. At present, Nepal is facing political crisis. On one hand there is civil war (war between Maoist and government) and on the other hand there is lack of rules and regulation in practice. The political instability has affected economy of Nepal and people's faith in the country's future. Likewise, the open border with India and China also motivate for the criminals works. The open borders to India are another supporting factor for the trafficking. Nepal has 1,740 mile-long open border with India and people usually cross the border without any restriction. The security in the check post of border is so weak. Traffickers are taking benefit of this weakness and selling girls to Nepal. The government is inefficient to bring rules and regulation into strict practice. Even police officer who are responsible to check the rules and regulation are helping sex trader taking the bribe. In many cases where sex trader are caught, but they are not given hard punishment.

While some of these proposed causes can be said to increase vulnerability specifically to trafficking, the rest are part of changes happening globally that are leading both to the increased feminization of poverty and to increased female migration. Hence, they are factors that lead to the desire or need to migrate. Again, it is perhaps misleading to single these factors out as being fundamental causes of trafficking per se. Rather, these factors underlie the phenomenon of increased migration, with some people being trafficked as a result. Dominant representations of trafficked "victims" in Nepal usually depict innocent village girls who are suddenly tricked by a stranger and sold into sexual slavery.

HUMAN RIGHTS-BASED APPROACH
TO TRAFFICKING

Sex trafficking violates women's right to life, liberty, and security of person. The fundamental individual right to life, liberty, and security of person is reflected in Article 3 of the Universal Declaration of Human Rights (UDHR) and Article 6 of the International Covenant on Civil and Political Rights (ICCPR). The Inter-American Convention on the Prevention, Punishment and Eradication of Violence against Women (Convention of Belém do Pará), chapter 2, Article 3 provides for the right of women to be free from violence within both the public and private spheres, specifically listing trafficking in persons as a form of violence against women regardless of whether it involves the knowledge or acquiescence of state agents. Sex trafficking is often referred to as modern-day slavery. Many countries have ratified various international conventions that create obligations to prohibit slavery and slavery-like practices. While some sex trafficking situations may not involve the permanent ownership historically associated with slavery, they can involve exploitation and deprivations of liberty that render the situation tantamount to slavery. Slavery-like practices that can manifest in sex trafficking situations, including servitude, forced labor, debt bondage, and forced marriages, are also prohibited. Some acts of sex trafficking involve conduct that can be understood as a form of torture, inhuman or degrading treatment, which is prohibited under the Convention against Torture and Other Cruel, Inhuman or Degrading Treatment or Punishment (CAT), Article 5 of the UDHR and Article 7 of the ICCPR, and has attained the status of a jus cogens norm. The failure to protect women from sex trafficking also represents a failure to ensure women's right to equal protection under the law. This is a well-enshrined principle of international law. The Convention on the Rights of the Child, Article 35 states that states parties shall take all appropriate national, bilateral and multilateral measures to prevent the abduction of, the sale of or trafficking in children for any purpose or in any form.

A human rights-based approach is a conceptual framework for dealing with a phenomenon such as trafficking that is normatively based on international human rights standards and that is operationally directed to promoting and protecting human rights. Such an approach requires analysis of the ways in which human rights violations arise throughout the trafficking cycle, as well as of states' obligations under international human rights law. It seeks to both identify and redress the discriminatory practices and unjust distribution of power that underlie trafficking, that maintain impunity for traffickers and that deny justice to their victims. While the link between human rights and human trafficking is clear, it does not necessarily follow that human rights will naturally be at the center of responses to trafficking. Both the Charter of

the United Nations and the Universal Declaration of Human Rights confirm
that rights are universal—they apply to everyone, irrespective of their race,
sex, ethnic origin, or other distinction. Trafficked persons are entitled to the
full range of human rights. Even if they are outside their country of residence,
international law is clear that trafficked persons cannot be discriminated
against simply because they are nonnationals. In other words, with only
some narrow exceptions that must be reasonably justifiable, international
human rights law applies to everyone within a state's territory or jurisdiction,
regardless of nationality or citizenship and of how they came to be within the
territory.

It has widely been accepted in modern times that trafficking entails a
human rights dimension. In addressing trafficking in human rights terms
it is likely to relay on existing human rights instruments. There is a wide
range of instruments both at a regional and international level, which can
be applicable to trafficking. The concept of a human rights-based approach
derived from the field of development, where it was employed to broaden
the focus from solutions based on traditional economical strategies to a more
overarching human rights perspective. Today, the use the human rights-
based approach has extended and is also applicable to human trafficking. A
human rights-based approach is a conceptual framework for dealing with a
phenomenon such as trafficking that is normatively based on international
human rights standards and that is operationally directed to promoting and
protecting human rights. Such an approach requires analysis of the ways in
which human rights violations arise throughout the trafficking cycle, as well
as of states' obligations under international human rights law. It seeks to both
identify and redress the discriminatory practices and unjust distribution of
power that underlie trafficking, that maintain impunity for traffickers and that
deny justice to their victims.

A rights-based approach also requires addressing the root causes of trafficking, including discrimination and other social, economic and cultural factors, and ensuring that approaches to trafficking are sensitive to the women
and girls from different age groups and backgrounds. A comprehensive
rights-based approach to trafficking must encompass prevention, protection
and empowerment measures built upon women's rights in accordance with
the convention on the elimination of all forms of discrimination against
women and other human rights instruments. These measures must be interrelated and mutually reinforcing. Without detracting from the significance of
the promising practices undertaken by states in establishing anti-trafficking
measures, one must bear in mind that they are based on the laws and policies
of the respective states. In Nepal, the Plan of Action for Combating Trafficking in Women and Children for Commercial Sexual Exploitation adopts
a human rights approach to trafficking, emphasizing the need to advocate

for children's rights to education, survival, and development within anti-trafficking strategies. It promotes the establishment of policy, research, and development strategies. Among its components are: promoting and asserting women's legal rights; social mobilization; training children to become trainers and youth leaders; improving media awareness; promoting reproductive health education; developing databases and referral systems; rescue and reintegration strategies, including counseling and free primary health care for rescued girls; promoting international strategies and cooperation; and monitoring and evaluation. A holistic approach involves developing a broad range of measures that go beyond prohibiting trafficking. Such measures ought to address the links between trafficking and exploitation, abuse, violence and discrimination. They should also promote cooperation between and among professionals working with women and children, such as medical personnel, social workers, teachers and law enforcement officials. It is also important to assess existing plans and determine gaps in their coverage. Measures and activities need to be coordinated, integrated, and fully implemented so that all children are protected—those who have been trafficked and those who are at risk.

First, it is important to recognize that the essential feature of the approach is to ensure and protect the human rights of the victims of trafficking. The victims, who in this specific context are women and children who have been trafficked, and their human rights are at the very focal point of the perspective, which is also called a victim-centered approach. According to the approach, trafficked persons should first and foremost be seen as rights-holders, and not as merely instrumental to investigations or prosecutions. Secondly, determining the identity of the entitled rights-holders and obligated duty-bearers are essential to a human rights-based approach. In a general human rights-based approach, the rights-holders are considered to be every human being since human rights are entitled to every person. However, there are requirements that the rights-holders must be able to exercise rights, formulate claims and seek redress. Thirdly, the principles of universality, inalienability, indivisibility, interdependence, interrelatedness, nondiscrimination, equality, participation, inclusion, accountability, rule of law, and the best interest of the women and children are all necessary to take into consideration when applying a human rights-based approach on anti-trafficking efforts aimed specifically at trafficking of women and children. The principles form a base for examining the human rights violations occurring in cases of trafficking. Among these are the violations of the right to life, physical and mental security, self-determination, health and development. The violations actualize the victim's right to an effective remedy. However, in the human rights-based approach this does not only entail the right to prosecute the offenders but also the right to medical care, protection and rehabilitation if needed. Thus, the approach equalizes the importance of criminalizing the perpetrators with the need for the enforcement of the human rights of the survivors of trafficking.

Treaties are the primary source of obligations for states with respect to trafficking. By becoming a party to a treaty, states undertake binding obligations in international law and undertake to ensure that their own national legislation, policies or practices meet the requirements of the treaty and are consistent with its standards. Nepal is a party to several of the treaties, which form part of the current international human rights framework. Out of the now nine core international human rights treaties, Nepal has ratified six. By ratifying the international instruments, Nepal has undertaken obligations to also enforce the regulations in its domestic setting. One aspect, which might affect the efficiency of the implementation, is the unclear position of ratified international treaties in relation to national law in Nepal. Nepal is not categorized as either a monist or dualist state. In other words, it is not clear if an international treaty is directly applicable when ratified or if it requires a transformation into domestic law before it is enforceable. The Nepal Treaty Act, which was adopted first in 1990, gives prevalence to international treaties in case there is a conflict with domestic law. However, this does not reveal anything about the status of international law within the domestic system as such, and clear, guiding precedents from the Nepali courts has been absent thus far. Despite the uncertain status of ratified international treaties, the international legal framework of human rights has had an impact on the domestic legislation in Nepal. From the practice of the Supreme Court, one can discern an increasing liberal approach toward applying the provisions in the ratified conventions indirectly, namely by viewing constitutional provisions in the light of the human rights provisions. However, if the Supreme Court finds a conflict between domestic law and a treaty rule, it refers the issue to the GoN for appropriate alteration of the national law. Thus, while the latter process has a dualistic character, the actions of the Supreme Court suggest a system closer to monism. Consequently, there exists a high uncertainty of the status of ratified international legal instruments in the domestic legislation in Nepal which could have an effect on the implementation of the actual human rights standards laid down in some of them. A frequent explanation used by the GoN to explain the poor implementation of the trafficking legislation is that the country is in a transitional period after the civil war. It is, therefore, justified that focus is entirely directed toward ensuring the success of the peace process and the completion of the new constitution. The strengthening of the implementation of legislation on trafficking is thus not a priority. As much as this is the reality at the moment for Nepal, one could question how long the GoN can blame its passivity on this issue on the process of drafting a constitution, which parenthetically should have been adopted years ago.

METHOD

Women and girls who have been trafficked for sex trade may not recognize themselves as such through panic of revenges from their employers; fear of social stigma from involvement in sex work; and embarrassment of their activities being revealed to family members. Therefore, identifying sex trafficked women and girls and acquiring access to them for interview is highly complex. In view of these difficulties, the target population for this research were 158 Nepali women and girls who had been sex trafficked from Nepal to India. The researcher adopted both purposive and convenience sampling methods due to the nature of the problem under investigation and scanty possible sources of information.

This study used a combination of qualitative interviews and quantitative case records to identify the process, context and experiences of sex trade. A quantitative approach was most appropriate given the exploratory nature of this research among an understudied population sub-group. The Stata—data analysis and statistical software version 10.0 was used for quantitative analysis. Qualitative interviewing was also suitable for eliciting contextual, descriptive, and process-oriented information and for allowing respondents to identify issues from their own perspectives. The sensitive, and sometimes illegitimate, nature of the research theme also required a vigilant interpersonal approach whereby good rapport and trust was developed between the interviewer and respondent. The study was designed to examine demographic and social characteristics of the victims; causes of trafficking; process, routes, and transport; mode of operation of the traffickers; and types of sexual exploitation and experiences of violence from employers and clients toward the trafficked victims. All interviews were conducted from February 2013 to May 2013 in three major red-light districts in India. Before interviewing participants, a participant information sheet was provided to them, which described the study in detail. The interview process did not include the name or address or any other identifiable information of the participants. The confidentiality and privacy of the participants was strictly followed. The participant information sheet explained to participants that access to the transcripts and data were limited to the researcher. The researcher asked whether the participants had any questions or concerns regarding this research or their participation. If potential participants had questions, the researcher discussed them carefully; participants who agreed to participate voluntarily were included in the research. No women or girls refused to participate in the interview. Either a verbal or written consent was taken before proceeding with interviews. There exists no information on the population of sex trafficked woman as a whole, so this limitations cannot be verified; however, the specific nature of this target population must be highlighted as it may influence the pattern of results observed in this study.

FINDINGS

Demographic Characteristics

The trafficking victims who participated in the study were between 14 to 38 years aged (mean =31.3 and standard deviation = 4.9) and the experiences of vulnerability to sexual exploitation were for less than a year to more than nine years (mean=7.4 and standard deviation = 3.1). About 69.6 percent of the respondents were illiterate while 15 percent of the females had education beyond primary level (P<0.001). A few (4.4 percent) trafficking victims had completed their secondary school which indicates that victims of trafficking may be an educated one. Out of the 158 sample surveyed study shows that 45 percent were trafficked by their close friends or near relatives while 38 percent of victims were trafficked through the criminal networks. The number of victims lured by pimps was twenty-seven. Family-based trafficking occurs when families send or take their young girls to places of forced labor or prostitution where they are sold or trafficked. In these cases the trafficker is often a close relative such as father, uncle, or aunt and the movement or migration may be under family pressure or voluntarily. In cases where families push women or girls into trafficking circumstances, some do not rationalize this as detrimental, as they are considered chattels for the family, which clearly demonstrate gender discrimination and low status of women and girls in the society. These attitudes create an atmosphere of impunity for many traffickers who feel free to seek out those most marginalized and vulnerable as the hard trafficking more precisely exemplify. That's why the demand for unmarried young girls in the study was 70 percent (P<0.001). Table 8.1 shows that 51.9 percent of victims had more than three family members (P<0.001) and 45.6 percent of the trafficking victims were sexually exploited for one to three years while 5.6 percent was victimized for more than nine year (P<0.001). The number of years working in the sex trade was significantly associated with experiencing sexual coercion from clients. Given the high correlation between the age of women and the number of years working in the sex trade, these variables were not adjusted in a logistic regression model; instead, crude associations between the variables of interest were examined for exploratory purposes. The results of bi-variate analysis show that women who had been in the sex trade for one to three years had almost four times the odds of being sexually coerced by clients compared to women who had been in the sex trade for nine or more years (crude odds ratio: 3.9, 95 percent confidence interval: 1.1–17.2). Similarly, women who were aged 17–21 years had more than three times the odds

Table 8.1 Distribution of Demographic Characteristics for Three Types of Trafficking Victims

		Victims Trafficked By				
Variable	*Variable category*	Close friends and relatives N=71 (percent of N)	Gang and criminal networks N=60 (percent of N)	Pimps N=27 (percent of N)	Total N=158 (percent of N)	Chi-square test for trend
Age group in years	14–18	12 (16.9)	16 (26.7)	08 (29.6)	36 (22.8)	P<0.001
	19–23	29 (40.8)	18 (30.0)	06 (22.3)	53 (33.5)	
	24–28	16 (22.5)	13 (21.7)	08 (29.6)	37 (23.4)	
	29–33	08 (11.3)	06 (10.0)	01 (3.7)	15 (9.5)	
	34–38	06 (8.5)	07 (11.6)	04 (14.8)	17 (10.8)	
Educational level	Illiterate	56 (78.9)	39 (65.0)	15 (55.6)	110 (69.6)	P<0.001
	Primary education (class IV standard)	13 (18.3)	11 (18.3)	09 (33.3)	33 (20.9)	
	Above primary education	02 (2.8)	10 (16.7)	03 (11.1)	15 (9.5)	
Marital status	Married	12 (16.9)	13 (21.7)	07 (25.9)	32 (20.3)	P<0.001
	Separated	18 (25.4)	09 (15.0)	09 (33.3)	36 (22.7)	
	Divorced	04 (5.6)	06 (10.0)	01 (3.7)	11 (7.0)	
	Widow	03 (4.2)	04 (6.7)	02 (7.4)	09 (5.7)	
	Never married	34 (47.9)	28 (46.6)	08 (29.7)	70 (44.3)	
Number of the family member(s)	2	06 (8.4)	04 (6.6)	01 (3.7)	11 (7.0)	P<0.001
	3	31 (43.7)	28 (46.7)	06 (22.2)	65 (41.1)	
	More than 3	34 (47.9)	28 (46.7)	20 (74.1)	82 (51.9)	
Number of year(s) working in sex trade	Less than 1	17 (23.9)	09 (15.0)	08 (29.6)	34 (21.5)	P<0.001
	1–3	30 (42.4)	34 (56.7)	08 (29.6)	72 (45.6)	
	4–6	14 (19.7)	11 (18.3)	07 (26.0)	32 (20.3)	
	7–9	05 (7.0)	04 (6.7)	02 (7.4)	11 (7.0)	
	More than 9	05 (7.0)	02 (3.3)	02 (7.4)	09 (5.6)	

Table 8.2   Social Profile of Trafficking Victims

	Number of Respondents N=158 (percent of N)
Caste/Ethnicity	
Brahmin	14 (8.9)
Chettri	28 (17.7)
Tamang	57 (36.1)
Dalit	32 (20.3)
Other (Rai, Magar, Tharu)	27 (17.0)
Geographical origin	
Central	28 (17.7)
Eastern	43 (27.2)
Western	30 (19.0)
Mid-western	22 (13.9)
Far-western	12 (7.6)
Kathmandu valley	23 (14.6)
Pre-trafficking occupation	
Agricultural labor	47 (29.7)
Domestic worker	21 (13.3)
Rural artisan	12 (7.6)
Student	11 (7.0)
Workless	67 (42.4)

of being sexually coerced by clients compared to women who were aged 31 years or older (crude odds ratio: 3.1, 95 percent confidence interval: 1.2–15.6).

Social Characteristics

Table 8.2 shows the social characteristics of trafficking victims. Traffickers often target socially underprivileged groups.

Interestingly 36.1 percent of the women were from the Tamang ethnic group. 8.9 percent of the women were Brahmin and 20.3 percent were from the *Dalit* community, 5.4 percent were *Chettri* and 17 percent were from other ethnic groups. Data reveal that trafficking victims moved from all development regions in Nepal with highest from Eastern region. This is followed by Western (19 percent), Central (17.7 percent), Kathmandu valley (14.6 percent), mid-western (13.9 percent) and 7.6 percent for far-western region. It is found that the majority of respondents had no job opportunity (42.4 percent). Most of the employed women were engaged in agriculture (29.7 percent) followed by serving as domestic workers (13.3 percent). There are also trafficking victims who at the time of trafficking were studying in school (7 percent).

Causes of Trafficking

Different theorists attribute different factors to the causes of trafficking depending on their theoretical approach to the issue of trafficking itself. A migration-based approach, for example, will focus on such issues as policies on migration and migrant labor, availability of work opportunities in various countries, globalization of the economy and development strategies. A criminal justice-based approach focuses on legislation and its implementation, policing strategies, impediments to prosecution, and the involvement of organized crime. A human rights-based approach acknowledges the importance of criminal justice, but will situate the causes of trafficking in issues such as the abuse of power, corruption of authorities, discrimination, and state failure to protect civil, political, economic, and social rights. Structural factors include issues of economic deprivation and market downturns, the effects of globalization, attitudes to gender, the demand for prostitutes and situations of conflict. Proximate factors include lax national and international legal regimes, poor law enforcement, corruption, organized criminal entrepreneurship, and weak education campaigns. The overarching argument is that the interaction between structural factors or variables (such as economic deprivation and market downturns, social inequality, attitudes to gender, demand for prostitutes) and proximate factors (such as lax national and international legal regimes, poor law enforcement, corruption, organized criminal entrepreneurship, weak education campaigns) is key to understanding why some individuals are vulnerable to trafficking through the use of deception and coercion (Sarkar 2013). The study shows that economic depression or poverty was the main reason behind trafficking from Nepal to India (97.4 percent) followed by better living conditions with high wages in the destination country (95.6 percent). The in-depth interviews reveals that women and girls from Nepal migrated independently to seek better job opportunity in urban areas and it was after this process that they were sex trafficked (89.9 percent). The other causes of trafficking cited by the respondents include gender discrimination (29.7 percent), primitive conditions (24.7 percent), social benefit and protection (49.4 percent), better chances of finding courtship (40.5 percent) and so on (table 8.3).

Routes and Transport

Trafficking is not a mechanical process of transportation from a place of origin to a specific destination. Rather it occurs through multiple routes and modes of transportation. Nepal and India share an open border, which spans about 1,000 kilometers on the South and Southwest. The major transit points from Nepal to India include Pasupati Nagar (Ilam) (14.6 percent), Kakarbhitta (Jhapa) (27.8 percent), Biratnagar (Morang) (19.6 percent), Bhantabari (Saptari) (7.0 percent), Birgunj (Parsa) (8.2 percent), Bhairawa (Rupandehi) (10.1 percent), Nepalgunj (Banke) (7.6 percent) and Mahendra Nagar (Kanchapur) (5.0 percent). Long distance buses (41.1 percent) and trucks (13.3 percent) were used for illegal transportation. Sometimes a combination of bus and train was widely used for trafficking to the destination (45.6 percent) (table 8.4). Generally travel by train was preferred by the traffickers after crossing the border. Some

Table 8.3   Causes of Trafficking

	Number of Respondents N=158 (percent of N)
Push factors	
Abject poverty or economic depression	154 (97.4)
Gender discrimination	47 (29.7)
Political instability	29 (18.4)
Disintegration of the family structure	129 (81.6)
'Primitive' conditions	39 (24.7)
Pull factors	
Job opportunities	142 (89.9)
Better living conditions with high wages	151 (95.6)
Political and/or religious freedom	41 (25.9)
Social benefit and protection	78 (49.4)
Better chances of finding courtship	64 (40.5)

Table 8.4   Routes and Transport of Trafficking

	Number of Respondents N=158 (percent of N)
Routes	
Pasupati Nagar (Ilam)	23 (14.6)
Kakarbhitta (Jhapa)	44 (27.8)
Biratnagar (Morang)	31 (19.6)
Bhantabari (Saptari)	11 (7.0)
Birgunj (Parsa)	13 (8.2)
Bhairawa (Rupandehi)	16 (10.1)
Nepalgunj (Banke)	12 (7.6)
Mahendra Nagar (Kanchapur)	8 (5.0)
Mode of transport	
Bus	65 (41.1)
Truck	21 (13.3)
Both bus and Train	72 (45.6)

key informants including long distance truck and bus drivers as well as border security personnel told that many traffickers make transport arrangements with long distance truck drivers. These trucks stop infrequently at public places such as bus stops and cities, and are not always strictly inspected by police. Even in cases police uncover illegal merchandise, bribes can often persuade them to overlook the infraction.

Trafficking Trail: Broker Sources, Involvement, and Destination

Table 8.5 shows that 36.1 percent of the trafficking victims were sold by their uncle, aunt, brother-in-law or neighbor to the pimps in the destination

Table 8.5   Trafficking Path: Sources and Working Places

Broker at source	Number (N=158) (percent of N)	Source location	Broker at destination	Working place
Relatives via criminal network	57 (36.1)	Village	Pimps	Brothel
Boyfriends	34 (21.5)	Village	Hotel manager or taxi driver	Pub, bar, hotel
Father via criminal network	42 (26.6)	Village	Pimps	Brothel
Girls run away from home	18 (11.4)	Village	Village friends	Private house
Local criminal gang	7 (4.4)	Village	Pimps	Brothel

country. Girls are recruited in a number of ways. Village girls and their families are often misled by smartly dressed young men who arrive in the village claiming to have come from the city and offering marriage and all the comforts of modern urban life. They go through a local ritual and disappear from the village. The girls end up in Indian brothels. Local criminal gang often sells the girls directly to a broker in the destination country (4.4 percent). Boyfriend sold the girls to the hotel manager or taxi driver for sexual service in cabin, pub, and dance bar (21.5 percent). Generally father sold his daughter to a broker to pay off debts (26.6 percent). If there is an economic crisis at home, it is more common. Local women who have returned from India are also employed as recruiters. These women are exceptionally well-placed to identify potential trafficking victims because they already know the local girls and their families. Many girls ran away from home with their girl-friend who in reality acted as a broker cum sex worker for a long time in the destination country (11.4 percent).

Modus Operandi of the Traffickers

Girls are lured with a range of techniques and promises, depending on the circumstances. According to one key informant, most traffickers possess an in-depth knowledge of local customs, the prevalence of poor and vulnerable households, and the aspirations of families and their daughters. Some agents pretend they are in love with the girls and make promises of marriage, other promise employment, while some lace food with drugs. In a few cases, parents are contacted and a direct negotiation is made. The majority of the respondents in the survey were trafficked with a promise of better employment (36.7 percent). This suggests that one of the most important means by which girls are trafficked is through hopeful offerings of economic improvement. Agreement with parent, mostly with father stands out as the second

Table 8.6   Mode of Operation of the Traffickers

	Number of Respondents *N=158 (percent of N)*
Commitments/promises	9 (5.7)
Better employment	58 (36.7)
Fake marriage	31 (19.6)
Drugs used	4 (2.5)
Coercion	6 (3.8)
Agreement with parent	38 (24.1)

leading means for trafficking girls (24.1 percent) followed by fake marriage (19.6 percent) (table 8.6).

Typology of Sexual Exploitation

Table 8.7 reveals that brothel-based sexual exploitation was probably the most widespread type of prostitution in India where 49.4 percent of the trafficking victims were engaged. Many respondents were engaged in cabin, pub, and dance bar-based sex services (24.7 percent). They regarded this form of sex work as undesirable because of the danger of violence and other forms of social hostility. Nevertheless some were recruited as call girls (17.7 percent). Client contacts them by phone or via brokers. It is the most clandestine form of sex work and relatively expensive because of low client mobility. Service is provided at client's home or hotel room. In an alternative of settings street-based sex work was considered by the respondents as more lucrative, however there is every possibility of aggression from the clients. 8.2 percent of the respondents served as floating sex workers.

Experiences of Violence from the Employers and Clients

Experiences of verbal and physical violence by the employers and clients were assessed in the study. Verbal abuse was assessed with one item that

Table 8.7   Mode of Sexual Exploitation

	Number of Respondents *N=158 (percent of N)*
Brothel complex-based	78 (49.4)
Street-based or floating	13 (8.2)
Cabin, pub and dance bar-based	39 (24.7)
Home-based or call girl	28 (17.7)

Table 8.8   Experiences of Verbal and Physical Violence from Employer and Client

Type of Violence	Violence from Employers N=158 (percent of N)	Violence from Clients N=158 (percent of N)
Verbal aggression	143 (90.5)	138 (87.3)
Minor physical assault	132 (83.5)	98 (62.0)
Severe physical assault	154 (97.5)	92 (58.2)
Yelled or shouted at	143 (90.5)	145 (91.7)
Hit with fist or something that could hurt them	112 (70.9)	72 (45.6)
Slapped or had something thrown at them	129 (81.6)	111 (70.3)
Pushed, pulled, or held down	78 (49.4)	87 (55.1)
Kicked or dragged	67 (42.4)	21 (13.3)
Tried to burn or strangle	47 (29.7)	8 (5.1)

examined shouting, and moderate physical violence included slapping or throwing, pushing, pulling, and hitting with fist while severe physical violence included kicking or dragging and trying to burn. Additionally, the frequency of each of the acts of violence was also assessed. The Cronbach's alpha for the abuse items for this sample was 0.67 for employers and 0.61 for violence from clients. Variables for experience of violence from employers and clients were coded as four-level categorical variable: 0=no violence, 1=verbal violence, 2=moderate physical violence, and 3=severe physical violence. Exploratory analysis, that is, crude associations and chi-square test were conducted to investigate the potential factors associated with experiencing forced sexual exploitation from the clients. Experience of violence either from employer or client was a criterion for participation in the study. Table 8.8 shows that all participants experienced some form of violence either from employer or client. While all the victims experienced some type of violence, significantly more experienced severe physical assault (97.5 percent), from employers and minor physical assault from clients (98 percent). Specifically, 47 percent reported that their employers had tried to burn or strangle them if they sometime denied working, and eight women reported these experiences to burn with a cigarette from clients. Further, significant proportions of the women experienced severe physical assaults from many times, including being shouted at (90.5 percent and 91.7 percent), slapped (81.6 percent and 70.3 percent), kicked (42.4 percent and 13.3) and so on. On the other hand, the most common form of abuse from clients was verbal aggression (87.3 percent). In addition, the study finds that victims who were physically forced by clients to have sex were more likely to also report experiencing verbal or moderate physical violence from clients compared to those who were not forced to have sex (χ^2=4.93, p=0.026).

CASE STUDIES

Case 1: After completing primary education, Gouri (aged 17) helped her parents to do some domestic chores and worked in the agricultural field in Bharatpur. One day her friend told that she was going to Darjeeling for work and persuaded Gouri to go with her. She decided to go with her. When Gouri, her friend, and another girl arrived in Darjeeling the climate was so cold. From Darjeeling, an agent chose Gouri and her friend and sent them to Gangtok. The other girl was sent to Kalimpong. The agent told them that each of them owed him ₹10,000. They were taken to a bar where inside they could notice eight Nepali women were singing and talking to customers. The manager of the bar told them to sit with one of the customers who had already paid ₹3,500 to the bar manager. After that he directed Gouri to go out with that customer. Sometimes, while Gouri was staying with a customer in a room, she heard her colleague screaming for help in Nepali language from a nearby room. But the customer forbade Gouri to do anything like that otherwise she herself would receive the same awful treatment.

Case 2: A group of five Nepali girls, aged between 18 and 24, desired to earn some money so they could continue their studies. They were recruited by a temporary employment agencies owned by a Nepali national, who was subcontracting Nepali girls to work in various call centers in Siliguri. On arrival they were put to work in a call center for ₹100 per day and provided a free dwelling. On third day of arrival in the evening the agent went to their house and gave them some fast-food to eat. They ate and did not remember what happened afterward. When they regained consciousness, they found that they were staying in a red-light district and a woman was asking them to satisfy the customers. It was like a shock for them. They refused to work there but the brothel owner beat them with a stick and told them that they were sold and must work as a prostitute. They wept a lot but it had no effect. Ultimately, they were forced for sex trade.

Case 3: Puspa (aged 19) from a poor family of Puma village was in need of work for others on ill-paid daily wages. So she came to Pokhara with her cousin brother in search of better job. She searched for better jobs but could not get any job there due to her illiteracy. She started selling of artisanal handicrafts to the tourists with a boy from her village during the day time. One day, the boy told her that he could send her to India for work where his uncle was working. There she could get a lucrative salary. It was a good proposal and Puspa decided to follow the boy. The boy asked her to call other friend also so that Puspa would have friends even if she feels alone. Then Puspa talked to one of her friends about the work in India. Her friend was also ready to go with her. The boy took them by bus to Kakarbhitta and told them that if border security officials stop them, they should say that they are brother and sister going to visit their aunt in Siliguri. All did as the boy said and crossed the border. The boy then took them to Siliguri by bus. Thereafter, they traveled to Kolkata by a train. Next morning, they reached a small house in a narrow lane; the accompanying boy told them that it was his sister's house and told them to live there with his sister. The boy then told them that he had to go out to ring his family in Nepal and buy some food and clothes for them. They waited for him but he did not come back. Puspa and her friend did not know about the brothel until that woman told them to get ready for prostitution. They refused to do so and did not eat anything for next three days. The brothel keeper told them that she had bought them for ₹45,000. They had no option except to involve in forced prostitution for their survival.

Case 4: Sanam (aged 27) and her friend Sima (aged 29) women from Lalitpur were interested to become actress in their life. One day Sanam along with her friend met a person in a restaurant who introduced himself as a make-up man in Bollywood film industry in Mumbai. The man offered them to move to Mumbai for better future. They could not refuse his request, as the man claimed with interpretation that he knew their parents. After a few days, they initially caught a bus thereafter traveling by a train eventually reached Mumbai with that man. Initially they stayed at a hotel and then they were taken to a place where they saw many girls who looked younger than 16 years of age. They had never seen before girls ornamented with expensive dresses (short skirts), much make-up, and bright red lipstick. There they met a lady who introduced herself as a film producer. The lady acted with them very gently so that they might be impressed. The accompanying man told them to relax there as he had an urgent work at the shooting spot and he would come back in the evening. The man never returned. The lady told them to take a shower, and gave them some clean clothes for wearing. When they asked the lady where they would go, the lady just laughed and walked away saying that they had been sold by the man for ₹1,00,000 for sex trade.

ANALYSIS

The Government of Nepal actively endorses cross-border labor migration in the acknowledgment of significant remittance inflows to Nepal, but at the same time this stream of cheap labor migration supply is exploited by traffickers who fish out the most vulnerable women and children for sex trade. As the countries into which Nepali girls and women are trafficked, among others India is expected to enforce its laws against exploitation of children and trafficking in persons. None of the major laws, however, has made the least dent in trafficking in persons anywhere in India.

The study showed that participation in rural-urban migration increased the risk of being trafficked for many girls and women from Nepal. They were either sent from rural areas to cities to work under the arrangements of a recruiter, or they keenly migrated in search of better employment. The girls were pulled by the lure of promises of love, entertainment, and so on and with hopes of economic benefit. Either way, the girls found themselves without a support network of family, relatives, or friends, making them more vulnerable to being pulled from their new and uncertain circumstances to the sphere of trafficking, and consequently sexual exploitation.

The majority of the parents of the trafficking victims conferred implicit consent or were involved in the trafficking of their daughters. Once girls were sold, they belonged to the brothel owner until they pay back the amount paid for them. The reasons behind trafficking and sexual exploitation were enumerated as poverty, illiteracy, lack of awareness, lack of employment opportunity, low social status, and so on. A range of social, religious, and cultural factors were also consistently cited, including family disorder, food scarcity, violence in the family, patriarchal society, decline in moral values, as well as the general exploitation of girls in the form of sexual abuse.

The duration of stay in sex trade varies with the age at the time of trafficking. The younger the girl is at the time of trafficking, the greater the likelihood that she will be exploited for a much longer period. At the risk of repeating a notion that is frequently cited but little researched, it seems that there is a higher demand of younger girls, and that brothel keepers also prefer to recruit teenagers as they make high profits. The survey states that there were a substantial number of girls who have spent more than a year being sexually exploited in a brothel and the majority of the girls experienced the first sexual victim between ages of fourteen to sixteen.

The study shows that the mean hours engaged in sex service reported was fifteen with a minimum of twelve hours to a maximum of twenty hours a day. On average, a girl was forced to serve average six clients per day with a minimum of five customers to a maximum of eight. As congregated from the interviews, there were cases in which the girls did not receive any money during the period of sexual exploitation. The study reveals that, in reality, after covering their expenses, majority of the victims received between 5 and 7 percent of the money they earned. The rest of their earnings were distributed up the ladder. In addition to the money from the victimized girls, the criminal organizations drew money from the independent pimps through racketeering.

Respondents were asked how many days after their arrival they were forced into sexual exploitation. The girls reported that this generally happened within a day of their arrival. One victim explained "if any girl refused and attempted to run away they were badly beaten and kept in a gloomy room without food and water until they were finally forced to serve the clients." The majority of victims believed "how the process of returning home is a complex phenomenon, with a multitude of mechanisms and actors involved. They reported that the girls who returned home after rescue are not having a normal life due to the perceived beliefs and social stigma towards such girls in the society." In terms of their economic status it seems that some of the trafficked girls are in a situation that is even more miserable than in sex trade. A few reported that they were much better off in brothel, and it seems likely that there is a risk of revictimization such as commercial sexual exploitation. Often, victims did not even have basic control over their daily decisions such as when to sleep, eat, or rest. Their lives were at the mercy of the traffickers who subject the victims to physical violence, repeated rape, torture, forced drug use, forced abortions, and psychological manipulation.

CONCLUSION

Human trafficking is driven by demand and supply. If there is a demand for forced sexual services, traffickers use all means to meet those demands by targeting vulnerable people. The government of Nepal has an obligation to do everything in its power to check the trafficking and sale of Nepali women and girls from its territory and to protect them from the violation of human rights. Nepal should comply with the international instrument most relevant to the trafficking in women and girls—the Convention for the Suppression of Traffic in Persons and the Exploitation of the Prostitution of Others. The government of Nepal should ensure that all reports of trafficking or attempted trafficking be promptly and thoroughly investigated and that those found guilty are prosecuted. The government of Nepal has a special obligation to investigate reports of official corruption and complicity in the trafficking and sale of persons and should hold all persons alleged to have involvement with the industry to the same legal standards. This includes police officers, government officials, and influential private citizens. Negotiations between Nepal and India regarding the status of their shared border should include establishing systems for monitoring the trafficking in women and girls and investigating and prosecuting the traffickers to the fullest extent of the law.

On the other hand, the demand for Nepali girls and women in India's brothels drives the trafficking from Nepal. The government of India should move to reform its prostitution and trafficking laws to ensure they are nondiscriminatory and in line with international human rights standards, particularly those designed to protect the victims of trafficking. Long open border with India and Nepal makes it essential that both countries give priority to strict monitoring efforts to guard against the trafficking in women and girls, including the inspection of vehicles. Special training should be given to law enforcement officials at the border in the problem of trafficking and their obligation to protect trafficking victims and investigate those who engage in such exploitation. The government of India should actively investigate and prosecute all those involved in trafficking and brothel operations, with particular attention to its own police and officials. Any case involving the detention of a Nepali woman or girl following a raid on an India brothel should be given particular attention with a view toward the speedy release of anyone found to be a trafficking victim. All laws which can lead to the prosecution of all others involved in trafficking and brothel operations, including recruiters, agents, brothel owners, and pimps, should be strictly enforced. The Indian government should ensure that arrangements with the government of Nepal for the safe return of trafficking victims make sure the protections guaranteed by the Convention on the Suppression of Traffic in Persons.

Increasing international and domestic pressure on both the governments to focus on safe migration will encourage adoption and enforcement of anti-trafficking frameworks that are more comprehensive, user friendly, and transparent. Integrating anti-trafficking measures into economic and development planning would help address both supply and demand. In addition, thinking about ongoing and potential policies, plans, and projects from an anti-trafficking movement in Nepal would entail assessing how the most vulnerable could become trafficked as a consequence of those efforts. This would enable development planners to adjust program design to mitigate effects or to include additional preventive attention to vulnerable subgroups. Schemes that require displacement could be designed to minimize the effect and mitigate vulnerabilities that arise, and post-conflict assistance could be designed to ensure that the social dislocation does not lead to vulnerability to trafficking, especially for women and girls, in already high-risk situations.

The implications of human trafficking research create opportunities for future research. This study is preliminary and seeks to promote future research in this particular field. Hopefully, through this research a greater understanding of the causes of the human trafficking from Nepal to India can be spread to those who can make positive change and bring about greater human rights for victims. Further research on this topic is socially and politically necessary. The issue of human trafficking from Nepal to India continues to be a major concern. This study was limited to a particular cohort of survivors in three major red-light districts in India. Research must be conducted on more red-light areas and rescue centers, include more types of victims, and delve deeper into ways for lessening this crime.

REFERENCES

Ali, A. K. M. M. 2005. "Treading along a Treacherous Trail: Research on Trafficking in Persons in South Asia." *International Migration* 43(1–2): 141–164.
Bashford, P. 2006. *A Sense of Direction: The Trafficking of Women and Children from Nepal.* Kathmandu: Asha-Nepal.
Brown, L. 2006. *Sex Slaves: The Trafficking of Women in Asia.* London: Virago Press.
CCWB, and the Save the Children Alliance. 2005. *An Increasing Wave: Migration of Nepalese Children to India in the Context of Nepal's Armed Conflict.* An Unpublished Research Report, Kathmandu.
Child Work in Nepal. 2002. *Facts about Human Trafficking.* Kathmandu: Child Work in Nepal.
Ekberg, G. and Manandhar, M. D. 2005. *Review of the Office of the National Rapporteur at the National Human Rights Commission Kathmandu, Nepal.* Kathmandu: National Human Rights Commission.
Evans, C. and Bhattarai, M. P. 2000. *Trafficking in Nepal – Intervention Models: A Comparative Analysis of Anti-trafficking Intervention Approaches in Nepal.* Kathmandu and New Delhi: The Asia Foundation and Population Council.
Ghimire, D. 1994. *Girl Trafficking in Nepal: A Situation Analysis Red Light Traffic.* Kathmandu: ABC Nepal.
Ghimire, D. 1997. *Sexual Exploitation of Nepalese Girls.* Kathmandu: ABC Nepal.
Gupta, R. 2010. "Human Trafficking in Asia: Trends and Responses." In *Migration Challenges in the Indian Ocean Littoral*, edited by E. Laipson and A. Pandya. Washington, DC: The Henry L. Stimson Center.
Hennink, M. and Simkhada, P. 2004. "Sex Trafficking in Nepal: Context and Process." *Asian and Pacific Migration Journal* 12(3): 305–338.
Human Rights Watch. 1995. *Rape for Profit: Trafficking of Nepali Girls and Women to India's Brothels.* New Delhi: Human Rights Watch.
Huntington, D. 2002. *Anti-trafficking Programs in South Asia: Appropriate Activities, Indicators and Evaluation Methodologies.* Summary Report of a Technical Consultative Meeting. New Delhi: Population Council.
Mahendra, B. S., Bhattrai, P., Dahal, D. R., and Crowley, S. 2001. *Community Perceptions of Trafficking and Its Determinants in Nepal.* Kathmandu: The Asia Foundation.
Maiti Nepal. 2012. *Maiti Nepal News Letter.* July-September, Kathmandu.
Mukherjee, K. K. and Mukherjee, S. 2007. *Girls and Women in Prostitution in India: A Report.* Ghaziabad, Uttar Pradesh: Gram Niyojan Kendra.
NHRC. 2008. *Trafficking in Persons, Especially on Women and Children in Nepal.* National Report 2006–2007. Lalitpur, Kathmandu: NHRC.
NHRC. 2011. *National Human Rights Commission-Nepal and OHCHR-Nepal Observations on the National Human Rights Commission Bill 2009.* Lalitpur, Kathmandu: NHRC.
NHRC. 2012. *Trafficking in Persons, Especially on Women and Children in Nepal.* National Report 2011. Lalitpur, Kathmandu: NHRC.

O'Dea, P. 1993. *Gender Exploitation and Violence – the Market in Women, Girls and Sex in Nepal: An Overview of the Situation and a Review of the Literature.* Kathmandu: UNICEF.

Paudel, P. and Carryer, J. 2000. "Girl Trafficking, HIV/AIDS, and the Position of Women in Nepal." *Gender and Development* 8(2): 74–79.

Pradhan, G. 1994. *The Road to Bombay: Forgotten Women Red Light Traffic.* Kathmandu: ABC Nepal.

Prasai, S. B. 2008. *Call for Global Action to Halt Nepalese Women and Girls Trafficking.* American Chronicle National Media Network, February 11.

Rao, A. 1996. "Girls Trafficked from Nepal into Indian Brothels." *Reclaiming Children and Youth* 5(2): 114–117.

Sarkar, S. 2011a. "Engendering Trafficking and Human Security: A Comparative Study of India and Hungary." *International Journal of Development Research and Quantitative Techniques* 1(2): 25–42.

Sarkar, S. 2011b. "Trafficking in Women and Children to India and Thailand: Characteristics, Trends and Policy Issues." *International Journal of Afro-Asian Studies* 2(1): 57–73.

Sarkar, S. 2013. *Trade in Human Beings: An Empirical Study of Trans-border Human Trafficking for Sexual Exploitation into India and the UK.* Unpublished Research Report, University of London, London School of Economics and Political Science and Cambridge University.

Sarkar, S. 2014a. "Trans-border Sex Trafficking: Identifying Cases and Victims in the UK." *Migration and Development* 3(1): 95–107.

Sarkar, S. 2014b. "Rethinking Human Trafficking in India: Nature, Extent and Identification of Survivors." *The Round Table: The Commonwealth Journal of International Affairs* 103(5): 483–495.

Scarpa, S. 2008. *Trafficking in Human Beings.* New York: Oxford University Press.

Seddon, J. D., Adhikari, J., and Gurung, G. 2002. "Foreign Labour Migration and the Remittance Economy of Nepal." *Critical Asian Studies* 34(1): 19–40.

United Nations. 2000. *United Nations Protocol to Prevent, Suppress and Punish Trafficking in Persons Especially Women and Children.* New York: United Nations.

US Department of State. 2009. *Trafficking in Persons Report 2009.* Washington, DC: US Department of State.

US Department of State. 2013. *Trafficking in Persons Report 2013.* Washington, DC: US Department of State.

Wilson, T. 1997. "Rape for Profit: Trafficking of Nepali Girls and Women to India's Brothels." *The International Migration Review* 31(2): 490–491.

Index

About the Author

Siddhartha Sarkar (b.1973), *PhD (Economics), PDF (The Netherlands and Hungary), CAF (London, UK), MISPCAN (USA)* is Principal and Executive Head at Ananda Chandra College of Commerce, West Bengal, India, and Founder and Director of Centre for Human Trafficking Research. He has previously been a Post Doctoral Fellow and Visiting Professor (2006) in University of Amsterdam, The Netherlands, a Senior Post Doctoral and Professorial Fellow (2010) in Thammasat University and Asian Institute of Technology, Thailand, Senior Post Doctoral Fellow and Visiting Professor (2011) in Corvinus University and Central European University, Hungary. He was also a Commonwealth Academic Fellow (2013–2014) in SOAS, University of London, London School of Economics and Political Science, Cambridge University, United Kingdom, and European Commission Erasmus Mundus Visiting Professor (2015) in University of Warsaw, Poland. Sarkar is nominated as a working committee member of the *"National Institution for Transforming India"* (NITI Aayog), Government of India and the recipient of India Leadership Award 2018.

www.ingramcontent.com/pod-product-compliance
Lightning Source LLC
Chambersburg PA
CBHW022315280326
41932CB00010B/1109